When Children
ABUSE

CAROLYN CUNNINGHAM
KEE MacFARLANE

When Children
ABUSE

Group Treatment Strategies For
Children With Impulse Control Problems

WITHDRAWN

Safer Society Press

PO BOX 340
BRANDON, VERMONT 05733-0340
PHONE (802) 247-3132

Cover Design: Barbara Poeter, Pittsfield, VT

Photos: Steven Larese, Corrales, NM

PTSD Workbook Illustrations: Cathy Detzer, Laser Image

Editor: Euan Bear

ISBN: 1-884444-23-7

Order from:
The Safer Society Press,
PO Box 340, Brandon, VT 05733-0340,
(802) 247-3132
$28.00

The authors thank the following for permission to reprint and/or adapt copyrighted material:

"Assignment One/Assessment Questions for Older Children" from *Informational Guide on the Juvenile Sexual Offender* by A. Stickrod, J. Hamer, & B. Janes. Published by The Oregon Adolescent Sex Offender Treatment Network, © 1984. Permission granted by Alison Stickrod Gray. // "Stop and Think Award," "Dealing with Feelings Award," & "Dealing with Stress Award" from *Skill Streaming the Elementary School Child* by E. McGinnis and A.P. Goldstein, 1984. "Student Gus the Dragon Cue Pictures" reproduced from *Think Aloud Classroom Program Grades 5-6* by Mary Ann S. Bash & Bonnie W. Camp, © 1985; "Social Cue Cards" & "What Might Happen Next Peanuts" reprinted with permission from *Think Aloud Primary Level* by Bonnie W. Camp & Mary Ann S. Bash, © 1981. All permissions granted by Research Press. // "Group Evaluation" excerpted from *Self-Esteem, A Classroom Affair, Volume 2* by Michele and Graig Borba. Copyright © 1978 by Michele and Graig Borba. Reprinted by permission of HarperCollins Publishers. // "It's Me," "Me Badge," "Being Me Means," & "Counter It" reproduced from *Helping Yourself to a Healthier You*, by Ann Vernon, © 1988, by permission of Burgess International Group, Inc. // "The Little Red Fire Engine" reprinted from *Color Us Rational* by Virginia Waters, © 1979, by permission of the Institute for Rational-Emotive Therapy. // "My Strength Book," "Goal Results," "Goal Wheel," "Recording Friendly Deeds," & "Friendship Goal" reproduced with permission from *Esteem Builders* by Dr. Michele Borba, © 1989. B.L. Winch and Associates/Jalmar Press. Used with permission from B.L. Winch Associates/Jalmar Press. // "Aggression," "Fight Form," & "Responding to Aggressive Behavior" from *Creative Conflict Resolution*, by William Kreidler, © 1984 by William Kreidler. Reprinted by permission of Scott, Foresman and Company. // "Who Controls Me," "It Makes Me Angry," "Ring Around of Temper," "Who Needs It," & "What Should I Do?" from *Creative Conflict Solving for Kids*, by Fran Schmidt and Alice Friedman, © 1985, reprinted with permission from the Grace Contrino Abrams Peace Education Foundation, Inc., 3550 Biscayne Boulevard, Suite 400, Miami, FL 33137. // "Eency Weency Spider" song words and worksheets reprinted from *Creative Problem Solving for an Eency Weency Spider* by Gretchen A. Duling, © 1983; "Sticks and Stones" reprinted from *Explore* by Jay Cerio, © 1983. Permission for both granted by DOK Publications, Buffalo, NY. // "Roadblocks to Resolving Conflict," "Conflict Situations," "Emotional Wheel," & "Gilbert and the Color Orange" excerpted from *Teaching Peace* by Ruth Fletcher. Copyright © 1987 by Ruth Fletcher. Reprinted by permission of HarperCollins Publishers. // "Tom and Bill Solve a Problem" & "George Feels Better" reprinted from *That's Not Fair* by Larry Jensen, © 1977; "New Crayons" from *Responsibility and Morality* by Larry Jensen & Karen Hughston, © 1979; permission granted by Brigham Young University Press. // "Tell My Story Chart" adapted from *Treating the Young Male Victim of Sexual Assault* by Eugene Porter, © 1986, with permission from The Safer Society Press. // "Signs of Stress" & "Desensitization" from the book, *Coping for Kids* by Gerald Herzfeld, Ph.D. & Robin Powell, Ph.D., © 1986. Used by permission of the publisher, The Center for Applied Research in Education, West Nyack, NY. // "What Was Going On Inside of Me Before I Was Hurtful," "Danger Sign Thoughts," and "Vulture Back-Talk" reprinted from *Steps to Healthy Touching* by Kee MacFarlane and Carolyn Cunningham, © 1990, 1988 MacFarlane, Cunningham, & KIDSRIGHTS. Reprinted with permission of KIDSRIGHTS, 3700 Progress Blvd., Mount Dora, FL 32757, 1-800/892-5437. // The "Sexual Abuse Cycle Diagram" and "Steps to Getting in Trouble" adapted with permission from *The Sexual Abuse Cycle in the Treatment of Adolescent Sexual Abusers* (Video & audiotape reference materials), by permission of authors Connie Isaac & Sandy Lane, © 1990 by The Safer Society Press. // "Appreciating Others" from *Tribes—A Process for Social Development & Cooperative Learning* by Jeanne Gibbs, © 1987, with permission from Center Source Publications, Santa Rosa, CA. // "You Are Important Too" reprinted from *Caring*, by Mary Anne McElmurry, © 1986, by permission of Good Apple Press, Carthage, IL. // "My Body ... Continuums," "Selection Ladder," "Relationship Collage," "I Feel," & "Discussion Sheets," reproduced from *Taught Not Caught*, Clarity Collective, © 1983, by permission of Spiral Education Resources, Fitzroy, Australia. // "Weekly Evaluation Form: Children's Group" and "Progress Evaluation and Treatment Needs: Children's Group" adapted by C. Cunningham & K. MacFarlane, 1987, from "Individual Implementation Plan Assessment Sheet" developed by G. Freitag, Ph.D. & D. Kingdon, Ph.D., Dubnoff Center for Child Development and Educational Therapy, North Hollywood, CA 91606, © 1986.

Thanks to all of our colleagues who contributed suggestions, donated their time to read and comment, field-tested the exercises and granted permission to reprint their work in the first edition of this book.

For their assistance and contributions to this revised edition, we would like especially to thank:

Alison S Gray, MA, of the Center for Prevention Services in Underhill, Vermont;

Fire Marshall Charles Campbell of Eugene, Oregon;

Ann Welty, MD of the Greater Long Beach, California Child Guidance Center;

Tim Boatman, M.A., of the National Resource Center for Youth Services at the University of Oklahoma;

Lynne Namka, Ed.D., of Talk Trust & Feel Therapeutics; and Kimberly Fill, M.A., of the Children's Protection Center

Thanks also to the Safer Society Press for providing the opportunity to expand our first volume to include a much broader population of children who are in trouble and in need of help.

—*Carolyn Cunningham, Ph.D.*   —*Kee MacFarlane, M.S.W.*

About the Authors

Carolyn Cunningham, Ph.D. is the Director of Psychological Services at the Children's Protection Center at Long Beach Memorial Hospital. In addition, she is adjunct faculty in child therapy at California Family Study Center, a graduate school awarding the masters degree in psychology.

Dr. Cunningham is a national consultant regarding children with sexual behavior problems and therapy with traumatized children. She is the author/co-author of three other publications addressing the issues of children who are sexually acting out or who have separation problems.

She is the former executive director of the Children's Center of the Antelope Valley, a comprehensive child abuse prevention, assessment, and treatment center. She has worked with children, adolescents, and families for over 15 years, including 9 years in the field of child sexual abuse treatment.

She is a member of the National Task Force for the Adolescent Perpetrator Network.

Kee MacFarlane, M.S.W., is Director of the Education and Training Department at Children's Institute International in Los Angeles. She has been an Associate Clinical Professor in the Department of Child Psychiatry at the University of Southern California School of Medicine, where she taught courses on the evaluation and treatment of child abuse. Prior to moving to California, she spent six years as the Child Sexual Abuse Specialist for the National Center on Child Abuse and Neglect in Washington, D.C., where she also served as the first director of the US office on Domestic Violence.

Kee has served as a consultant and advisor board member to the numerous national organizations including: the American Professional Society on the Abuse of Children, the National District Attorney's Association Center for the Prosecution of Child Abuse, the U.S. Army, Navy, and Air Force, the F.B.I. Police Training Academy, the Denver Research Institute, the Barbara Sinatra Children's Center, and the national board of Parents United, Inc. She is on the editorial and review boards of two professional journals.

She has received several Congressional commendations as well as state and national awards for her contributions to the field of child abuse. In 1994, Kee received the award for Outstanding Professional from the American Professional Society on the Abuse of Children. She was appointed to the Los Angeles Superior Court Expert Panel, and received Governor's appointments to the California Commission on the Enforcement of Child Abuse Laws and the Honorable Order of Kentucky Colonels. She received her Master's Degree in Social Work from the University of Maryland, and has worked in the field of child abuse for more than 20 years. Her clinical work has focused on the evaluation and treatment of young children. She has delivered more than 1,000 presentations and has co-authored four books and more than 50 journal articles and chapters on the subjects of child abuse and molestation. Her books include: Child Sexual Abuse: Selected Readings (1980), Sexual Abuse of Young Children (MacFarlane et al., 1986, Guilford Press), Steps to Healthy Touching (MacFarlane & Cunningham, 1988, Kidsrights), and When Children Molest Children (Cunningham & MacFarlane, 1991, Safer Society Press).

Preface to the First Edition

This book is full of simple therapeutic activities designed to engage children aged 4 to 12 in their own treatment. It is designed to be practical for therapists and fun for children. What isn't fun is its subject matter.

To put it in terms that are stark and easily understandable, this book is for and about sex offenders. No, not the ones in trenchcoats who hang out in playgrounds. This book is for the ones who go to playgrounds to play ball and swing on the swings. It is about the young ones, the not-yet-adolescents, the kids whom none of us wants to see labeled with pejorative terms like "offender" or "perpetrator." And yet, these are children whose behavior can be defined by these terms.

The fact is, we don't yet know what to call them, how to explain them, or what to do with them. Most are too young for criminal justice solutions, too high risk for foster homes with other kids, and too unsettling to ignore. They make all of us uncomfortable—so uncomfortable we've had to deny their existence and/or minimize their behavior until now. We've called their behavior "exploration" or "curiosity" until they were old enough for us to comfortably call it what it is: sexual abuse of other children.

These are not children out to explore the wonders of the human body. They aren't even old enough to engage in legally consensual sexual relations, yet their sexual behavior can involve coercion, force, intimidation, and secrecy. Their victims, whose participation is usually obtained through threats or trickery, are younger, smaller, weaker, or in some way disadvantaged in relation to themselves. Like their adult counterparts, their behaviors include everything from voyeurism to rape: acts of violence, seduction, rage, confusion, sexual gratification, and the abuse of power.

Who are these kids and why do they do the things they do? No one has good answers to those questions yet. What we know is that seeing some of them led us to develop this book. There was Teddy—a freckled Tom Sawyer look-alike, except that Teddy ruptured his younger brother's rectum with a stick. And 8-year-old Willy, who tied a little neighbor girl to a bench in a shed and left tape on her mouth and bruises between her legs. They didn't find her for nearly two days, and Willy didn't tell them where to look. Then there was a bright and charming 10-year-old who used his parents' reward system to bribe his sisters into performing oral sex—and then said he'd kill their kitten if they told his secret.

And what of the girls we've seen? There was 11-year-old Myra who bullied and molested children in her mother's daycare center. Susan had fantasies about sex with adult women and forced her young cousins to serve as substitutes. Among the toughest (and most adorable) of the young abusers we've seen were previously molested 6-year-old twins who nearly bit off the penis of their 18-month-old brother.

These cases are extreme examples of a problem we must force ourselves to examine. The extreme cases are easier for us to see and act upon but, too often, they are the end result of less dramatic but no less harmful forms of sexual acting out. We must identify these children sooner when there is more hope for change and less stigma and shame attached to what they've done. Who are they? So far, relatively few have come to our attention. We still may know little about what makes them tick, but we're beginning to learn what they look like.

They are every age from 5 to 12 or 13. They are male and female; they are black and white and brown. They live in the inner city, the best suburbs, and every place in between. Their parents may be insensitive, immature, abusive, or absent—or they may look like Ozzie and Harriet, the Huxtables, or the people next door. Some of these children are withdrawn and uncommunicative, others are outgoing, charming, and eager to please. Many have been sexually abused themselves, but some have not. Most reveal some history of physical, sexual, or emotional abuse, while others have been exposed to neglect or inappropriate behavior by adults or older siblings. Some have been raised in sexually overstimulating environments, some in homes where rigid sexual boundaries, strong religiosity, or unspoken family prohibitions left little room for the expression of conflicted thoughts or feelings.

Of all the potential contributing factors in the development of a child who molests other children, we continue to return to the presence of some form of maltreatment or traumatic influence during the early years of these children's lives. It may not have been overtly sexual (or even overt) but its imprint remains nonetheless. Whether it's a definitional issue or simply our own discomfort with the prospect of labeling these children within existing categories intended for adults, we call them "abuse-reactive" because it fits our sense of who they are.

Most of us work with or within social service systems that have yet to understand or address this population of 4- to 12- year-olds who molest other children. Usually young sexual abusers slide into the cracks between the child protection and juvenile justice systems, often leaving the families of their victims enraged and their own parents in confusion, denial, or despair. If we are to interrupt the cycle of abuse that usually begins before we ever see these children, we must take care not to participate in the collective paralysis and minimization that frequently accompany their detection. Effective intervention in these cases usually involves as much advocacy and interaction with other agencies and professional disciplines as it does actual clinical work.

In our experience, the degree of child and family resistance to long-term therapy argues for court-mandated participation in treatment. Accomplishing this may be no simple matter, depending on the laws, policies, and resources of your community. When younger children in the home have been victimized or are at continuing risk, it is often necessary to find alternative living arrangements for the perpetrator child, arrangements that may not currently exist for children in this age group. Unlike society's usual unequivocal reaction to adult sex offenders, such actions are far from automatic in most communities. It often takes creative intervention and advocacy with Child Protective Services, the police, the Dependency or Juvenile courts, and the families themselves.

In cases where children are very young and families are not very cooperative, it may require a Dependency Court petition regarding neglect, failure to supervise, or other category addressing parental responsibility in order to compel parents to cooperate with recommended living arrangements and treatment plans. Aside from requiring parents or caretakers to *bring* children to therapy, a court order provides a means of eliciting their participation, an aspect of treatment we emphasize throughout this text.

Sexual victimization and perpetration by children are *family* problems and should be regarded as such by treatment providers. Exploring the family's feelings about the child client, their ability to receive help, their need to minimize, and their use of blame or guilt as defense mechanisms should be an ongoing process throughout treatment. As with most therapeutic interventions, if a child begins to grow healthier within an environment that remains static and dysfunctional, the ultimate benefit is likely to be minimal.

When Children Molest Children does not label, categorize, or predict the extent of future pathology in children with sexual behavior problems. Like most treatment manuals, it provides no promise of cures, estimates of prevention, or outcome data on the ultimate effectiveness of the techniques and activities it contains. Therapists who are uncomfortable with a structured activity format may find that its contents seem foreign and incomplete. For these colleagues, we stress two points: first, the manual is not intended to represent an all-inclusive approach to treatment or to replace individual or family therapy (although many of the activities can be used in an individual therapeutic setting, most have been designed for a group therapy format); and second, it has been our continuing experience and firm opinion that structure helps impulsive children to bind their anxiety in appropriate and predictable ways, freeing them (and their therapists) to deal with difficult underlying issues. As with all clinical materials, the concepts, language, and activities in this manual may have to be modified to fit a particular child's developmental needs.

We have learned much in the four years it has taken to write this manual. It was not a fun process for two people with other jobs and obligations that always seemed to take precedence over this task. It has sorely tested our friendship, our patience, and our tolerance for living with piles of draft chapters constantly underfoot. We did it so that others like us wouldn't feel as lost as we did when we began to treat these children. We did it to provide a place to start, a foundation for others to build upon, a challenge for those who are willing to take on these kids while they're still young enough to benefit from our intervention.

Now we can clean out our closets and boxes and piles of stuff. Now we can pass on these materials like a baton in a relay race, hoping that they will be taken for what they are—a first step in a much longer quest to discover how to put abuse-reactive children on a different path, a path to healthy development.

—Kee MacFarlane, M.S.W.

Dedication

To the clinicians and families with whom we have worked who are helping to build the fences which will help to safeguard our youth:

An Ambulance Down in the Valley

'Twas a a dangerous cliff as they freely confessed,
Though to walk near its edge was so pleasant,
But over its edge had slipped a Duke,
And it had fooled many a peasant.

The people said something would have to be done,
But their projects did not at all tally.
Some said, "Put a fence around the edge of the cliff,"
Others, "An ambulance down in the valley."

The lament of the crows was profound and loud,
As their hearts overflowed with pity;
But the ambulance carried the cry of the day,
As it spread to the neighboring cities.
So a collection was made to accumulate aid,
And dwellers in highway and alley,
Gave dollars and cents not to furnish a fence,
But an ambulance down in the valley.

"For the cliff is all right if you're careful," they said,
"And if folks ever slip and are falling;
It's not the slipping and falling that hurts them so much,
As the shock down below when they're stopping."

And so for the years as these mishaps occurred,
Quick forth would the rescuers sally,
To pick up the victims who fell from the cliff ,
With the ambulance down in the valley.

Said one in his plea, "It's a marvel to me
That you'd give so much greater attention,
To repairing results than to curing the cause;
Why, you'd much better aim at prevention.
For the mischief, of course, should be stopped at its
source;
Come friends and neighbors, let us rally!
It makes far better sense to rely on a fence,
Than an ambulance down in the valley."

"He's wrong in his head," the majority said.
"He would end all our earnest endeavors.
He's the kind that would shirk his responsible work,
But we will support it forever.
Aren't we picking up all just as fast as they fall,
And giving them care liberally?
Why, a superfluous fence is of no consequence,
If the ambulance works in the valley."

Now this story seems queer as I've given it here,
But things oft occur which are stranger.
More humane, we assert, to repair the hurt,
Than the plan of removing the danger.
The best possible course would saferguard the
source,
And attend to things rationally.
Yes, build up the fence and let us dispense,
With the ambulance down in the valley.

— anonymous

Use of These Materials

Since the initial publication of When Children Molest Children in 1991, we have received feedback from many professionals who have used it. They have pointed out that many of the activities and resources designed for use with children who molest also apply to children who exhibit a variety of acting out behaviors. Indeed, most of the skill-building categories, e.g. anger management, self-esteem, problem-solving, empathy development, etc., are basic elements in treatment planning for a wide range of childhood disorders especially those associated with emotional deprivation, early traumatic experiences and attachment disorders. Our own continuing use of these materials with different populations of children also has taught us how easily the activities can be adapted for use in addressing other clinical issues with young children.

We have responded to this feedback by expanding and revising this manual to encompass other types of problematic childhood behaviors, particularly those associated with a lack of impulse control. These include: excessive physical aggression or violence toward other children or adults, fire setting, rage/acts of hatred toward members of the opposite sex or others who are "different" in some way, and cruelty or torture involving animals. Due to time constraints, we could not rewrite the existing activities to address each of these specific conduct problems; however, we have added a few new activities in this volume. At the beginning of each section we've added new suggestions on ways to expand or adapt the material for use with other populations of children aged 4 to 12. We also have expanded the theoretical section (to reflect our own expanded thinking on the subject), and we've included some additional hands-on material for use with children who have sexual behavior problems as well as other issues.

We hope that this revised and expanded edition will be helpful to a broader range of professionals who work with troubled children, such as teachers, school counselors and child care workers. We encourage all who use these materials to be creative in their application; we hope you will use our ideas to create new applications which will touch these children in ways that may truly make a difference.

Carolyn Cunningham
Kee MacFarlane

Contents

Introduction and Theory

Background and Knowledge Base

Social workers, therapists, and researchers have learned much in the past two decades about the sexual abuse of children. Foremost in our education has been the realization that it is a more pervasive and complex problem than anyone realized. The myths and preconceptions that preceded professional interest in this subject (along with those that evolved from our early attempts to generalize findings from limited data) are being replaced with new discoveries and theories which continue to expand.

Initial intervention efforts were aimed at the victims of father-daughter incest, most of whom were thought to be adolescents. Even with the infusion of federal funding and the strengthening of state reporting laws in the 1970s, treatment programs were still primarily focused on incestuous families and, occasionally, on incarcerated adult offenders. The population of sexual abusers was regarded as composed almost exclusively of males, and male children were rarely reported or thought of as victims. The long- and short-term effects of sexual abuse were a matter of debate, while sibling incest and abuse of children by adolescents were acknowledged but rarely addressed in a specific or uniform way.

Expanded clinical experience and the targeted research efforts of the 1980s have changed the picture considerably and broadened our view of the problem. Sometimes it seems that the more we learn, the less we can be certain of—or at least, the more complicated the puzzle becomes. Child victims are being identified at younger and younger ages, and the more we learn about the nature of their abuse, the more difficult it is to contemplate or understand. Some professionals believe that boys may be victimized as frequently as girls (Porter, 1986), though most agree that boys are still at far greater risk of not being *identified* as victims. Treatment programs for child victims and their families have taught us a great deal about the effects of sexual abuse (Conte & Berliner, 1988; Wyatt & Powell, 1988), as have research and treatment of adult survivors, both male and female (Briere, 1989; Briere & Runtz, 1988; Lew, 1990).

Despite these gains, we still have much to learn about the differential effects of sexual victimization. We know that its impact varies greatly depending on such factors as the nature and duration of the abuse, the age of the child at onset and at disclosure, the degree of violence or coercion, the relationship between the child and the abuser (including the child's needs for affection, approval, etc., that are being met and manipulated by the abuser), and the actions and reactions that follow discovery. We do not know how these various factors relate to one another or how to assess their potential impact in relation to a particular child. We do not know all the reasons why some victims seem to recover or respond better to treatment than others, or why some who were less "severely" abused may suffer more than others who appear to have been more traumatized over longer periods of time. We know that many adult perpetrators were sexually abused as children (Groth, 1979). However, given the high prevalence of abuse indicated by retrospective research (Peters, Wyatt, & Finkelhor, 1986; Russell, 1984), we can only assume that most victims do not become perpetrators. We don't have the answers yet to why some child victims grow up and become abusive while others do not. We also don't know why some offenders appear to have no sexual abuse or maltreatment of any kind in their backgrounds. Our knowledge about those who are sexually attracted to and take advantage of children who are younger, weaker, smaller, or more naive has increased enormously in the past 20 years, but it is a field of study and practice that is still young.

Program Development

Therapists working in treatment programs designed for child molesters and rapists soon discovered that many adult offenders began their sexually abusive behavior when they were adolescents (Longo & Groth, 1983). Longo and McFadin (1981) reported that the majority of the adjudicated sex offenders they studied began their deviant sexual behavior as early as age 7. It also became apparent that the addictive, compulsive quality of the behavior associated with child molestation usually occurs for years prior to its identification (Abel, Becker, Cunningham-Rathner, Rouleau, Kaplan, & Reich, 1984). In addition, increasing numbers of victims began to report abusive situations involving perpetrators who were not yet adults. Thus, even as the number of treatment programs for both confined and nonincarcerated adult offenders began to expand, specialized adolescent programs also began to develop.

Many of the same dynamics observed in adult offenders also occur with adolescent offenders. However, adolescents need treatment approaches and therapeutic techniques that apply to their developmental levels. In addition, clinicians recognized the need for treatment models involving the adolescent's family or support system in the process of treatment. In response to these needs, many innovative adolescent sex-offender treatment programs have been established throughout the country during the last decade. Because so little is currently published on the specific subject of *preadolescent* offenders, we encourage readers to familiarize themselves with the many excellent publications describing treatment programs and issues for the adolescent counterparts of the children who are the subject of this manual.[1]

In 1984, several young children who had been placed in foster care due to physical abuse or neglect were brought to the Child Sexual Abuse Diagnostic Center at Children's Institute International in Los Angeles. Although to our knowledge they had not been sexually abused prior to placement, they were subsequently molested by other children placed in the same homes. Some of the victims were as young as 4 years old. Some of the perpetrators were as young as 6 and 7. Some of the abusive acts were as serious as those committed by adolescents. The child victims were removed from the homes where they had been victimized, and treatment was initiated. However, an exhaustive search for appropriate treatment resources for the young *perpetrators* of this abuse revealed that no such programs existed in the Los Angeles area (or anywhere that we could locate). The few sex-offender treatment programs for adolescents were not available for children so young, and the juvenile courts and juvenile justice facilities were designed for children over the age of 12.

Therefore, early in 1985 the first specialized program for young "child perpetrators" of sexual abuse was founded at Children's Institute under the direction of Kee MacFarlane, with initial funding from the California Youth Authority. The program, aimed at children ages 4 through 12, was

---

[1]For descriptions of programs and/or treatment issues with adolescent sex offenders, see Bera, 1990; Briere & Runtz, 1988; Heinz, Gargaro, & Kelly, 1987; Isaac & Lane, 1990; Kahn, 1990; Knopp, 1982, 1985; Ryan & Lane, 1991; National Adolescent Perpetrator Network (NAPN), 1988; Salter, 1988; Steen & Monnette, 1989; and Stickrod, Hamer, & Janes, 1984.

called SPARK (Support Program for Abuse-Reactive Kids). The term "abuse-reactive" was coined to describe children who have been abused *in some way* and are reacting to their early trauma in abusive, aggressive, and inappropriately sexual ways.[2]

Since the inception of the SPARK program, other similar programs aimed at this population were developed in Glendale and Lancaster, California, by Carolyn Cunningham, and by other practitioners in Denver, Sacramento, San Diego, and elsewhere.[3] Although this area of study and treatment is still new, the progress so far and recognition of the need for more resources and early intervention is most encouraging.

Who and Why: Theoretical Considerations

As mentioned in the Preface to the First Edition, we are beginning to get a clearer picture of these children in terms of their demographics and family backgrounds. Research findings from the SPARK program and other similar groups have shed some light on the small population of abuse-reactive children that has been identified, studied, and treated so far (Johnson, 1988; Johnson & Berry, 1989; Green, 1985). But recognizing what these children look like or even knowing what they have experienced in the past is a far cry from understanding why they feel and behave the way they do. Following are some of the theoretical formulations we have used in the development of three separate treatment programs and of the activities and materials we have adapted for this volume. As will be apparent, we have combined and borrowed theories from various aspects of the fields of child maltreatment and sexual assault. Until such time as more is known, we use it as a framework for our understanding of these children.

Theories of Cause and Effect: A Brief Review

Post Traumatic Stress Disorder (PTSD)[4]

Although post traumatic stress reactions have been documented and observed in adults for many years, the recognition of PTSD in children is a relatively new phenomenon. In their landmark volume *Post Traumatic Stress Disorder in Children* (1985), Eth and Pynoos define the disorder in terms of the following components:

1. Existence of a recognizable stressor that would evoke significant symptoms in children.

---

[2]The term "abuse-reactive" is not intended to imply a direct cause-and-effect relationship between victimization and perpetration or to de-emphasize accountability. It *is* an attempt to find a linguistic middle-ground in the dilemma of what to call these children. Some colleagues want to avoid unnecessary labeling or stigmatizing of children so young and suggest calling them "children with sexual behavior problems." Other colleagues are concerned that the term "abuse-reactive children" may tend to minimize or excuse the abusiveness of the child perpetrator's behavior. The choice of terminology may reflect the differing perspectives of mental health and criminal justice professionals. Our approach is primarily developmental, and our terminology reflects this perspective. For us, the use of the term "abuse-reactive" has never served to lessen or minimize our awareness of the considerable harm done to their child victims, whom we also treat.

[3]For information concerning specialized treatment programs and providers, contact Gail Ryan, Facilitator, The Perpetration Prevention Project, c/o the C. Henry Kempe National Center for the Prevention of Child Abuse and Neglect, 1205 Oneida St., Denver, CO 80220 / phone: 303-321-3963.

[4]See the *Diagnostic and Statistical Manual of Mental Disorders*, Fourth Edition (American Psychiatric Association, 1994), pp. 424-429.

These include: physical victimization, natural disasters, and observing violence, such as homicide, suicide, and war.

2. Re-experiencing the trauma in at least one of the following ways: a) recurrent and intrusive recollections, b) recurrent dreams or nightmares, and c) suddenly re-experiencing the traumatic event because of an association with an environmental stimulus.

3. Numbing of responsiveness or reduced involvement with the external world.

4. Presence of at least two of the following symptoms not present before the trauma: hyper-alertness, sleep disturbance, guilt about surviving, trouble concentrating, and avoidance of activities that arouse recollections of the trauma.

When theoretical explanations involving PTSD are applied to child perpetrators, they obviously apply to children who, themselves, were traumatized at very young ages. Their sexually aggressive behavior is viewed as a trauma response to their own previous abuse (Green, 1985). Breer (1987) applied this conceptual model to adolescent sex offenders when he described their behavior as an attempt to recreate their own traumatic molestation or abuse in ways that allow them to develop mastery and control over their feelings.

Several authors have theorized about the reason a smaller percentage of adult females become sexually abusive than do their male counterparts, despite the fact that they appear to be molested in higher numbers (Finkelhor & Russell, 1984; Russell, 1984). Many have noted that males tend to cope with abuse by externalizing their behavior, while females usually cope through internalization (MacFarlane, Cockriel, & Dugan, 1990; Porter, 1986; Summit, 1983). In other words, boys appear to be more likely to turn their pain into rage and project it outward onto others, while girls typically convert pain into depression and turn it inward on themselves.

The tendency of some children to identify with those who abused them also contributes to this theoretical framework. Projective identification with the aggressor is a maladaptive defense mechanism used in situations where anxiety is provoked by fears of attack or abandonment. This defense permits the child's feelings of helplessness and annihilation (experienced during the original abuse) to be replaced by feelings of power and omnipotence (Green, 1985). Breer (1987) describes identification with the aggressor as a form of relief from having to identify as a victim (clearly a more difficult identity issue for males than for females in our society). The compulsive, repetitive quality of the sexually assaultive behavior engaged in by some abused children suggests that identification with an aggressor also is used to relieve tension, counter painful affect, and renew a pathological form of self-esteem (van der Kolk, 1987).

Failure to master a childhood trauma can create a need to repeat or re-enact the trauma throughout developmental life stages. For abuse-reactive children, the unresolved emotional pain from their own victimization may vary widely. For some children, this pain may be so intense that aggressive acting out becomes the compulsive behavior used to rid themselves of their feelings of shame and helplessness, or to compensate for feelings of inadequacy. This may take the form of sexual acting out, fire setting, torturing animals or physical aggression. Of course, their abusiveness may be experienced as shameful as well, but too often it is not enough of a deterrent to inhibit their compelling need to protect themselves from the residue of vulnerability left by their victimization. Once the initial reaction to trauma becomes repetitive, it not only may become more difficult to extinguish, but the sexual stimulation itself becomes a powerful reinforcer, and it may progress to compulsivity.

Addiction Model

The addiction model traces its roots to learning theory. There is no doubt that sexual orgasm is a powerful reinforcer of behavior. According to Breer (1987), reinforcement can occur as a result of actual behavior (e.g., masturbation or sexual touching with another child) or in response to a fantasy about molesting behavior. In addition, Breer hypothesizes, adolescent sex offenders seem to work themselves up to acts of molestation in reality by creating them first in fantasy.

Carnes (1983) has applied the addiction model directly to disorders of sexuality. In his book *Out of the Shadows*, he lists the following signs of sexual addiction:

1. Preoccupation with sex or sexual thoughts

2. Ritualization

3. Sexual compulsivity

4. Secretivism

5. Pain relieving quality

6. Sex activity devoid of a caring relationship

7. Despair and shame

8. Progressive addictions

9. Massive denial

The addictive behavior model has its place in the dynamics of child sexual offending. Sexual preoccupation is one of the common reasons these children come to our attention in the first place; family secretivism and massive denial keep too many children from getting the help they need. While concepts of addiction usually are associated with adults as well as with items or substances outside our behavior, they may also apply to the behavior of children. It is our hope that by identifying and treating children in the early stages of repetitive sexual acting-out, we may deter the likelihood and/or minimize the development of compulsive/addictive sexual behavior before it becomes intractable.

While characterizing sexually abusive behavior as "addictive" (a term associated with the disease model originally related to the treatment of alcoholism) versus "compulsive" (a term derived from psychoanalytic theory) is currently controversial, we use some language and elements of both schools of thought. In our view, neither model provides a sufficient framework for understanding the sexually inappropriate behavior of young children. While we believe that the behavior of abuse-reactive children includes psychological, physiological, behavioral, and environmental components, no one has had enough experience with this population to know how these factors influence sexually abusive behavior. Therefore, our use of the terms "addictive" and "compulsive" interchangeably reflects our reluctance to embrace any single approach. Finally, regardless of the connotations these terms may have in other contexts, our choice of terminology is not intended as a statement regarding the degree to which children are responsible for their behavior.

Sexual Abuse Cycle Theory

Sandy Lane, treatment coordinator of Redirecting Sexual Aggression,[5] has described youthful offenders as each having a unique "sexual abuse cycle." The cycle includes antecedent thoughts, feelings, and behaviors culminating in sexually abusive acts as a response to situations the child perceives as threatening (Lane, 1991). It consists of: 1) an event that is—or is perceived as—threatening in some way; 2) an emotional response representing an intolerable set of feelings for that youth; and 3) an attempt to compensate for the initial reaction with substitute feelings of rage and revenge, allowing the youth to feel in control again. The youth then makes a conscious or unconscious decision to increase his/her sense of being in control through actions that include molestation or rape. Upon completing the assault, the young offender rationalizes the reasons for the offense.[6]

This theory, in part, also describes the younger child-offender or abuse-reactive child perpetrator. In our work with over 100 of these children we have found that they generally suffer from low self-esteem and feelings of inadequacy; they struggle against intolerable feelings of vulnerability and victimization; and they attempt to compensate in front of others by exhibiting sexual or physically aggressive behavior. It should be noted that aspects of this theoretical model involving the role of sexual fantasy may or may not prove to be applicable, since the sexual fantasy development of very young children (whether or not they have been abused) is still unclear.

Theoretical Summary

From our review of the literature on adolescent and adult sexual offenders and from our practical experience with this specialized population, it seemed relevant to incorporate aspects of all three of these theories, as well as Finkelhor and Browne's (1986) "Four Traumagenic Dynamics" of child sexual abuse (discussed in Chapter Eight-B of this volume) and Finkelhor's (1984) "Four Preconditions of Abuse" (explained and applied in Chapter Nine). Our efforts to translate theory into practical application are summarized as follows:

1. The *Trauma Model* is used throughout the manual to address the potential history of victimization in both the child and in his/her family. This perspective influences Chapter Two (assessment), Chapter Six (anger management), and Chapter Eight-B (victimization)—the latter particularly emphasizing PTSD and desensitization.

2. *Addiction Theory* is reflected throughout the text in exercises focusing on denial, taking responsibility for one's actions, making amends, scapegoating, and ritualization/compulsivity (see Chapters Eight-B, Nine, and Ten).

3. *The Sexual Abuse Cycle* contributes to exercises that deal with self-esteem (Chapter Five); the development of social skills, empathy, and morals (Chapters Six, Seven, and Ten); and anger, authority, and healthy sexuality (Chapters Six, Seven, Ten, and Eleven).

Obviously, theories of causation contribute to the theoretical basis of treatment, although the developmental capabilities of the client and the applicability of existing resources also play a role.

---

[5]RSA, Inc., located in Denver, Colorado, is a community-based program to assess and treat adult, adolescent, and preadolescent sex offenders.

[6]Isaac & Lane's (1990) adaptation for preadolescents of the original "assault cycle" is shown in Chapter 9.

Following is a brief summary of some of the treatment theory that underlies the methods reflected in this manual.

Theoretical Basis of Treatment

During the past five years, we have observed and experimented with various treatment modalities in an effort to determine which approaches appear to be most effective in engaging this population of children in treatment. Because abuse-reactive children are often initially impulsive, angry, and highly anxious, traditional therapeutic methods are usually difficult to apply. For example, many of these children are too young, too anxiety-ridden, or too unused to verbalizing their feelings to tolerate traditional "talking therapies," particularly in early stages of treatment. We have learned the hard way that premature confrontation or directly verbalizing their victimization, perpetration, or inner fear and shame too soon can actually intensify children's feelings of being out of control and increase their acting-out behavior. Timing is a crucial element to consider when approaching these issues directly.

Although many of these children have been victimized, including them in a victims' treatment group can be problematic because there may be marked differences in the ways they have integrated their experiences as victims. For example, a goal for most sexually *abusive* children is to *reduce* their anger and aggression toward others. In contrast, for many molestation *victims* who have *not* expressed feelings or acted out sexually, the task is to *encourage* the appropriate expression of anger. Similarly, while many abuse-reactive children have the same issues as adolescent offenders, their developmental and cognitive levels differ, as do their attention spans and tolerance for confrontation. Therefore, while treatment content may be parallel, methods must be geared to their level—with particular respect for children with strong defenses and fragile egos.

From the perspective of traditional psychotherapy the question arises, "Over time, will the transference between client and therapist heal most of these children?" It is our belief that, while the value of a trusting and consistent relationship is extremely important to abuse-reactive children, it is not enough—by itself—to stop the abuse cycle once it has begun. In fact, there is some disincentive in the process because, with young children, the more they like and identify with the therapist, the more difficult it may be for them to address perpetration issues for fear of disapproval or rejection. Another major treatment dilemma is the question of how to approach the emotionally charged issues of victimization and perpetration in ways that allow young children to focus on them without totally losing control.

Cognitive-Behavioral Theory/Approach

The techniques and goals of cognitive-behavioral therapy are directed toward remediating children's deficiencies and correcting their distortions in cognitive processing of events (Kendall, 1991). In relation to this population, Cognitive-Behavioral therapy focuses upon the perceptions and thoughts of aggressive children as they counter perceived threats and frustrations.

Cognitive-Behavioral methods of treatment, conducted in a small group setting, appear to be an effective approach to working with aggressive children. An array of structured, topic-based exercises that address cognitive-behavioral issues are included throughout the book. We have found that progressing from general or neutral to specific subject matter (i.e., approaching topics through the "back door") is the least threatening and most successful way to ease into the material.

Using stories or analogies that initially address the young offenders' *issues*, rather than what they have *done*, works better than focusing too soon or too directly on their acting-out behavior (an approach that, we discovered, only raises anxiety and causes chaos in the therapy session). Later on, therapy can become more direct, still keeping in mind the child's developmental capabilities.

Cognitive-Behavioral approaches with abusing children include the following:

Social Problem Solving. An example of a social problem solving program is an approach call Interpersonal Cognitive Problem Solving (ICPS). This technique, developed by Spivak, Platt, and Shure (1976), and described by Hoghughi (1988), also highlights cognitive elements of behavior. This technique emphasizes that children should learn and practice the following kinds of thinking: 1) *causal thinking* about events and their consequences; 2) *consequential thinking* of the costs and benefits of various actions; 3) *means-end thinking* to master the skills to achieve goals; 4) *perspective taking* to recognize the different views and problems of different people; and 5) *alternative thinking* to recognize the various ways of dealing with the same problem.

The ICPS technique is used in various ways throughout this manual. Helping abuse-reactive children to identify and understand the causes and consequences of their behavior and its effects on others and themselves is a theme of many of the activities, particularly those focused on morality development and empathy building.

Social Skills Training. Emotional loneliness increases the probability that a person will engage in aggression toward others. Aggression resulting from loneliness has been observed in children (Marshall, Hudson, & Hodkinson, 1993.)

Seidman, Marshall, Hudson and Robertson (1994) in a recent study have observed that emotional loneliness is a crucial common factor among incest perpetrators. It is important not to assume that group therapy itself will teach social skills. Social skills training should be a specific component within the therapy process.

Many abuse-reactive children have difficulty with basic social interactions ranging from the inability to initiate or carry on conversations to highly inappropriate social skills. Research on social functioning suggests that, while socioeconomic and personality variables are important, social know-how is a significant factor in gaining social success. As the term implies, "social skills" are "learned patterns of successfully manipulating the environment to the person's greatest benefit without negative consequences for others" (Hoghughi, 1988, p. 144).

The difference between social skills training and the acquisition of other skills lies in a greater emphasis on social experiences, modeling, and feedback in social settings. According to Hoghughi, the basic components of social skills training include "instruction and discussion, modeling, practice and role-play, feedback, social reinforcement, and the adoption of appropriate techniques for generalizing the learned skills to a wider social setting" (p. 144).

This approach is used in a variety of ways with different subjects throughout this volume. It relies heavily on the role of discussion with and among the children in terms of identifying their skill deficits, defining alternatives, practicing new behaviors, and examining consequences. Simplistic as this approach may seem at times, improvement can be seen, even by child clients, when the therapist provides the opportunity for repeating the same stimulus-response sequences with appropriate rewards in the group setting and followup at home. The success of this approach, like that of most activities contained in this manual, depends on practice and repetition. The younger or more dysfunctional the child, the more important it is to return to specific skills for practice.

Self-instruction and Stress Inoculation. Self-instruction techniques employed in both this volume and our 12 Step treatment manual *Steps to Healthy Touching* (MacFarlane & Cunningham, 1988) emphasize internal "self-talking" skills as a way of engaging children in a process of cognitive restructuring. "Self-talk" involves teaching children, through the examples given in the exercises, to develop their own ongoing self-instruction programs that can be adapted to specific situations as they arise. One goal is to train them to train themselves to think and respond to stimuli in particular ways. Self-instruction, including the ability to diagnose and self-reward your own progress, is especially helpful for children who receive little support from the adults in their lives.[7]

Self-instruction training with children emphasizes the development of personal skills in four major areas (Meichenbaum & Asarnov, 1979, cited in Hoghughi, 1988). Self-instruction exercises are interspersed throughout this manual and employ the following skills:

1. Problem-identification and self-interrogation skills ("What is the problem? What should I do?").

2. Attention-focusing and responding skills ("Pay attention. What are the alternatives/consequences for me and the others?").

3. Self-reinforcement skills ("Good, I'm doing well. I just need to keep at it.").

4. Self-correction and coping options ("I didn't do so well that time. I'd better stop doing *this* and try *that* next time.").

Exhibiting thoughtful and appropriate behavior involves more than just the development of applicable skills—it also includes the ability to respond appropriately under stress or to a stressful stimulus. This means that in the course of treatment, children need help with and practice at dealing with stress. The kinds of coping skills that will assist them include: preparing for provocation by anticipating difficult situations; confronting and coping with the difficulty through awareness and control of physical responses to stress; and reflecting on the positive or negative consequences of various behavioral choices. This type of "stress-inoculation training" (Hoghughi, 1988, pp. 164, 167-168) provides young children with the frame of reference and self-control they usually need in order to apply the more concrete behavioral and social skills they are learning simultaneously.

Psychodynamic

As discussed in the beginning of this section, therapy with aggressive and impulsive children should be "systemically eclectic." That is, while there may be no single method that works best, a structured and deliberate approach is still very much needed. It is possible to view abuse-reactive children psychodynamically, yet still employ cognitive-behavioral techniques. The crucial point is to know why you are doing what you are doing, rather than initiating techniques without understanding the theory behind them.

Techniques used in psychodynamic therapy are directed toward discovering repressed conflicts and bringing them into the client's conscious awareness (Thompson & Rudolph, 1982). The

---

[7]See Hoghughi (1988), pp. 165-167 for more on self-talk techniques.

primary goal of psychodynamic therapy is to work with unconscious material and bring it to conscious awareness.

With adult clients, therapists use psychodynamic techniques that include catharsis, free association, interpretation, and dream interpretation. These techniques are often too sophisticated for children because of children's limited cognitive development. Play therapy is the primary technique used in psychodynamic therapy with children for two reasons: 1) because children's limited cognitive development limits their ability to verbalize their thoughts and feelings, and 2) because play is their natural mode of expression and communication. Storytelling, metaphors, bibliotherapy, sandtray work, and art and dollhouses are among the media utilized in play therapy.

According to Murdock (1991, p. 102), the goals of play therapy for abusive or impulsive children include:

1. To assimilate what goes on around the child into his/her present scheme of knowledge.

2. To master both him/herself and the environment.

3. To transcend situations.

4. To increase relatedness.

5. To express feelings.

6. To master threats to self-esteem and anxiety created by unconscious conflicts.

The use of bibliotherapy, art, metaphors, and sandtray are discussed throughout *When Children Abuse*. An important step in the treatment of these children is assisting them to make conscious their unconscious conflicts. Cognitive-behavioral techniques can then be incorporated into treatment with an increased chance of success.

Attachment Theory

Another important theoretical model applicable to children who abuse other children is Attachment Theory. A high percentage of children who have sexual behavior problems have disruptions in their attachment to a significant caregiver. This disruption in early life often leads to emotional loneliness and an inability to develop appropriate relationships with peers.

Attachment has been defined as a "lasting psychological connectedness between human beings" (Bowlby, 1969). Attachment, according to Bowlby, is the bond between child and caregiver. It is that relationship which provides the child with a secure base.

Securely attached children have positive internal working models. They see themselves as worthwhile and competent and caregivers as consistent and trustworthy. They have experienced soothing by significant caregivers during times of distress, as well as receiving empathetic responses from them. As a result, securely attached children have learned the ability to self-soothe in times of distress, have developed self-empathy and empathy toward others, and will be able to form intimate, positive relationships with others.

Children with insecure attachments develop negative working models about themselves and the world. They see themselves as worthless and powerless and caregivers as unavailable, unreliable, and rejecting (Delaney, 1991). In times of distress, these children are unable to self-soothe, so and have not developed self and other-directed empathy. They are more likely to be at risk for victimization because of their emptiness and feelings of self-loathing.

When experiencing trauma, particularly sexual victimization, an insecurely attached child is more likely than a securely attached child to compensate and self-soothe in a self-destructive manner, including sexual acting out, fire setting, torturing animals, or physically abusing other children. Traumatized, acting-out children lack the foundation of attachment and relationship skills that would serve as deterrents to aggressive behavior that harms others.

Although early childhood trauma can contribute in large measure toward later behavior problems, not all children with sexual behavior problems have been abused themselves. As Marshall, et al. (1993), write, "insecurely attached children do not grow up devoid of needs for affection and love, they simply lack the capacity to meet these needs, or they are afraid to seek it from others" (p.174). Unattached children and adolescents are emotionally lonely. They may engage in self-stimulation designed to relieve their loneliness and self-soothe their distress; however, this activity does little to meet their additional needs for intimacy and love. As a result, they may turn to younger children to meet these needs.

Attachment issues are so basic that they must be addressed during the assessment phase as well as throughout treatment.

These theoretical approaches have been used with children as young as 4 years old and as old as late teens. They are relevant to children from the time they are able to contemplate various responses to circumstances. Although we advocate and use an holistic approach to treatment of abuse-reactive children, the younger or more developmentally delayed the children are, or the more their moral development is focused on punishment/consequences rather than empathy/compassion, the more concrete and externally enforced the treatment process must be. Cognitive restructuring, especially the use of techniques that involve insight, perspective-taking, and self-instruction, appears to be most successful with children who are at least school age and have average abilities in verbal and cognitive skills. Most of the exercises in this volume can be easily "scaled up" or "scaled down" to match the cognitive and developmental abilities of the children: for younger children, simplify the language, break tasks down into the simplest possible steps, and focus on one task at a time.

John B. Murdock, in *Counseling Children: Basic Principles for Helping the Troubled and Defiant Child* (1991, p. 48), delineates treatment goals that should be used as guidelines regardless of one's theoretical orientation. They are:

1. Strengthen relationships with caregivers.

2. Improve reality-testing.

3. Reduce excessive and unrealistic self-preoccupations and increase understanding and acceptance of self.

4. Increase understanding of the feeling world.

5. Increase understanding of choices and consequences.

6. Fortify defenses that are weak and ease others that are rigid.

The treatment approaches we have identified as a basis of treatment were developed to provide the clinician with a framework for understanding and developing treatment techniques in working with children who have exhibited abusive behaviors.

Organization of This Manual

This manual was developed as a "hands-on" tool to help therapists in existing comprehensive programs treat children aged 4 to 12 who molest other children, physically abuse animals or other children, or set fires. It is not, in itself, an outline of a comprehensive treatment program. It presents structured activities in the areas of self-esteem, problem-solving, anger-management, sexuality, victimization, and perpetration. Each of these areas is crucial for young offenders to address. Because this material can evoke such anxiety for child clients, the activities presented move from general to specific. In other words, a structured activity may be presented that is not directly related to sexual acting out. During or after the activity, the therapist should draw parallels or guide the discussion to specific issues relating to sexual behavior. The reason for this approach is to avoid overstimulation or barraging young children with material they cannot handle. The goal, of course, is to eventually transfer the feelings and information gleaned from the indirect material to direct and concrete acknowledgment of specific treatment issues.

The manual also addresses the issues of intake, assessment, and evaluation by providing both guidance and written forms to assist the therapist. In addition, group management issues and techniques for leading parents' groups are discussed. The activities in the manual may need to be repeated over the course of treatment in order for children to grasp the concepts and internalize the issues presented. Therapists should feel free to change or adapt any of this material in order to fit a child's cognitive or developmental level. Although age ranges are suggested for each activity, every child is different; therefore, intellectual and emotional abilities should be taken into consideration.

Some activities use stories, books, or workbooks that could not easily be excerpted; therapists will need to acquire these books to complete these activities (marked with a 📖 symbol). Many activities have been gathered from widely disparate sources; all reprinted activities are so marked, and we encourage therapists to acquire these valuable resource books for additional relevant exercises. All activities not credited to another source have been developed in clinical practice by Carolyn Cunningham and/or Kee MacFarlane. Complete Reference and Resource listings have been included at the end of the text.

In conclusion, although the problems of children molesting children, physically abusing other children or animals, or setting fires are not new, organized efforts to treat this population represent a new and rapidly developing area of intervention. Because so little has been published to assist in these efforts to date, other treatment professionals probably feel as tentative and exploratory as we did in developing and adapting the materials that follow. The activities presented in this manual have all been field-tested in group settings where they have worked well for our purposes. However, most of them can easily be adapted for individual or family therapy settings. Many abuse-reactive children benefit from individual, family, *and* group therapy. Many need one-on-one support and attention from their own counselor; for others, their families are half the problem. We have focused this manual on group treatment because: 1) groups are so valuable to the development of interactive skills; 2) groups offer relief from the isolation and "damaged goods" syndrome that are so pervasive with abuse-reactive children; 3) groups are the mode of treatment most reliant on structured activities; and 4) group treatment provides a cost-effective option for families and agencies with limited resources.

We recommend that treatment groups meet for approximately 90 minutes, and that the structured activity be presented at the beginning of the group when the children are most focused. The ensuing discussion can be followed by free play or a less anxiety-based structured activity. We also recommend that boys and girls be treated in separate groups due to the different sexual issues that arise and their tendency to act out in front of each other (though boys also tend to act out for their peers, it is a simpler dynamic to control). Co-therapists (a male and female, if possible) can provide feedback to each other, consistency if one is absent, and role modeling to group members. The group's size should be kept to no more than eight or nine children. It is also highly recommended that a parallel parents' group be conducted at the same time that the children's group meets. The parents must be aware of the material being presented to their children so they can reinforce progress at home. Further, some parents who otherwise might not bring their children to therapy will attend regularly in order to get support for themselves.

We encourage therapists to be flexible and imaginative when using these materials in working with these children. It was the children who initially taught us what not to do, what techniques not to use if we wanted to reach them. It is they who now teach us what gets through. This area of treatment for this particular age group is too new to be able to assess the effectiveness or ultimate impact of our efforts. We still have much to learn about these children. Our education, training, and previous experience may not hold answers in this arena. For now, we must rely on the children themselves and on our own creativity to guide us.

<u>CHAPTER ONE</u>

Children's Sexual Development

When treating abuse-reactive children, professionals in the field are faced with two questions: what is normal sexual play, and when is sexual acting out between young children considered abuse.

This chapter briefly compares what is considered "normal sexual behavior" with abnormal sexual acting out during the stages of preschool, latency, and preadolescence. It provides the reader with guidelines to assess whether or not a child's sexual behavior is abusive or age-appropriate.

Stages of Sexual Development

Ages 0-5

Children at this stage have intense curiosity about the world around them and about their bodies. Masturbation normally begins in early infancy and continues through the preschool years as a self-soothing behavior. During this time children are generally not discreet and masturbate in front of others.

Ilg and Ames (1982) state that children aged 2 and 3 are intensely interested in looking at others' bodies and are extremely interested in the bathroom activity of others. At this stage there is also verbal play around the theme of elimination. Preschool children take advantage of opportunities to touch others' genitalia if permitted or allowed to. However, they take redirection quickly and respond to limit-setting about touching others' bodies. This touching is of an exploratory rather than a coercive nature. Sexual exploration games begin during this stage and reach heightened activity during latency years. Children at this stage may show their genitalia to peers—again, in a curiosity-seeking way—and respond to adult limits very quickly.

To summarize, during this stage, sexual play is part of infants' and toddlers' curiosity about the world around them as well as about their own body parts. Sexual play can be considered *abnormal* when curiosity becomes obsessive preoccupation, when exploration becomes re-enactment of specific adult sexual activity, or when children's behavior involves coercion toward others or injury to themselves.

Latency Age (6-10)

Latency-age children continue to touch and fondle their own genitals, evolving into masturbation, and they become more secretive about their self-touching. Interest in viewing others' bodies continues although it changes from curiosity-seeking to game-playing. Games such as "I'll show you mine, you show me yours" and "doctor" begin. Latency-age boys also start comparing penis size. During this time children become extremely interested in sex words and dirty jokes. At ages 9 and 10, children begin seeking information about sex and look for books and diagrams that explain their own organs and functions. "Swearing" begins during this stage. Touching others' genitalia usually takes place in a game-like atmosphere and involves stroking or rubbing.

Sexual penetration, genital kissing or oral copulation, and simulated intercourse would be considered abnormal at this age.

Preadolescence (10-12)

Masturbation continues as a sexual behavior for preadolescents. Developmentally, preadolescents are focused on establishing relationships with peers. Many preadolescents, and certainly adolescents, engage in sexual activity with peers, including kissing, fondling, and sexual penetration. While most of these experiences are heterosexual, it is common for preadolescents and adolescents to have some same-gender sexual experiences (Kinsey, Pomeroy, Martin, & Gebhard, 1953).

During this time there may be intense interest in viewing others' bodies, especially members of the opposite sex. This may take the form of looking at photographs or published material, including pornography (Sgroi, 1988). However, Sgroi concludes that it is highly unusual for preadolescents and adolescents to become involved in sexual play with younger children.

Guidelines for Assessing Sexual Behavior

What, then, denotes sexually *abusive* behavior among young children? While there is still limited research on sexually inappropriate behavior among children, a review of the available literature indicates that any sexual behavior involving coercion, threats, aggression, secrecy, or developmentally inappropriate (precocious) sex acts between younger children, or where one participant relies on an unequal power base, is considered abusive. Most of these criteria involve the abrogation of the participant's right to give or withhold *consent*.[8] But since children do not have the knowledge to give informed consent to sexual acts, additional criteria must be used to ascertain whether or not a sexual act is abusive.

In their preliminary report (National Adolescent Perpetrator Network, 1988), the Task Force on Juvenile Sexual Offending states, "Sexual interactions involving children with peers or younger children are problematic if the relationship is coercive, exploitive or aggressive or threatens the physical or psychological well-being of either participant." The report further declares that "the exploitive nature of child sexual offending is measured in terms of size and age differential; power or authority differential; lack of equality and consent; and threats, violence or aggression" (p. 42).

In her book, *Vulnerable Populations* (Vol. 1, 1988), Sgroi uses similar criteria in suggesting that answers to the following questions indicate whether a sexual activity may be considered abusive:

---

[8]The National Adolescent Perpetrator Network's Task Force on Juvenile Sexual Offending (1988) defines *consent* as: "agreement including all of the following: 1) understanding what is proposed based on age, maturity, developmental level, functioning and experience; 2) knowledge of societal standards for what is being proposed; 3) awareness of potential consequences and alternatives; 4) assumption that agreements or disagreements will be respected equally; 5) voluntary decision; and 6) mentally competent." *Compliance* is defined as "passive action without overt resistance in spite of opposing beliefs or desire," and it "may occur without consent." *Cooperation* is defined as "participation regardless of beliefs or desire, may occur without consent" (p. 8).

What are the power positions of the participants?
Is force or intimidation used?
Is ritual or sadistic abuse involved?
Was secrecy involved?
How developmentally appropriate are the sexual acts?

Berliner, Manaois, and Monastersky (1986) developed a set of diagnostic criteria for *child sexual behavior disturbance*. They view this disturbance as having three levels, the first level being the most severe and definitely considered abusive.

Level One: Coercive Sexual Behavior

Level one involves *aggressive sexual contact,* including physical force; attempted or actual intercourse; touching genitalia in a forceful way; hitting, choking, or using a weapon or threat of a weapon to obtain submission.

Also considered level-one behavior is *socially coercive sexual contact,* defined as the use of threats or social coercion where an inequality of size, age, or developmental sophistication exists, or where bribery is used.

According to Berliner et al., level-one behavior should be considered serious and abusive, and any child exhibiting it needs immediate assessment and therapeutic intervention.

Level Two: Developmentally Precocious Sexual Behavior

Level-two behavior involves attempted or completed intercourse, including vaginal, anal, and oral penetration with or without objects. The difference between the apparently similar *behaviors* of level one and level two is that in level two no *coercion* is involved.

Berliner et al. caution that "these behaviors are not always evidence of psychological disturbances, but definitely require further evaluation, because they are developmentally out of the ordinary. These evaluations should address such variables as the age of the child, family context, how/where learned, and access to sexually explicit materials" (p. 8).

Level Three: Inappropriate Sexual Behavior

Level-three behaviors include persistent masturbation (particularly in public), touching breasts/genitalia, excessive interest in sexual matters, sexualization of nonsexual situations, and sexualized content in play, art, or conversation.

Again we are cautioned that these behaviors are "not necessarily evidence of psychological disturbances unless they occur in inappropriate situations, they frequently interfere with other activities, or persist in spite of intervention" (Berliner et al., 1986, p. 9).

In their study "Normative Sexual Behavior in Children" (in press), Friedrich, Grambsch, Broughton, and Kuiper indicate that aggressive sexual acts—including oral copulation, insertion of objects in vagina/anus, touching animals in sexual ways, and masturbation with objects—were "infrequent" (not "normative") for children aged 2 through 12.

In summary, both the literature and direct experience suggest we should assess as abusive any sexual act between children that is coercive; uses aggression, bribery, or secrecy; involves a significant age or power difference; and is developmentally inappropriate.

In response to reports of sexual abuse between young children, professionals and nonprofessionals alike often dismiss this abuse as "just playing doctor" or playing sexual games. In some cases these statements are due to public and professional ignorance of the severe abuse children can inflict upon each other. More often however, this response stems from a continuing societal need to deny that this problem exists. It is our hope that professionals reading this material will gain understanding into the severity of the problem of abuse-reactive children and the need for early intervention by first realizing that the kinds of sexual behaviors addressed in this manual are *not* within the realm of normal sexual development.

PART I

PLANNING INTERVENTIONS

CHAPTER TWO

Intake and Assessment

The initial intake assessment is a vital part of treatment for the abuse-reactive child. A thorough history and astute clinical observations enable the clinician to formulate an individualized treatment plan for the client and his/her family.[9]

When conducting an initial assessment, it is important to interview the parent or guardian of the identified client, the client, and the entire family unit if possible. The intake process may take several sessions to complete. It is advisable to work slowly, respecting the fear and initial denial prevalent in abuse-reactive children and their families.

When interviewing the *parents* of abuse-reactive children, remember that they are often in a state of denial associated with feelings of fear and guilt. The therapist can help alleviate their initial anxiety by reinforcing them positively for being there and reassuring them that they are not alone. Following is a suggested list of information to gather from the parents or caretakers. Diagnostic information is best obtained via an in-person interview.[10]

Parents' Information

1. Parents' names, ages. With whom is the child currently living?

2. Status of parents' marriage.

3. Length of time married.

4. Reason for separation or divorce.

5. Custody arrangements.

6. Parents' own history of childhood molestation or physical abuse. Description of abuse.

7. History of exhibitionism, abusiveness, or sexual deviance.

8. History of alcoholism or drug abuse.

9. Previous psychotherapy received by either parent. Name and address of therapist.

10. History of mental illness in the family. Describe.

11. Religious preference.

12. Parents' reactions to child's sexual offense.

13. Parents' values about sexuality, nudity, masturbation, etc.

---

[9]For information on specific interviewing techniques, see *Sexual Abuse of Young Children* (MacFarlane & Waterman, 1986), or *Response to Child Sexual Abuse: The Clinical Interview* (videotape; MacFarlane, 1986) and its accompanying *Syllabus* (MacFarlane & Feldmeth, 1989).

[10]As it becomes available, therapists may want to add questions from the "Child Sexual Behavior Inventory" (Friedrich, et al., in press).

Child Client Intake Information (provided by parent)

1. Client's name, age, birthdate.

2. Names and ages of siblings.

3. Names and ages of others living in the home.

4. Name of school and current grade level.

5. Referral source and reason client was referred (parent's perception).

6. Type of sexual acting out/abuse.

7. Type of violence or coercion involved.

8. Name of victim(s), age, relationship.

9. Additional aggressive behavior (fire-setting, killing animals, assaults, oppositional behavior, etc.).

10. Name of probation or social worker, police officer (if applicable).

11. Court date (if applicable).

12. School performance and behavior, teacher.

13. History of medical problems and medications taken.

14. Name and address of physician.

15. Developmental milestones (ages walked, talked). Normal? Abnormal? Describe abnormality.

16. Child's history as a victim of sexual or physical abuse:

    When and how often?   Age of client at the time?

    Report filed?   Yes   No   Approximate date filed?

17. Previous psychotherapy? Name of therapist.

18. Current life stressors (parents' divorce, alcohol abuse, death in family, death or loss of a pet, change of schools or neighborhood, etc.).

19. Extracurricular activities (clubs, scouting, sports, music or dance lessons, band, etc.).

20. Does child have adequate peer relationships?

21. Describe child's best friend.

In addition to obtaining this factual information, it is equally important to observe the parents' possible defense mechanisms, level of anxiety, relationship to each other, feelings about the identified client, protectiveness, and willingness to participate in therapy, in order to develop an effective treatment plan for the client and family.

Interviewing Children

When interviewing abuse-reactive *children*, it is important initially to establish rapport and positively reinforce the child when he/she is honest in answering difficult questions. Because abuse-reactive children generally have power and control issues, it is equally important not to *force* the child to talk. When the therapist engages in a power struggle to seek information, the future therapeutic relationship may be jeopardized. More information can be obtained at a later time. Prior to the actual interview, ask the child to draw a picture of his/her family doing something, then ask the child to explain the drawing to you (i.e., who the people are, what are they doing, etc.). This activity provides information about the family structure and serves as an ice breaker.

Intake Guidelines for Assessment of Abuse-Reactive Children[11]

Child's Perception of the Interview:

Why does the child think he/she is here?

- What was he/she told about you or the purpose of the interview?

- Does the child think he/she has a problem (other then being here, being accused, being in trouble, etc.)?

- Does he/she readily admit to the sexually inappropriate, coercive, or abusive behavior of which he/she is accused? If yes, see *Behavior Acknowledged* section.

Sample Introductory Statements

- "I talk to lots of kids who have problems: problems with grownups, problems with being in trouble, problems with touching other kids, problems with their families, problems with sexual things ..."

- "There isn't any kind of problem that I don't already know about ... so you should know that nothing you say can surprise me."

- "There are lots of reasons why kids have problems or do things that are not okay or get them into trouble. Sometimes they find themselves in trouble for stuff they didn't do. I'm here to sort out the reasons why you're here ... but I need your help to do it."

- "I want this to be a place where you can say anything, use any kind of language, express any kind of feelings about anyone or anything ... I just want you to know that no matter what we talk about or what you tell me, I'm still going to like you. I'm on your side."

Behavior Acknowledged: Interview Guidelines

Details of Incident(s)

- Description of participants
  Who was touched/molested (names, ages, relationship)

---

[11]Some of these questions have been incorporated (with permission) from the personal data form and the initial assignment form developed by the Oregon Adolescent Sex Offender Treatment Network. For further information on this program, refer to the *Informational Guide on the Juvenile Sex Offender* (Stickrod, Hamer, & Janes, 1984).

- Description of behavior
  What, how, where, duration, # of times (if child is young, uncommunicative, embarrassed, or has a language difficulty, anatomically detailed dolls can help a child demonstrate what occurred)[12]

- Description of circumstances
  Location of incident(s); where were adults? What triggered (led up to) the incident(s)? Why did you stop? How did you get caught? What were your parents' reactions when they found out? (Parents' attitude now? Reaction of victim's parents?)

- Assess degree of coerciveness
  Was it a secret? Was victim told not to tell? If yes, what were threatened consequences? Use of physical force, restraints, actual harm? Tricks, bribes, special favors, special relationship?

- History of similar behavior
  Have you done this kind of thing before? If yes, describe. Have you been caught/reported before now?

Child's Reactions to Behavior

- Assess child's feelings/thoughts:
  - remorse (what was wrong with behavior?)
  - guilt/blame (whose fault is it? how much of it was your fault? least=0/most=10)
  - shame (child's feelings about self)
  - empathy (child's feelings about victim)
- Feelings during/after incident
- Feelings about being caught
- Who else knows about this?
- How has disclosure affected the child?

Discuss/Assess Fantasies

i.e., "thoughts, ideas, dreams that excite you, scare you, get you angry, turn you on, things you can't stop thinking about," etc.

Future Thoughts

- What will/should happen now?
- What are you afraid of most?

---

[12]Interviewers are cautioned not to draw conclusions from play behavior with the dolls and should avoid making diagnostic interpretations in the absence of verbal explanations by the child. See White, Strom, Santilli, & Halpin (1986).

Behavior Denied

Potential Reasons for Denial of Abusive Behavior

- Child has been falsely accused (didn't do it).

- Fear of: punishment, being blamed, removal from the home, incarceration, wrath of God, etc.

- Shame, guilt, regret, fear of therapist's reaction/rejection.

- Fear of being labeled "bad," or in same-gender abuse, "queer."

- Fear of loss of love/emotional abandonment by family and/or friends.

- Minimization or unconscious blocking of behavior.

- Behavior misinterpreted by other child or adult; parental over-reaction to sexual behavior within range of normal development; miscommunication.

Potential Questions for the Child

- Why does ___(the victim or others)___ say it happened?

- Why are you in trouble?

- Do your parents believe you? Does anyone?

- How do you feel about being accused?

- If you were to say, "Yes, I did it," what would happen to you? (assess fears, threats, homophobia)

Keeping the Door Open

Sometimes it's best just to go with the child's resistance and come back to the difficult material either later in the session or another time:

"If you think of anything else that you've forgotten to tell me or are too uncomfortable to discuss right now, you can tell me later."

The "Assumption of Guilt" Approach

Rather than putting children on the spot by asking them to "admit" or "confess" to you what they have done, it is easier for some children (especially where there is credible evidence that the molest occurred or the child has acknowledged the behavior to someone else) to approach the interview with the attitude that you assume that it occurred and now you want to talk about it. For example:

"You know, little kids rarely ever lie or make up stories about this sort of thing, so I tend to believe them unless I can find some reason not to. Why don't you tell me how this happened so that we can work on what to do next."

"I've talked to ___(victim's name)___ about what happened" (usually a helpful step if you can get access to the victim), "and I believe what she told me. Now I want to hear your side of it so we can figure out how I can help you and your family."

"I've read the report and talked to _(your parents, the police, etc.)_ about what took place between you and ___(victim's name)___. Now that I have a general idea about what happened, maybe you and I can talk about what we can do about it."

"I wasn't there when this happened, so I don't know exactly what took place between you and ___(victim's name)___. It may have happened the way he tells it or in some other way ... either way, it looks like you have a problem. I'm here to help you with it."

History of Abuse

Because published materials are already available on techniques for interviewing/diagnosing child sexual abuse and violence (Boat & Everson, 1986; Jones & MacQuiston, 1985; MacFarlane, 1986; MacFarlane & Feldmeth, 1989; Pynoos & Eth, 1986), this section highlights only a few of the issues to be addressed.

Secrets/Threats

- Has the child ever had secrets (anything happen to him/her) that he/she was afraid to tell?
- Has anyone ever forced the child to keep a secret he/she wanted to tell?
- If yes, did he/she ever tell? If the child didn't ever tell, what were the reasons?
- If he/she were to tell now, what does he/she think will happen? (fears, threats)

Direct Inquiry

- Has anyone ever hit, kicked, or touched the child in a way that left him/her marked or hurt afterward?
- Is there anyone of whom the child is physically afraid?
- Has anyone ever touched the child in a way he/she didn't like? (... in a sexual way? ... in his/her private parts?)
- Has anyone asked the child to keep a secret about touching?

Suggestive Approach

"Sometimes kids who have problems with touching other kids were touched themselves by someone. They usually have lots of feelings about being touched in ways that make them uncomfortable but they don't know how to talk about it. One way they try to tell us about what happened to them is by touching other kids in the same way. I wonder if this is what's going on with you?"

This list is simply a range of approaches for getting at hidden or repressed material on possible victimization of the child perpetrator. Depending on the child's responses to these types of inquiries, the interviewer would usually go on to ask for more details, i.e., who, what, where, how many times, circumstances, previous reports, feelings, etc. This information may take a long time to come out; interviewers are cautioned not to pressure the child for answers during the initial intake session.

With older children, the therapist might give a homework assignment to help them tell you about themselves in areas other than the abuse, as in the suggested questions on the following page.

Rather than having children or parents fill out forms (except, of course, for any homework assignment), we suggest that therapists ask the questions themselves. Observations of the child's and family's affect, defense mechanisms, and anxiety constitute an important part of the therapeutic evaluation. In addition, latency-age children sometimes get so caught up in spelling correctly, putting down the "right answer," or in avoiding mistakes that much of the essential information may be lost or overlooked.

The last portion of the evaluation process is a family assessment. This is an important observational tool for the therapist. Questions may be asked of family members together or individually. Assessing the appropriateness of family hierarchies, boundaries, sibling relationships, and power/control issues provides invaluable information when formulating a treatment plan. Often therapists get caught up in "getting the facts" and may forget the power of clinical observation. Following are family assessment questions combining facts with observations.

Sexual Dynamics of Family and/or Environment

The following issues can be discussed with each member of a family as part of a family assessment. Often you will find very different perspectives on the same information.

General Questions

- Why do you think you are here?

- What do you think happened?

- How do you feel about it?

- What do you think will/should happen to _____ ?

- Who has the most problems in your family?

- Who has the least problems in your family?

- Who obeys the most in your family?

- What is the best and worst thing about your family?

- What do you like about each person in your family?

- What would you like to change about each of them?

- If you could change one thing about your family, what would it be?

- "Generally, I am/am not happy with my family life."

More About Me

Name _____ Birthdate _____

School _____ Grade _____

I have attended _____ schools in my life.

My favorite year in school was _____

because _____

_____

My least favorite year in school was _____

because _____

_____

I have lived in _____ places in my life.

I am / am not happy with my family life. (circle one)

If I could change one thing about my family, I would _____

_____

My most important goal in life is _____

_____

The saddest time in my life was when _____

_____

The happiest time in my life was when _____

_____

Some other things I think are important to know about me are _____

_____

_____

_____

_____

(add more pages or write on the back if you like)

_____

Adapted from Assignment One, developed by the Oregon Adolescent Sex Offender Treatment Network, *Informational Guide on the Juvenile Sex Offender* (Stickrod, Hamer, & Janes, 1984).

Sexual Attitude Questions

- What are the family's attitudes/"rules" about:
    - nudity, privacy, people seen without clothes?
    - bathing or toilet habits or procedures?
    - bedroom or bathroom doors being open or closed?
    - masturbation, sibling sexual activity, virginity?
    - who sleeps where, number of people living in home?
    - talking/joking about sex? are people uncomfortable?
    - teasing the child in a sexual way?
    - homosexuality?
    - punishing children for any sexual activity?
    - how you first learned about sex?
- Have children been exposed to adult sexual activity:
    - was a child ever present when adults were having sex? If yes, circumstances, reactions?
    - does a child have access to sexual material in the home (books/magazines about sex or with nude photos, X-rated videos, cable TV, etc.). For example, ask children, "Have you seen any books, magazines, or movies that show naked people touching each other?"
    - is this material hidden or are kids allowed to see it?
    - what sexual materials or activity has the child been exposed to outside the home/without parental knowledge?
    - was the child ever caught with sexual material? Reactions?
- Does the family know of other people who have been sexually abused:
    - any friends who have been sexually abused? who?
    - do you think any member of the family has been molested, raped, or otherwise sexually abused? You think this because ...

At the end of the interview, reframe the individual issues as family issues and correct myths or factual errors. This will help the family to avoid further scapegoating the identified child client. While interviewing the family, observe the methods of communication between family members, i.e., who controls the family, the types of defense mechanisms family members use, and secretive attitudes shown by family members.

These issues/questions can be used as guidelines for initial assessments. It is presumed that each therapist will use his/her own techniques and methodology in conducting the initial intake. We have found that two successful ingredients of effective intake interviews are confrontation mixed with support. It is equally important to respect defense mechanisms and avoid power struggles. Information that is not obtained at the intake can be gained later on in therapy as the child becomes more comfortable with sharing feelings and experiences.

The Use of Medication and Psychiatric Consultation

Some children continue in therapy for a considerable period of time and show no real improvement. They may continue to have symptoms of anxiety, depression, continual sexual acting out, poor impulse control, anger, or aggression that are not improving with therapy. These problems tend to interfere with the child's ability to function at home and/or at school. There also may be sleeping problems, appetite changes, and suicidal ideation. If these symptoms are not alleviated with therapy, a consultation with a child psychiatrist may be necessary. The child psychiatrist's task will be to identify whether the child's problems may be helped with medications.

A typical case scenario of a child who as been referred to a child psychiatrist follows:

T. is an eight year old boy who was referred for evaluation by the child psychiatrist for continued angry outbursts, crying spells, nightmares, and sexualized behavior with his younger sister. He had been therapy for six months for a prior history of sexual abuse victimization by his mother's boyfriend. The mother chose to stay with her boyfriend, and T. was being raised by an aunt. T. was doing poorly in school and was assaultive with his peers. Prior to the referral to a child psychiatrist, T. was diagnosed with ADHD by his pediatrician and was taking Ritalin. During the evaluation, T. crawled under the table, curled up into a ball, and cried.

It was decided that T. suffered from an agitated depression. He was started on a low-dose antidepressant and began to improve within two weeks. His temper outbursts decreased dramatically, and he was less anxious. He began to socialize more with his friends at school, and was less aggressive. His sexualized behavior decreased dramatically. The sexual abuse issues as well as the abandonment issues were then addressed in therapy, and T. was able to respond to therapeutic interventions.

Antidepressants are used successfully in children with both depression and symptoms of PTSD, including anxiety, agitation, depression, poor anger control, irritability, or apathy. In addition, these children may have trouble sleeping, with frequent awakening or severe nightmares.

Antidepressants must be taken daily, sometimes several times a day, for several months at a time. Common side effects may include sleepiness, dry mouth and constipation. If improvement is going to occur, it should appear in about 3-4 weeks. Antidepressants will improve the child's energy level, reduce depression, improve frustration tolerance, reduce sexual acting out that is a result of PTSD, and reduce anxiety. These medications need to be handled and supervised carefully, as they can be toxic and even lethal if taken in high doses, as in a suicide attempt.

Aggressive, hyperactive behaviors, especially behaviors which may have been present prior to any trauma, may respond to stimulants, such as Ritalin or Dexedrine, rather than antidepressants.

Another medication which is very helpful in decreasing aggression and problems related to impulse control is Clonidine. This medicine helps reduce impulsive behavior, distractibility, poor concentration, aggression, and hyperarousal. These medicines need to be given daily. There is a patch that can be utilized in place of oral medication. Side effects may include appetite suppression, headache and stomachache.

The combination of psychotherapy and pharmacotherapy can greatly improve your client's prognosis especially if the symptoms have not been alleviated by therapy alone. Often clinicians, due to either lack of knowledge or their own personal bias, do not consult a psychiatrist, when in fact medication can be lifesaving for children or a useful adjunct for psychotherapy.

Ann Welty, M.D., Child Psychiatrist,
Medical Director
Long Beach Child Guidance Center

CHAPTER THREE

Group Behavioral Management

In group therapy, behavior management is a vital part of the therapeutic process. Abuse-reactive children often lack both impulse control and the skills to be able to contain their behavior or their emotions. The results of uncontained behavior or feelings can be frightening for the child and upsetting for the group therapist. In order for children to benefit from the therapeutic process, they must be able to feel safe in the group. They must feel that *someone* will be able to set limits and control their behavior. Therefore, when beginning the group therapy process some behavioral management skills are essential.

It is important to remember that abuse-reactive children are in therapy because they have acted out in an aggressive, coercive manner. To allow unmanageable behavior to continue is to give them the message that their aggressive behavior is acceptable and/or truly uncontrollable. It is not until after these children gain some control over their behavior that therapy actually begins. Only then will they feel safe enough to expose their vulnerability; only then will they know that if they begin to feel anxious and agitated, someone will be able to help contain their behavior.

One of the first group activities should be the establishment of group rules, developed with the children's participation and agreement. The following list contains suggestions for basic group rules:

1. Respect the body space of all group members: no hitting or hurting other group members.

2. Stay together: no leaving the room, unless given permission by an adult.

3. Respect others' property: no breaking toys or furniture in the room or the room itself; no taking toys or other group items.

4. If you begin to feel anxious or angry, you can talk about it, ask a therapist to take you to a quiet place, write about it, or draw a picture about it.

5. Listen and take part during a structured activity.

Positive reinforcement is extremely important when dealing with abuse-reactive children. ***Reinforcement is needed every 15 minutes to begin to shape young children's behavior.*** For example, if children are taking part in a structured activity and acting appropriately or if they *talk* about their anger instead of acting it out, reward them with colorful stickers placed on the backs of their hands or in a sticker book as an effective way to reinforce appropriate behavior. Placing marbles in a jar is another effective technique for managing the behavior of the group as a whole. All you need is a glass jar and a bag of marbles. Every 15 minutes (for young people) or every half hour (for older children), several marbles should be dropped in the jar as a means of rewarding the group for following the group rules. When the jar fills up with marbles, the kids can have a party, go on a picnic, see a video, or some other positive reinforcer. These reinforcement techniques can be used in combination as well as alone. The advantage of the marble jar is in the group's working together on a goal. Special awards can be given to individual children who have improved their behavior (see, for example, the following illustrations reproduced with permission from *Skill*

Stop and Think

Award

to

_____

for using the skill of

_____

Date _____

From *Skill Streaming the Elementary School Child* by E. McGinnis and A.P. Goldstein, 1984. Champaign, IL: Research Press. Reprinted by permission.

Dealing with Feelings Award

to

_____

for using the skill of

_____

Date _____

From *Skill Streaming the Elementary School Child* by E. McGinnis and A.P. Goldstein, 1984. Champaign, IL: Research Press. Reprinted by permission.

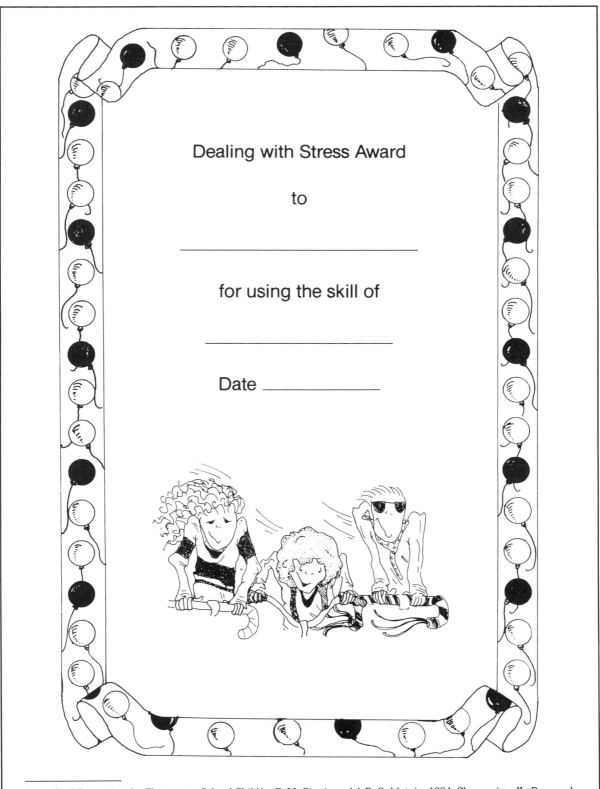

Dealing with Stress Award

to

_____

for using the skill of

_____

Date _____

From *Skill Streaming the Elementary School Child* by E. McGinnis and A.P. Goldstein, 1984. Champaign, IL: Research Press. Reprinted by permission.

Group Evaluation

Name _____

Group _____

Problem _____

Date _____

1. How did you work?	😊 Well	😐 So-So	😞 Not So Well
2. Did you wait your turn?	😊 Yes	😐 Sometimes	😞 No
3. Did you help someone?	😊 Yes	😐 A Little	😞 No
4. Did you help the group?	😊 Yes	😐 A Little	😞 No
5. Did you like the activity?	😊 Yes	😐 So-So	😞 No
6. Did you have enough time?	😊 Yes	😞 No	

Streaming the Elementary School Child by McGinnis & Goldstein, 1984). Children of all ages love to get awards like these and will be motivated to continue the appropriate behavior.

Behavioral contracts are particularly helpful with children having difficulty with containment. The contracts can be signed by the child, therapist, and parent. If the child follows the contract, the therapist and/or parents should always positively reinforce the child. The contract should be specific and concrete with concentration on one behavioral task at a time.

A group evaluation should be done at the end of each session to help children evaluate their own behavior (a sample evaluation sheet precedes this page). This process helps children recognize their own behaviors and assess those of others; it also helps to unify the group.

When a group rule is broken, a consequence should occur immediately. A time-out is often the most effective, immediate consequence. For a time-out the child is taken to a separate area and asked to sit and think about why he/she is there. If the child refuses to sit alone, or if the behavior begins to escalate, he/she may need to be gently held in place. While some therapists feel that physically holding a child who has been abused is traumatizing, our experience suggests that abused children need to know that someone can hold them or touch them in a nonsexual and nonabusive way. A time-out done correctly can give them this message. It can also be very comforting for children to know that someone can help them control themselves.

It is important *not to talk to the child* during his/her time-out. Explaining repeatedly why the child is in time-out can act to reinforce or even escalate the child's behavior. A simple statement of 10 words or less, such as, "I am going to hold you to help you stay safe," or "I am going to help you control your behavior," will suffice. The time to talk about why he/she is there and what rules have been broken is after the child has calmed down, when he/she can hear and respond to you. The child is much less likely to be able to respond to you during the escalated period of emotional upset.

When one or more children become assaultive in the group, it is important for the therapists to get a co-therapist to help. One therapist can take the children involved in the conflict to a different part of the room and talk about what happened. Assaultive behavior should not be permitted in the group. Along with immediate restraint, withholding stickers or other positive reinforcers should be the other consequence of not following the rules. When children see their peers receiving awards while they are left out, they will be less likely to repeat the behavior, although they may say they don't care.

Consistency is the key to behavior management. ***Continuing the same reinforcement schedule every week is vital.*** Since many of these children have not had consistent environments or authority figures, your consistency will help them learn to manage their own behavior.

Not only are appropriate behavioral standards necessary, but individual and group goals also should be implemented. Individual goals should be determined at intake and then reassessed during the therapeutic process. Below is a list of appropriate group and individual therapeutic goals for abuse-reactive children.

1. Expressing positive feelings in appropriate ways.

2. Expressing anger and negative feelings in appropriate ways.

3. Talking about why you are here.

4. Talking about victimization.

    –Who molested you?

    –What happened?

    –How did it happen (details)?

    –How you feel about it now?

5. Talking about perpetration.

    –Who did you molest?

    –How many times (years, months, etc.)?

    –What were you thinking just before you did it?

    –What did you do?

    –How did you get the other person to do it?

    –How did you feel after you did it?

    –How do you feel about it now?

    –Whose responsibility is it?

6. Talking about sexual fantasies.

7. Assuming responsibility for your own actions.

8. Developing assertion and victimization avoidance skills.

9. Learning to problem-solve and to negotiate.

10. Learning to wait (developing frustration tolerance).

11. Developing empathy skills.

12. Learning to deal with anxiety.

As the group and/or individuals accomplish these goals, give positive rewards. Encourage children to talk about difficult things. Tell them they will feel better after they do, and that there are no secrets in this group. It is important to remember that most abuse-reactive children have strong denial systems (as do their families). These children will continue to be at risk to re-offend if their victim/perpetrator issues are not addressed. Their reluctance to talk about difficult issues usually needs to be dealt with in order to get past the initial barriers of denial. In addition, their families often encourage secrets about a variety of family issues. To avoid dealing with pertinent issues in the therapy group is to imply and reinforce the idea that inappropriate secrets are okay.

Behavior Management is essential when working with impulsive children. The same basic principles apply whether the children are sexually abusive or have other impulse control problems. The same group rules and positive reinforcement are applicable to all impulsive disorders. The goals listed in this chapter may be revised depending upon the therapeutic goals of the child. Some examples of possible revisions include:

Fire Setting

Talk about why you are here.

Talk about victimization (if applicable).

Talk about the fire that you set.

Where did you set the fire?

What happened?

How did it happen? What did you do? (Details?)

How did you feel after you did it?

How do you feel about it now?

Whose responsibility is it?

Talk about power fantasies, or sexual feelings.

Hurting Animals

What kind of animal did you hurt?

What was the animal's name?

What did you do to it?

What happened to it?

What happened to you (if anything)?

How did you hurt the animal?

How did you feel after you did it?

How do you feel about it now?

The suggestions, rewards, etc., can apply to each of the behaviors that we have talked about. Containment must come before safety, trust, and insight can occur.

This chapter has offered a few basic guidelines that have been found useful in working with abuse-reactive children in groups. Unmanageable behavior and anxiety must be contained in order for learning to begin. Immediate time-out followed by loss of privileges when children re-enter the group is a useful technique. Awards and certificates given to children who talk about difficult issues can be very effective in overcoming communication barriers as well as in shaping behavior. In addition, gentle confrontation with young children can produce results without being unduly intrusive. Remember that goals for group behavior always have a dual purpose: to reshape inappropriate and unmanageable behavior patterns, and to develop and reinforce new patterns of communication and self-control. There is no better training ground for such tasks than a well-structured group, but it doesn't happen automatically or right away. Children's groups have evolutionary lives during which the children and the group leaders must learn to trust, respect, and care about one another. There may be many stormy sessions in which boundaries are tested. At times the most important therapeutic ingredient is patience.

CHAPTER FOUR

Working with Parents' Groups

It is essential that the parents of abuse-reactive children receive treatment at the same time the children do. If only the children receive treatment, they will be attempting to change themselves within an unchanging and often dysfunctional environment. Many parents of abuse-reactive children were molested in childhood, have substance abuse issues, and/or have undergone a divorce or separation. Most of the families have difficulty with family hierarchies and boundaries in addition to their problems in containing their children's impulses. Placing the parents in a group with other parents who have similar issues facilitates their acceptance and understanding of the issues, needs, and interventions with a child who has become abuse-reactive. This chapter addresses issues and techniques to be utilized in group treatment for parents; however, the need for and the value of individual, couples, and/or family counseling should not be underestimated.

Stages in Acceptance

Families in which children have been molested, especially those where children are sexually acting out and have begun to victimize others, often proceed through stages similar to those resulting from the loss of a loved one through death. In her book *On Death and Dying* (1969), Kubler-Ross identifies five stages of grieving: denial, anger, bargaining, depression, and acceptance. The grief process in this case is related to accepting the fact that a child has been molested and/or has begun abuse-reactive behavior.

Denial

Often when parents and their children initially seek treatment, they are in extreme denial. The children may have been given the message that they must keep secret what they have done. Because parents do not want to accept the fact that their child is in trouble, they frequently minimize what has happened: they may say that the children were "just being curious"; they may refuse to acknowledge the sexual content of an incident ("They were only playing doctor"); or they may insist, "It was nothing," or "No harm was done."

It is important for the therapist to remember that for many of these families, denial has operated pervasively for years, serving as a shield from some of their own issues such as alcoholism, molestation, and loss. Parents who themselves were molested in childhood may believe that such incidents are a "normal" part of growing up. The therapist must maintain a delicate balance in confronting parents' denial and nurturing the parents at the same time. Rushing the process or attempting to change the family system too quickly may push the family out of treatment or encourage the family to focus only on the identified client rather than on the family unit. During this denial period, therapists should positively reinforce the parents for attending group sessions and enlist the help of other parents who are further along in their process to confront the newer group members' denial system. Other parents in the group can supportively share their experiences about how they too were in denial, and that they too were terrified of dealing with the fact that their child molested another child.

Anger

The anger stage can be the most difficult stage for the therapist, as the parent often displaces all of his/her anger and guilt onto "the system" and the therapist as its representative. The therapist should allow the parent to air his/her frustrations, while at the same time making the parents aware that they are blaming others when the problem is actually *their* family's problem. Parents can be helped with anger-management techniques in much the same way their children are taught (see Chapter Six). During this stage, the therapist must be extra-sensitive to the possibility that the child client may be at risk of physical abuse at home; the parents may take their anger out on the child and blame him/her for making them face and deal with their problem. *Steps to Healthy Touching* (MacFarlane & Cunningham, 1988) includes a 12 Step program for parents of abuse-reactive children that assists them in working through their denial and anger.

Bargaining

During the "bargaining" stage of the grieving process, some parents may say to themselves, "If my child and I just come to these groups for a while, my child will be cured." Other parents may believe that if they pray hard enough or sincerely enough for guidance or deliverance, this problem will go away. During this stage parents tend to minimize their child's problem. It is the therapist's responsibility to explore with parents their fears about therapy and to reinforce the parents frequently for continuous attendance. Keeping parents focused on the reality of their situation is extremely important and will be an ongoing process during this stage.

Depression

When families begin to experience depression and pain at a deeper level, the therapy begins to stimulate change. In a group these feelings can be supportively accepted by other group members who have gone through similar pain and process. During this stage the reality of their children's victimization and/or perpetration finally begins to sink in. Parents may also experience fear and sadness. The therapist must be supportive in interpreting and helping the parents make sense of these mixtures of feelings.

Often family, marital, or individual therapy for the parents becomes necessary during this stage. The family unit has been disrupted and the marital dyad experiences conflict. If either or both of the parents are adult survivors of incest, individual or group support may become necessary for them. Offering this supportive therapy at the same agency can provide the family with continuity and the staff with additional data and team input.

Acceptance

During this stage, the parents have accepted that their child victimized another child and that this problem is a *family* problem not to be scapegoated onto one family member. Drug and alcohol problems, parenting skills, sexuality, and sex-role stereotyping are more successfully dealt with in this stage.

Parent education in such areas as behavior management, improving communication, and human sexuality should be an adjunct or ongoing part of the treatment process. Parents and caretakers need to be clear about the safety issues associated with their child's interactions with other children. Parents also need help in developing realistic expectations of their children: children should not be inadvertently "set up" (placed in situations providing an opportunity to abuse) because their parents have overestimated their ability to control their impulses and self-regulate their behavior. Parents should be taught how to: monitor behavior, protect other children in the home, identify pre-offense behavior, and intervene to prevent re-abuse.

An additional important issue to be addressed is whether and how parents are given feedback about their particular child individually or in group. The issue of confidentiality is always a difficult one when dealing with children. Many times therapists get so caught up in preserving client confidentiality that they fail to give the parents any feedback at all. It is crucial to remember that when working with children, parents should be given general feedback and specific information about the goals and purpose of the child's therapy in order to enhance the therapeutic process and relieve parents' anxiety. Otherwise they may consciously or unconsciously sabotage therapy. One of the therapists from the child's group may join the parents' meeting during the last 10 minutes to provide general information about that day's issues in the children's group. For example, if the issue was anger management, the structured activity and suggestions for follow-through at home would be discussed.

It is essential that parents and families learn how to accept and deal with the fact that their children are sexually victimizing others. It must be done in a way that combines support with confrontation and helps them acquire the knowledge, skills, patience, and understanding to support and foster their children's growth.

Working With Parents Groups

The purpose of this book is to assist clinicians by providing a brief theoretical background and some tools and techniques that will help them in working with impulsive children.

This chapter barely begins to communicate the importance of working with parents. Many parents of abusive-reactive children have insecure attachments with their own parents. As a result, they do not have the ability to form adequate and secure attachments with their own children. An important part of a parents' group is to be able to provide a "holding environment" that will model safety and trust for parents.[13]

---

[13] Since the initial publication of this text, a guide for parents of children with sexual behavior problems has become available. Entitled *From Trauma to Understanding*, it was written by Dr. William Pithers, Alison S. Gray, Dr. Carolyn Cunningham, and Sandy Lane. Available from The Safer Society Press, this simply written, 32-page booklet was developed to assist parents and clinicians in working together.

PART II

TEACHING SKILLS & COMPETENCIES

CHAPTER FIVE

Building Self-esteem

Abuse-reactive children generally have negative self-images and low self-esteem. Their lack of impulse control often leaves them feeling powerless and guilty. As they become increasingly self-critical, their sense of self-worth diminishes and their anxiety increases. Too often, the only coping mechanism they have for alleviating their tension is to continue acting out. This strategy works only for a short time and produces more adult disfavor, increasing the child's sense of powerlessness and enlarging the cycle of guilt, self-criticism, anxiety, tension, and acting out.

Children who have been sexually molested or physically abused often feel responsible for the victimization. They tend to polarize themselves and the other people in their lives into good and bad parts. The black-and-white (or polarized) quality of their world makes it difficult for these children to integrate realistic concepts of themselves or others.

It can be very painful and frightening for an abused child to become aware of feeling anger or rage toward the perpetrator, particularly when he/she is someone the child knew and trusted prior to the abuse. The child may try to maintain his/her image of the adult as "good" either by not seeing the "bad" side and denying the existence of the "bad behavior," or by changing his/her own self-image ("If a good adult is doing bad things to me, it must be because I'm bad"). Because a self-image of being totally bad is usually intolerable even for a young child, the child often assumes (or is told directly) that the abusive adult is responding to his/her two sides: he/she is "bad" when being abused and "good" when not being abused. This type of black-and-white thinking can be the basis of "splitting" in the personality development of a young child.[14]

The child may take this black-and-white perception process one step further in thinking, "I have to keep doing what this person wants or something worse will happen, and that will be my fault, too." While a child may arrive at such a conclusion on his/her own, it is equally likely that the perpetrator has taught this lesson with explicit messages.

In abuse-reactive children, black-and-white thinking is usually quite pronounced. Their feelings of fear or vulnerability increase their sense of powerlessness and being out of control. For them, one way to avoid these feelings is to begin to identify with their abusers. They may make an emotional leap from a position of total fear to one of rage, then proceed to act it out. This transition may take them from feeling totally vulnerable and powerless to feeling an intense need to control their environment and others and to feel powerful. One way they may achieve this feeling of power is to make another person the victim, reinforcing their denial of their own victimization.

This chapter suggests activities to develop a positive sense of self or "positive self-esteem." We have positive self-esteem when we feel competent, cherished by some, worthwhile to others, secure, and accepting of ourselves. We have negative self-esteem when we feel incompetent, unworthy, out of control, rejected, invisible, and discouraged.

---

[14]For more information on the concept of "splitting" in children, see Kluft, 1985; Kreisman & Straus, 1989; and Terr, 1990.

The activities in this chapter can be used with all children. Low self-esteem and feelings of powerlessness are issues that children with impulse problems suffer from, regardless of how they are manifested.

Again, change the activity to fit the particular issue of your client. Some examples are:

1. **Joe's Angry Secret**—If the child has been sexually abused, the first portion of the story can stay the same. The second part can be changed, depending upon the issue. For fire setting, for example, it might read like this:

   "One day on the playground, Joe found some matches. He couldn't stop thinking about setting a fire on the playground. He begin playing with the matches during lunchtime. The noon lunch monitor saw him and began talking to Joe about the dangers of fire setting. Joe began to cry, and started to talk to her about having a secret he feels badly about. She helped Joe join a group of boys who had similar problems. He learned that what happened to him and that others are available to help him. He also learned it's better to talk about your anger rather than to hurt people or burn down property."

2. **Counter It**—Sentences 8 and 9 can be changed to fit the issue. For example, if the issue is hurting animals, an exercise might include: "If someone finds out I hurt my dog, they'll hate me" or "they will think I'm a bad person because I hurt my cat."

In order to increase the abuse-reactive child's self-esteem, the following issues need to be addressed: 1) changing negative self-images into positive ones; 2) forgiving oneself for mistakes; 3) adjusting black-and-white thinking toward more realistic shades of gray; 4) increasing autonomy and individuality; and 5) learning to assess strengths and weaknesses realistically.

Below are specific activities geared to the self-esteem issues that pertain to abuse-reactive children.[15]

Activity: *I'M A PIECE OF THE PUZZLE* [16]

Ages: *4-8*

Materials: *One piece of construction paper; a pair of scissors; crayons or markers*

Procedure: Take a standard-sized sheet of light-colored construction paper, and cut it into enough puzzle pieces of various sizes to match the number of people in the group, including group leaders. Distribute the puzzle pieces, and have the members and leaders write their names on their puzzle pieces. Then have them write something they do well underneath their names.

Next, as a group, try to put the piece of construction paper back into its original shape. To stress the importance of communication, have the group put the puzzle together without talking.

---

[15]There are many excellent resources for developing positive self-esteem in both children and adults. For additional activities, see *Liking Myself* by P. Palmer, *Helping Yourself to a Healthier You*, and *Thinking, Feeling, and Behaving* both by Ann Vernon (listed in Resources).

[16]This activity was originated by Tim Boatmun, M.A., The University of Oklahoma, National Resource Center for Youth Services, and published with permission from the author.

Discussion: The objectives of this activity are to help each group member understand his/her importance to the group process, and to address issues of universalization and identifying strengths.

Many times, when groups are first getting started, members might feel as if they have nothing important to say. This activity can help the group members focus on how everyone brings strengths to the group and how each individual member is needed to solve the puzzle.

Some suggested processing questions include:

- How did we solve the puzzle?

- What would have happened if one piece of the puzzle wasn't there?

- Were the smaller pieces or the larger more important? (Both are equally important to solve the puzzle)

- Are everyone's strengths important?

- How are we all different? How are we the same?

- Would it be good if we were all the same?

- How do differences make us special?

- Is it important to realize that some people have gone through some of the same things we have? Why?

- What can we learn from people who have gone through some of the same things we have?

Activity: *The Positive Box*

Ages: *5-11*

Materials: *A box; small pieces of paper; pencils*

Procedure: Have each child write his or her name on a piece of paper, fold it, and place it in a box. Explain to the children that the group members are going to think about and say nice things about the other members in the group. Pull a child's name from the box and have each group member say something positive about the person whose name was pulled out. Write them down on a separate page for each child. After pulling out all the slips from the box, have each group member tell you three of the nicest things that were said about them.

Discussion: It is commonly difficult for children to give and receive compliments, particularly for children with low self-esteem. There may be giggling and distractions. However, continue with this exercise and repeat it often, as it is an excellent way to enhance self-image.

Activity: *What I Like about Myself*

Ages: *6-13*

Materials: *None*

Procedure: Discuss with group members what it means to *like yourself*, i.e., that you accept yourself and can identify things about yourself that you like. Explain that this game will help each of us to identify things that we like in ourselves and others. Go around the circle and have the children state something that they like about themselves and something that they like about the person on their left or right.

Discussion: Talk with the children about what they were feeling during the activity. Is it hard to identify things that you like about yourself? How do you feel when you say nice things about someone else? Do you agree with what was said about you? Can you accept the things that other people say they like about you?

Activity: *Paddle Drums*

Ages: *7-12*

Materials: *Paddle Drums (available from many musical instrument stores).*

Procedure: Paddle Drums are real drum heads mounted on rackets, that when played produce wonderful sounds. A variety of balls are provided and drum rackets. Play as you would badminton, do relays or hot potato. Also, can be used to produce feeling sounds. For example, how do you make an angry sound? How do you make a sad sound?, etc.

Discussion: This is an excellent therapeutic tool that is fun yet therapeutic. Boundary issues, healthy catharsis, as well as social skills are benefits from the drum set.

Activity: *It's Me*

Ages: *5-10*

Materials: *One game board (pattern follows); set of question cards; dice*

Procedure: Draw the game board on oaktag or cardboard following the pattern. Make a set of question cards from the list on page 61, writing one question on each card. Play the game according to the directions on the gameboard in small groups of no more than four children. Allow groups to play at their own pace.

Discussion: When the game is done, ask the children questions: What were the hardest questions for you to answer? Why? Which was the best question, etc.?

It's Me

Questions for Cards

Make one of each sentence per set—each question on a separate strip

Sometimes I think I'm _____ .

I really am _____ .

People don't like me when I _____ .

People do like me when I _____ .

I feel happy when _____ .

I am excited about _____ .

Something I'd like to try is _____ .

Something that frightens me is _____ .

I feel hurt when _____ .

The thing about me that I'd like to change is _____ .

The best thing about me is _____ .

Something I have in common with others my age is _____ .

If I could be someone else, I'd be _____ .

Something I believe in strongly is _____

    (because _____).

When I talk in front of the class, I feel _____ .

I wish I _____ .

Tell the best thing that ever happened to you outside of school.

When I lose an argument or game, I feel _____ .

Share with each other something you do like about school.

Tell each other what you dislike most about school.

When I'm with friends, I like to _____ .

When I'm alone, I _____ .

Tell something that you do like about yourself.

One of my most frustrating experiences has been _____ .

A sad thing that happened to me is _____ .

One of my talents is _____ .

I'm good at _____ .

Something I need to improve on is _____ .

Something that's important to me is _____ .

If I could change anything about my family, it'd be _____ .

I think I'm capable in _____ .

If someone were to give me a nice surprise, it'd be _____ .

Being a (boy or girl) is nice because _____ .

An important decision I've made is _____ .

It's Me

Game Board Diagram

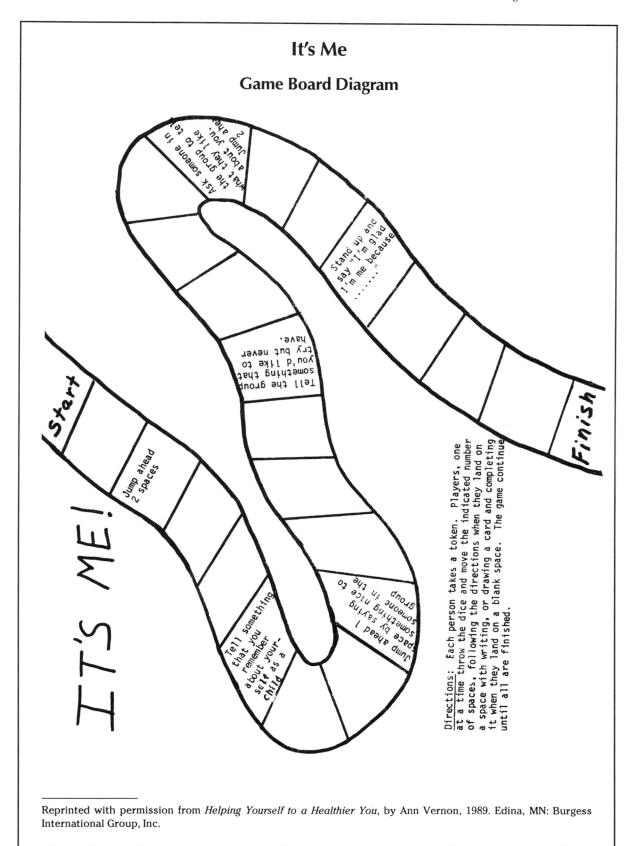

ITS ME!

Start

Jump ahead 2 spaces

Tell something that you remember about yourself as a child

Jump ahead 1 space by saying something nice to someone in the group

Tell the group something that you'd like to try but never have.

Ask someone in the group to tell what they like about you. Jump ahead 2

Stand up and say "I'm glad I'm me because ...."

Finish

Directions: Each person takes a token. Players, one at a time throw the dice and move the indicated number of spaces, following the directions when they land on a space with writing, or drawing a card and completing it when they land on a blank space. The game continues until all are finished.

Reprinted with permission from *Helping Yourself to a Healthier You*, by Ann Vernon, 1989. Edina, MN: Burgess International Group, Inc.

Activity: *My Inner Critic*

Ages: *7-12*

Materials: *Paper; pencils or crayons*

Procedure: Explain to the children that we all have a part of ourselves that says mean or critical things to us. Give examples: "John, you are ugly"; "Linda, you are too fat"; "Sheila, you are really dumb." Group leaders should use themselves as examples. Pass out writing materials. Have the children make a list of what mean things their inner critics say to them. Younger children may need help with their lists. Have the children compare lists.

The next week, teach the children to become aware and in control of their inner critics. Tell them that when they hear the critic saying mean things, they can tell the critic to stop. This can be done by visualizing a stop sign and then replacing the mean thing with a nice self-statement. Example: if your inner critic says you are stupid, you would say ***"Stop!"*** and replace that idea with a positive self-statement such as "I am smart in math," or, "I'm not stupid. I just don't understand this problem."

Discussion: With young children, self-critical statements often have to do with appearance and intellect. Since they avoid issues relating to their perpetration, it can be helpful to bring that up as an example. One group leader might say, "Sometimes a child's inner critic says to him/her, 'You are a bad, no-good person for touching your sister.' What does your inner critic say to you about your touching problem?" Most children will reply with such statements as, "You're stupid for doing that," or "You're a mean person." It is important to help children replace these statements with more positive statements such as, "You made a mistake, but you are still a good person," or "You are still okay, even if some of the things you do are not okay." On the next page is a list of some negative self-statements or cognitive distortions that abuse-reactive children say to themselves. You can use the method listed above to introduce the negative as well as the positive self-statements.

Activity: *Person of the Week*

Ages: *4-8*

Materials: *Picture of each child (either a photograph brought in by the child or a picture drawn by the therapist or child); construction paper; tape or glue; slips of paper; pencils*

Procedure: Each week introduce a different child as the person of the week. Make a construction paper poster of each child using a photograph or drawing of that child and put his/her name at the top. On slips of paper, have each person in the group write something nice about whoever is the person of the week. Tape or glue the slips of paper onto the poster. Hang each poster up in the group room until all children have their pictures on the wall. Then allow children to take their pictures and positive compliments home.

Discussion: This is an excellent activity to build self-esteem. Each week the child can look at him/herself and see all of the positive statements that were written.

Cognitive Distortions of Abuse-Reactive Children
Ages 4-11

Distortion	Coping Sentences
I am a bad person.	I am a loveable person.
I have no power.	I do have power over my body and myself.
It is my fault that adults touched me in my private parts.	It's always the adult's fault.
My body is dirty.	I like my body.
I cannot control touching others.	I can control my touching.
There is nothing I can do to protect myself.	I can say no and tell if anyone touches me again.
I can't feel anything.	I am aware of my five senses—seeing, smelling, tasting, touching, and hearing. I can feel my anger, fear, sadness, and happiness.
I shouldn't be angry at the person who touched me.	It's okay for me to be angry at the person who touched me.
When I get mad I have to hurt someone.	1. When I get mad I should talk about it or let my anger out in other ways.
	2. Hurting someone else is not going to take away my hurt.
When I get mad I have to get someone.	I don't need to hurt anyone when I get mad. I can let my anger out in other ways.
I shouldn't have told on the person who touched me.	It was very good that I told and got some help.

Activity: *Me Badge*

Ages: *4-8*

Materials: *"Me Badge" outline (following); construction paper or oaktag; pencils or markers; scissors; tape*

Procedure: Following the example, make blank "Me Badges," or have the children make their own. Explain to group members that these are special badges that will tell something about their lives. The group members then draw pictures or write answers to the questions in each section. Have the children share the information on the badges after they are complete.

Discussion: Compare badges and ask members if everybody has the same things in each space. If not, does this mean that some people are better than others? What would it be like if everyone had drawn the same things?

Me Badge

Draw pictures to fill in these spaces

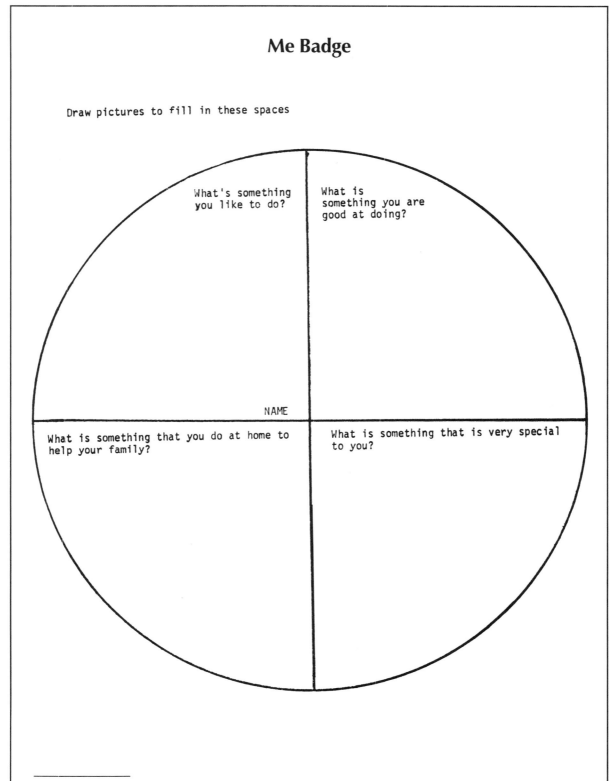

What's something
you like to do?

What is
something you are
good at doing?

NAME

What is something that you do at home to
help your family?

What is something that is very special
to you?

Reprinted with permission from *Helping Yourself to a Healthier You*, by Ann Vernon, 1989. Edina, MN: Burgess International Group, Inc.

Activity: *The Little Red Fire Engine*

Ages: *5-10*

Materials: *Story: "The Little Red Fire Engine"*

Procedure: Read the story "The Little Red Fire Engine." This story is about a little boy who steals a toy fire engine and gets caught. The lesson of the story is to acknowledge your mistakes, learn from them, and move on in your life.

Discussion: You can use this beautiful story as an analogy to talk about unwanted touching or "stealing" someone else's sense of privacy, safety, or self-control.

The Little Red Fire Engine[17]

Timothy Tyler loved fire engines.

"They're sooo big! And so shiny and red! And the way their sirens scream when they're racing to a fire is so neat! And most important of all, they bring firemen to fight fires! Fire engines are truly wonderful!" marveled Timothy.

Timothy loved to go to the firehouse to see the great big, red fire engines.

"Hello there, Timothy!" the firemen would call as they polished their engines. Sometimes they would even let him help shine up the fenders.

Timothy read all the fire engine books he could find. He daydreamed about fire engines.

"When I grow up, I'm going to be a fireman," he decided. "Gosh, maybe I'll even have my very own fire engine to take care of!"

"Timothy," said Mrs. Tyler one morning, "would you please go to Mr. Winterbottom's stationery store and buy ten postcards for me? Here is a dollar—it should be just enough to pay for them."

"Sure, Mom," replied Timothy, "I like to go to visit Mr. Winterbottom, and his store is really neat!"

As Timothy walked along, he thought of all the wonderful things in Mr. Winterbottom's store. Mr. Winterbottom sold not only stationery and postcards, but toys, and books, and candy as well. Timothy liked to look at all of them.

"Just imagine what I could buy if I had ten dollars!" he thought.

As Timothy pushed open the door of Mr. Winterbottom's store, familiar little bells tinkled. Mr. Winterbottom looked up.

---

[17]Reprinted with permission from *Color Us Rational* by Virginia Waters (1979). New York: Institute for Rational-Emotive Therapy. For more excellent stories contact the Institute for Rational-Emotive Therapy, 45 East 65th St., New York, NY 10021.

"Well, Timothy," said Mr. Winterbottom, "what can I do for you today?"

"My mom would like ten plain postcards," replied Timothy. "She gave me a dollar to pay for them. But I'd like to look around for a while first."

"O.K., be my guest," said Mr. Winterbottom. "I'll be in the back of the store—just let me know when you're ready to buy your cards."

Timothy wandered up and down the aisles.

"Gee, look at all this great stuff!" he thought. "There are party hats and streamers ... and party invitations ... and napkins that say 'Happy Birthday!' and 'Cheers!' ... and comic books and cookbooks ... and scotch tape and ...

"Wow!" he gasped. "Wowee! I've never seen anything as beautiful as that in my whole life!"

His eyes lit up, and his heart began to pound. He was gazing at a tiny red fire engine no bigger than his hand. He picked it up and examined it carefully.

"Gosh—you can crank the ladder up and down, and unwind this miniature hose! And when you open the doors, you can see mini-firemen inside!"

"I've just got to have this little fire engine," he told himself. "I want it more than I've ever wanted anything before."

"It's so small—Mr. Winterbottom will never even know it's missing. Besides, nobody could possibly want it as much as I do."

He glanced toward the back of the store. Mr. Winterbottom was out of sight. Timothy stuffed the fire engine into his left pants pocket. Then he looked down.

"It makes a tiny bulge," he noted, "but it's not enough of a bulge for anybody to notice." He tiptoed to the door and quietly started to open it.

"Tinkle-tinkle," sang the little bells over the door.

"Oh no!" thought Timothy. "I forgot about those noisy bells!"

"Timothy, is that you?" called Mr. Winterbottom from the rear of the store. "Don't forget your mom's postcards!"

"He sure has good hearing for an old man," thought Timothy.

"Oh, yes," answered Timothy, suddenly remembering why he had come to Mr. Winterbottom's store. "I guess I did forget." He kept his left hand over the fire engine in his left pants pocket while he carefully removed the postcard money from his right pants pocket and handed it to Mr. Winterbottom.

"Thank you, Timothy," said Mr. Winterbottom cheerfully. "Here are your cards. Come again soon—it's always good to see you."

"He wouldn't say that if he knew what I just did," thought Timothy, darting out the door.

"I sure hope I don't pass any policemen. They would probably guess what I've just done and arrest me." He ran as fast as he could, all the way home. When he reached his street, he stopped and thought about what he had done.

"Gosh, I've stolen something," he told himself. "I'm a thief, and a criminal, and I'll probably have to go to jail."

He no longer felt excited about the fire engine, and he no longer felt that he *had* to have it. He was too worried about the awful thing he had done, and too frightened of what might happen to him because of it.

"Here are your postcards, Mom," called Timothy as he walked into the house. He went upstairs to his room, closed the door, and slowly took the fire engine out of his pocket.

"Somehow it doesn't look as wonderful now as it did in Mr. Winterbottom's store," thought Timothy. "What an awful person I am to steal from nice old Mr. Winterbottom!"

"Timothy! It's time for dinner!" called Mrs.Tyler.

"I'll be right down, Mom," called Timothy, hiding the fire engine under his pillow.

Mr. and Mrs. Tyler were discussing the town's rising crime rate. Timothy's appetite got smaller as his guilt grew bigger.

"I don't know why these people go out and steal," said Mrs. Tyler, "but I think it's just terrible for anyone to do such a thing."

"I think they steal because they know they'll get away with it," said Mr. Tyler. "What we need are more policemen and tougher laws. All criminals should be locked up in jail for twenty years. They are bad people, and they should be punished."

"I'm a terrible person," thought Timothy. He was starting to feel worse and worse. "I probably deserve to go to jail for twenty years. Gosh, I wonder what it's like living in a tiny cell for twenty years—it must be awful!"

"I've got to figure out a way to avoid going to jail," he decided. "Maybe I could just throw the fire engine into a trash basket ... but then it'd still have my fingerprints on it. I could confess to Mr. Winterbottom ... but, no, even somebody as nice as Mr. Winterbottom could never forgive me for doing such a terrible thing. He might even call the police, and then I'd have to go to jail!"

"I guess the only thing I can do," he decided at last, "is to try to return the fire engine before Mr. Winterbottom realizes that it's missing."

The next morning, Timothy got dressed quickly and put the fire engine in his pocket. His heartbeat got faster and faster and louder and louder every step of the way to Mr. Winterbottom's store.

"I bet everybody else on the street can hear it pounding," thought Timothy.

"Tinkle-tinkle," rang the bells over the door as Timothy stepped inside Mr. Winterbottom's store.

"Good morning, Timothy," said Mr. Winterbottom, "what can I do for you today?"

"Uh, well, I think I'd just like to look around," gulped Timothy.

"Fine, fine," said Mr. Winterbottom. "I'll be in the back if you need me."

Timothy walked slowly up and down the aisles, to make it appear as though he really were just looking around. When he came to the shelf where the fire engine belonged, he stopped and glanced toward the back of the store.

"Good," he thought, "Mr. Winterbottom's out of sight, so I can just put back the fire engine, and he'll never even know I stole it."

Timothy reached quickly into his pocket and started to pull out the fire engine.

"Well, Timothy, I thought you might return."

Startled, Timothy whirled around to find Mr. Winterbottom standing right behind him.

"You see, Timothy," continued Mr. Winterbottom, "I saw you take the fire engine yesterday, but I didn't stop you because I wanted to give you a chance to work things out for yourself."

"Oh, Mr. Winterbottom," wailed Timothy, "I feel so awful. I must be such a rotten person to do such a terrible thing—especially after you've been so nice to me! I can't stand to have you feel disappointed and angry with me."

"I thought you might be feeling that way," said Mr. Winterbottom gently, "so I decided to come over and have a word with you about it. Actually, we're dealing with two separate issues here—and both of them are very important. Let's take them one at a time."

"First of all," he began, "you *have* done something that was wrong—but that doesn't mean that you're a rotten person. And it also doesn't mean that you should go around feeling guilty and punishing yourself for it."

"It doesn't?" asked Timothy.

"No, it doesn't," replied Mr. Winterbottom. "You've made a mistake. And the best thing to do when you make a mistake—even a serious one—is to admit it, try to correct it, and then stop worrying about it. Everybody does some things that are bad. But that doesn't mean that they are all bad people, because they also do many things that are good—just like you.

"Let me tell you a secret. Once, when I was a boy, I stole a bag of candy from a store. I think I must have gulped down that whole bagful of candy in about ten seconds. But it tasted terrible ... and I felt even worse, because I was telling myself the same things that you're telling yourself now. The best thing for you to do now is to admit that you were wrong, and forgive yourself."

"Wow!" cried Timothy. "You mean I'm not a bad person ... and I won't have to go to jail?"

"Not only that," replied Mr. Winterbottom, "but I still like you."

"And you mean that everybody sometimes does what I did, and that it's O.K.?" continued Timothy.

"No, that's not what I mean," said Mr. Winterbottom. "We have to make some important distinctions here. And that brings us to the second important issue I mentioned a while ago.

"You stole something ... and stealing is not O.K. You have to remember that stealing is against the law—it's a crime. I mean that what you did is not O.K. ... but to admit your mistake, and to try to correct it, and to forgive yourself is super O.K."

"I think I understand what you're saying," said Timothy thoughtfully. "I did do something that was bad ... but that doesn't mean that I'm a bad person because I did it. Mr. Winterbottom, do you really still like me?"

"More than ever," replied Mr. Winterbottom with a smile.

Timothy smiled too.

"Well," he said, "I really am sorry about what I did. Next time I want something, I'll try to think of a better way of getting it."

"You do that," said Mr. Winterbottom. "As a matter of fact, how about helping me out here in the store? You'll be able to earn that fire engine in no time at all."

"Gee, thanks, Mr. Winterbottom," replied Timothy. "I'd really like that! I feel better already."

Timothy and Mr. Winterbottom shook hands, and Timothy walked back home. As he walked along, he thought about all the things that Mr. Winterbottom had said.

"I'm going to try to remember not to blame myself—or other people—for doing bad things," he resolved. "From now on, if I make a mistake, I'm going to admit it, correct it, and forgive myself."

Activity: **Joe's Angry Secret**

Ages: **All ages**

Materials: **Story: "Joe's Angry Secret" (below)**

Procedure: Read the children the following story.

Discussion: Talk about Joe's feelings of helplessness, fear, and guilt. Help children to relate Joe's feelings to the feelings of the other children in the group. Ask children if they have ever felt like Joe.

Joe's Angry Secret

There was a little boy named Joe [change the name if there is a Joe in your group] who was angry a lot. He used to think about angry things in his head. Sometimes he'd imagine fighting with someone; other times he'd imagine hurting someone; sometimes he'd imagine touching other kids in ways they wouldn't like. Joe had a good reason to be angry. A couple of months ago someone touched Joe in a way that he didn't like. A neighbor man touched Joe's penis and made Joe touch his. Joe felt angry at his neighbor and blamed himself for the neighbor's touching problem. Joe was afraid to talk about it and he kept it a secret. The secret got harder and harder to keep and Joe felt angrier and angrier inside. His angry thoughts came more and more often until he began to act on his thoughts. He began to fight more often and hurt other people.

One day on the playground he touched another boy's private parts in a way that hurt the little boy. The teacher found out and talked to Joe about it. Finally, Joe told her about his neighbor who touched him. Joe joined a group of boys who had similar problems. He learned that it was not his fault that someone touched him. He also learned that it's better to talk about anger than to hurt somebody else. Has this ever happened to you?

Activity: ***Being Me Means***

Ages: *6-12*

Materials: *Spinner (buy or make out of cardboard; pattern follows)*

Procedure: The children take turns spinning the spinner. When the arrow stops in one of the categories, the child who spun states something about him/herself in that category.

Discussion: Ask children which category it was hardest for them to talk about. Talk about everyone making mistakes but also having strengths and talents. It is important for the therapists to acknowledge mistakes they have made.

Activity: ***Nobody's Perfect***

Ages: *6-12*

Materials: *The book,* Nobody's Perfect Not Even My Mother, *by Norma Simon (see Resources)*

Procedure: Read the story aloud to the children.

Being Me Means

Spinner Pattern

*Make a cardboard spinner, following this outline

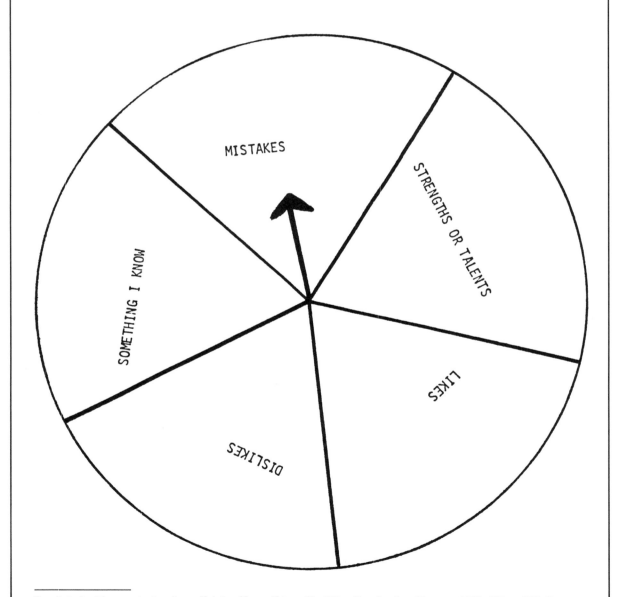

Reprinted with permission from *Helping Yourself to a Healthier You*, by Ann Vernon, 1988. Edina, MN: Burgess International Group, Inc.

Discussion: After reading the story, talk about the good things about their moms or the things they'd like their moms to change. Then have the same discussion about their fathers and perhaps other members of their families. Encourage them to talk about things they like about you, the therapist, and things they'd like to change. This exercise is difficult to do, but it's important for the children to know that everyone has good things about them and things that need changing. This also helps abuse-reactive children deal with black-and-white thinking.

Activity: *Changing Negative Thoughts into Positive Ones*

Ages: *8-10*

Materials: *Blackboard or flip chart; pencil and paper*

Procedure: Choose a bothersome situation that is likely to generate similar feelings among all of the children in the group. Try to choose a common situation, such as being told to clean up your room or having to do homework, so as not to create anxiety or escalate feelings and inappropriate behavior at the beginning of the exercise. Later, children can choose their own situations that bother them or make them feel bad about themselves.

Begin by writing the situation on the board, and then have the children answer the following questions while you record their answers on the board or flipchart: What are my feelings in this situation? What are my negative thoughts? What are some positive thoughts about this situation? Do I have any new thoughts that will help me with the situation? As an alternative, have the children write their answers on paper and read them aloud to the group.

Go back over the positive thoughts with the children, getting them to repeat them out loud to themselves as if they were trying to convince a friend who was discouraged.

You may want to use one or both of the sample exercises below to introduce the issue of sexual abuse into this activity after the children have had time to practice and are more familiar with the concept of changing negative thoughts into positive ones.

Situation: *Being touched in a sexual way by a grownup or a big kid*

Feelings: *Scared, upset, confused, nervous*

Negative Thoughts: *This is my fault; I can never tell anyone; I'm going to get in trouble; I must be bad for this to be happening; I hate myself.*

Positive Thoughts: *I didn't ask for this to happen; this is the other person's problem, not mine; this has happened to a lot of kids and they didn't like it either; I'm not going to carry this yucky secret around inside of me; I know a couple of people to talk to who will understand how I feel.*

New Feelings: *Less scared; less guilty feeling because I know that when this kind of thing happens, it's always the grownup's fault; glad that I can talk about my feelings.*

Situation: *Molesting another person*

Feelings: *Guilty, being ashamed, angry, turned on, powerful*

Negative Thoughts: *I'm stupid, I'm bad, I'm a pervert, I messed up, I can't control myself.*

Positive Thoughts: *I made a mistake, but I can learn from it; I can control my body; I'm learning to talk about my anger; I'm learning about myself, and this won't happen again.*

New Feelings: *More self-forgiving, understanding my anger, feeling more calm, less self-critical.*

Discussion: This exercise can be used to address many issues that come up in the group. It can help reduce negative thinking and can begin to alleviate depression.

Activity: *Five Things I Do Well*

Ages: *5-12*

Materials: *Paper and pencil*

Procedure: Have children fold a piece of paper in half lengthwise, then open it again. On the left side they are to list five things they do well. On the other side they are to list five things they'd like to do better. Compare lists.

Discussion: Done in a group, this exercise helps children see that everyone has strengths and weaknesses. Point out how people's strengths balance their weaknesses. Some children will have difficulty listing their strengths and prompting may be necessary. It's useful to repeat this exercise a number of times throughout the treatment process.

Activity: *Counter It*

Ages: *9-12*

Materials: *Copies of the "Counter It" worksheet (following); pencils or markers*

Procedure: Hand out the worksheet and have children pair up. Review the idea of negative thoughts or insensitive beliefs. Give an example, such as: "If I can't have my way in this game, I'll quit." Talk again about replacing these beliefs with more positive or sensitive ones. For example, replacing the "I'll quit" belief with something like: "Why should I always get my way? Will it do any good to quit? I'll only hurt myself." We've added three sentences specific to molesting to the list on the worksheet.

Discussion: This activity is an excellent one that can also be used as a diagnostic tool. It is important for therapists to understand the abuse-reactive child's belief system so they may initiate appropriate therapeutic interventions with the child and his/her family.

Activity: *Strength Book*

Ages: *5-11*

Materials: *Copies of "My Strength Book" cover (following); several blank pages; paper fasteners*

Counter It

Think of a question or statement as a way of showing how each of these sentences doesn't make good sense. Then come up with a more sensible statement.

1. You should feel bad because everyone doesn't like you.

   _____

2. Missing an answer to a problem makes you stupid.

   _____

3. If you can't figure that out, you're dumb.

   _____

4. If you don't do this for me, I'll tell everyone how awful you are.

   _____

5. I think your coat is ugly.

   _____

6. I'm afraid to call Bob — what if he says he doesn't want to play with me?

   _____

7. If I have to sit by her, I'll die.

   _____

8. If anyone finds out that I molested someone, they'll hate me.

   _____

9. I'm a bad person because I touched someone.

   _____

10. People will think I'm gay if they find out I was molested by someone of the same sex as me.

   _____

_____

Adapted with permission from *Helping Yourself to a Healthier You*, by Ann Vernon, 1989. Edina, MN: Burgess International Group, Inc.

Procedure: Make a booklet for each child using the illustration as a cover page. As a weekly ritual at the beginning or end of the group meeting, have the children write or draw one strength he/she has. You might ask younger children to draw something that is special about them.

Discussion: This exercise is terrific in helping children raise their self-esteem and gain a sense of mastery and nonabusive power. Boys in particular tend to think of strength as muscle or "outside" strength. As you continue to do this exercise every week, you can help the children focus on their internal strengths as well.

An important part of having a positive self-concept is feeling *mastery* over life skills ranging from simple environmental tasks all the way to experiencing, expressing, and controlling feelings relating to the emotions and the self. Abuse-reactive children tend to alternate between feeling totally out of control and feeling a need to totally control. They often have difficulty focusing and being successful in very simple tasks. Due to their lack of impulse control, they also have trouble finishing tasks they begin. When they see other children successfully completing tasks assigned to them, they feel even worse.

One therapeutic task in developing a positive sense of self is for abuse-reactive children to achieve a sense of mastery over single jobs. Various modalities can be used in this process, including simple board games (such as checkers, Battleship, and Life, etc.), that can be completed in one activity period. Activities dealing with the five senses help children feel more in control of their bodies. Simple craft projects that have never been tried before are another way to help children feel successful. Sewing and lacing together felt puppets is a favorite activity among latency-age boys. Since most boys have never attempted to sew, they feel a real sense of accomplishment when they find that they can sew a dinosaur puppet and take it home with them the same day.

Mastery over one's body is an important aspect of positive self-esteem, helping abuse-reactive children gain a healthy sense of control. Sensory awareness exercises, biofeedback, and activities that develop large and small motor skills help children develop mastery and a sense of internal control.

A sense of positive self-worth encourages personal growth and competence in all children. It is essential for abuse-reactive children to develop mastery over their daily lives, learn to control negative self-statements, and accept their strengths and weaknesses. The exercises included in this chapter encourage growth in each of these areas, helping the abuse-reactive child to develop positive self-esteem.

CHAPTER SIX

Managing Anger

Anger management is an essential part of a therapeutic treatment program for the abuse-reactive child. In an attempt to master the trauma of their victimization, many abuse-reactive children identify with their aggressors by acting out their anger and lack of control in coercive and destructive ways. These young perpetrators often feel powerless and do not yet have the social skills to get their needs met appropriately. Within their environments they often feel that they have no control over what happens to them. By committing sexually aggressive acts, many abuse-reactive children unconsciously translate their need to be in control of their lives into a need to dominate and exploit those who are less powerful or more helpless.

The major behavioral task for the therapist is to help the abuse-reactive child develop self-control methods in order to reduce their angry and aggressive acts. Some therapists believe that the best way to assist abused children in expressing their unresolved anger is to encourage them to use catharsis to "get rid of" angry feelings. It is crucial that therapists working with abuse-reactive children understand that when an *abuse-reactive* child is acting destructively to himself, others, or property, he/she is *being abusive*, i.e., he/she is *repeating the abuse cycle*, rather than using catharsis to express anger. When therapists allow an abuse-reactive child to engage in destructive behavior during the therapy session, they give that child the message that no one, not even a healthy adult, can control his/her destructive behavior. In addition, the therapist appears to be colluding with the child's inappropriate acting out.

Pioneers in the field of anger management, such as Feindler and Ecton (1986), Novaco (1975), and McGinnis and Goldstein (1984), employ a cognitive-behavioral approach when teaching anger management to both adolescents and adults. By combining several of these techniques, we have developed the following eight skills the abuse-reactive child needs to learn in order to control his/her angry and destructive acts:

Skills for Anger Management

The abuse-reactive child is able to identify a range of feelings, including feelings of anger. While this may seem simple at first, abuse-reactive children tend to react angrily to every situation, even when they may be feeling scared or sad. The task for therapists is to assist them in differentiating the four basic feelings (mad, sad, glad, and scared), and to help them identify what things or people in their lives they react to with anger. It is equally important to begin to interpret for abuse-reactive children when they are actually sad or scared and are using anger as a mask or defense.

The abuse-reactive child can identify aggressive acts exhibited by self and others. In this step, the therapist helps the child understand the meaning of "aggression," and identify it in him/herself and in others.

The abuse-reactive child can identify the potential consequences (to self and others) of aggressive behavior. This is extremely important during the early stages of treatment. Until children can monitor and control their angry outbursts, constant reminders of the consequences of aggressive behavior may be the only deterrent to further aggressive acts.

The abuse-reactive child can identify self-destructive behavior. Abuse-reactive children often believe they were victimized because they are bad. Therefore, they act in ways that elicit negative reactions and/or punishment. Due to their feelings of loss of control, abuse-reactive children engage in self-destructive acts (e.g., self-mutilation) as a way of gaining some degree of mastery over their bodies.

The abuse-reactive child can identify thoughts that occur prior to aggressive acts. The cognitive-behavioral method of anger management encourages children to attempt to identify the thoughts they have prior to their angry outbursts. Later, children are instructed on how to *change* their thoughts.

The abuse-reactive child can recognize and relate internal cues to feelings of anger. It is crucial to assist abuse-reactive children to learn to identify cues or signals in their bodies prior to their angry acts.

The abuse-reactive child has developed coping mechanisms to deal with anger and aggression. It is important for the child to be able to handle the anger of others without having to engage in power struggles or aggression. Two effective skill-building techniques in this area are modeling and role playing.

The abuse-reactive child can express anger without loss of control. This, of course, is the ultimate goal of anger management, and it may take a long time to achieve. However, with practice and consistent positive reinforcement by therapists and parents, it can be accomplished.

The activities in this chapter focus on building these eight skills.

Activity: *The Most Important Things to Remember About Getting Mad*[18]

Ages: *6 -12*

Materials: *Worksheet (following); index cards; marker*

Procedure: During group and as homework assignments have children repeat the phrases below. This needs to be reinforced and repeated throughout the duration of the group and at home. Reinforcement and repetition can be accomplished by copying the appropriate phrases onto index cards to be used like flash cards at home. This exercise should be repeated until the child internalizes these sentences as his/her own self-talk.

Discussion: Cognitive reframing is a crucial element in teaching children anger management. Repetition leads to internalization. The goal is to have these positive statements replace negative internalized statements that children often learn through poor role-modeling or witnessing family violence.

---

[18]This activity was contributed by Lynne Namka, Ed.D. from her *I Stop My Bully Behavior Kit.* See Resources.

The Most Important Things to Remember About Getting Mad Worksheet

I am in charge of my own feelings.

I own my feelings.

I feel them, name them and then tell them.

It is okay to feel angry.

I learn how to express my anger in ways that are helpful.

Anger is part of being a human being and that is a wonderful thing to be.

The more I learn about taking care of my anger, the more powerful I become.

I don't try to control my anger: I control what I do with my anger.

I gain control over how I let my anger out.

I watch my thoughts. Hot thoughts keep me angry. Cool thoughts calm me down.

I practice cooling off. I learn to chill myself out.

I remember that people are precious.

I stop hurting others or myself with my anger.

I watch my thoughts. I watch my words. I watch my actions.

I own the hurtful words and actions that I do to others.

I learn about things I do when I am stressed and threatened.

I stop hurting people with my words and actions.

Bully Behavior hurts two ways it hurts me and hurts the other person.

I stop blaming others and myself. Blaming does not solve the problem.

Blaming someone else only keeps me upset and angry.

Blaming others is a way of not respecting them.

Blaming myself is a way of not respecting myself.

I tell my feelings and then try to work things out.

I choose to feel good about myself through speaking out.

I express angry feelings in ways that are fair to others and myself.

I use my firm and fair words: "I feel when you ."

I don't have to hold on to my anger.

I find ways to let my anger go.

I talk about my hurt feelings and angry feelings.

I problem-solve things that make me upset.

I keep looking until I find someone safe to talk to about my anger.

I talk about my words and actions that hurt others.

I take my power!

I stand up for myself. I stand up for others who are being hurt.

I learn to break into my mean thoughts that I use to beat myself up.

I feel good about learning about myself.

I am powerful when I use my fair and firm words.

Activity: *What Makes Me Angry*

Ages: *All ages*

Materials: *Sheets of paper; crayons (for younger children) or pencils (for older children)*

Procedure: Have the children make a list, or, for younger children, draw the people and events that "make" them angry. After all the children have finished their lists, have them share the lists or pictures with the rest of the group members.

Discussion: Probe for reasons that these particular events and/or people "make" them angry. It is crucial for the therapist to validate the children's feelings of anger, particularly if they have been abused. Note whether children list the perpetrators of their own abuse. If the children omit people or events that the therapist feels are important, the therapist should gently confront or interpret the omission.

Activity: *Where Does My Anger Come From?*

Ages: *All ages*

Materials: *Photocopies of any diagram of the human body,[19] or drawings of gingerbread-type figures*

Procedure: Talk about body cues and how these cues let us know where we are feeling angry. Ask children to locate the places in their bodies they first begin to feel tension and anger. Discuss the fact that these are important messages letting us know that we need to find ways to express this anger without hurting ourselves or others. Have the children label or color in the place on the diagram that corresponds to where they feel their anger the most.

Discussion: After the children locate and color in their angry body cues, help them to develop ways to calm themselves down when they are feeling anger. This could be self-talk such as, "Calm down, it's no big deal," counting to 10, deep breathing, or physical exercise. Throughout this unit, help children develop a plan to manage their anger before it gets out of control. Set aside time in group for the children to practice their anger-management plans over and over again. This plan should be monitored by their parents and should include positive reinforcements given to children who begin to stop themselves prior to an angry outburst.

Activity: *My Angry Mask*

Ages: *5-12*

Materials: *Paper plates; marking pens; crayons*

Procedure: The purpose of this exercise is to help children identify when anger is used legitimately and when it is used to cover up feelings of fear and sadness. Talk about how we wear masks at Halloween to disguise who we are and that people also wear masks to hide how they feel. Give examples. Have the

---

[19]*Anatomical Drawings* (© 1984 by Forensic Mental Health Associates) provides simple, explicit line drawings of males and females in four age ranges and two races that can be photocopied (see the listing under Groth, A.N., in Resources).

children make an angry mask, put it on, and have them talk about what other kinds of feelings are hiding underneath the mask.

Discussion: Abuse-reactive children generally use anger as a way to block out feelings of fear, pain, or sadness. This is a powerful exercise to help children get in touch with feelings and events they have repressed.

Activity: *Aggression* [20]

Ages: *7-12*

Materials: *Chalk board; puppets (preferably people puppets)*

Procedure: Write the words "anger" and "aggression" on the board. Differentiate aggression from anger through the use of puppets or role playing. Discuss consequences of aggression.

Discussion: After using the puppets, ask the children why people behave aggressively. What are the results of behaving aggressively? Does aggression really help you get what you want? Clarify with abuse-reactive children how sexual acting out is a form of aggression. Explore with the group other ways to deal with anger instead of sexually acting out. This may need to be repeated often, because abuse-reactive children may not be conscious of the anger they harbor.

Activity: *Angry Picture*

Ages: *5-12*

Materials: *Cut-out magazine or newspaper pictures of people who look angry and people who are shown acting aggressively; large kraft or butcher paper for mural; glue; markers*

Procedure: Divide the mural into two parts, one part labeled "Angry," and one part labeled "Aggressive." Have the children glue the pictures into the correct columns.

Discussion: Talk about the differences in the pictures. Ask the group which pictures make them feel more comfortable. Ask them which person seems more in control. Ask each child to pick a picture and to make a cartoon or tell a story about what happens next in the sequence. Discuss the consequences of aggression with the group.

Activity: *Anger Game*

Ages: *6-12*

Materials: *Sets of questions (following) copied on index cards; tokens; dice; blank game board (any home-made board will do; optional)*

Procedure: Have children read game cards, and answer the questions on the cards. If the child attempts to answer the question, he/she gets a token. The child with the most tokens wins the game. In the game

---

[20]Adapted from *Creative Conflict Resolution*, by William Kreidler. Copyright © 1984 by William J. Kreidler. Used by permission of Scott, Foresman and Company.

board version, the board should include squares marked with a "?." Each player rolls the dice; the player landing on a "?" space draws a card and answers the question. Any good answer entitles the player to move one space on the board. The first player to the finish line wins.

Discussion: This is an excellent reinforcement for anger management skills that have been learned in the group. Games are a nonthreatening interactive way to teach necessary skills.

Questions for the Anger Game

1. How can you let out your anger without hurting someone else?
2. In this group who gets the angriest? Why do you think they get so angry?
3. A time that I stopped myself from hurting someone was when   .
   I did it by   .
4. A time that I didn't stop myself from hurting someone was
5. What do angry feelings and bad touching have to do with each other?
6. A friend borrows one of your favorite toys and breaks it. What can you say to yourself to keep from losing your cool?
7. You are watching your favorite television show. Your little brother switches the channel. You want to get up and kick him. What can you do to stop yourself?
8. What are some early warning signs in your body that make you aware that you are getting angrier and angrier?
9. What makes a person become a bully?
10. Whenever you think about the person who molested you, you begin to feel very angry inside. Instead of hurting someone, what can you do to deal with your anger?
11. Without using words, show how you feel when you get angry.
12. Draw or act out some of the things your anger tells you about yourself.
13. The angriest that I have ever gotten is when _____ .
14. I feel angry toward my father when _____ .
15. I feel angry toward my mother when _____ .
16. How do your parents act when they get mad?
17. A boy is angry at everyone. He is having thoughts about hurting people. He notices a younger child walking down the street. What is he thinking? What should he do?
18. How do bullies feel inside?
19. Tell about a time that you were talked into doing something that you really didn't want to do.
20. How do you feel when somebody criticizes you? A) Rejected. B) Fearful. C) Angry. D) Like a bad person. E) Don't care.
21. Here are some "not-okay" ways to react to feedback or criticism: A) Yell back at the person. B) Run away from the person. C) Hit or kick the person. D) Blame someone else. Have you ever reacted in one of these ways? Why doesn't it work?
22. Here are some good ways that you can deal with feedback or criticism: A) Agree. B) Disagree calmly. C) Say yes, that's a problem for me. D) Ask for advice on how to improve the problem. Have you ever reacted in any of these ways? What happened?
23. A time that I thought about hurting myself was_____ .
    These are things I can do instead of hurting myself: A)_____   B)_____
    C) _____ .
24. Where did you first learn how to act when you're angry?
25. Your anger is a way of protecting your fear inside. Is there another way of protecting yourself besides acting angry all of the time?

Activity: *Who Controls Me?*

Ages: *7-12*

Materials: *Copies of "Who Controls Me?" worksheet (following); string puppet or toy robot (optional)*

Procedure: Read "They Made Me." Discuss "Putting It Together." A string puppet or toy robot aptly illustrates the point.

Discussion: Talk about denial and how easy it is to blame the other person or avoid taking responsibility for our own actions. As an example, discuss how people who molest lots of different kids still blame it on the victims. Ask the group members if they have felt blamed or victimized for something someone has done to them. Clarify whose fault it really was. Ask the children if they have ever blamed their own victims. Discuss fairness. Is it fair to blame others for something you initiated?

Activity: *Power*

Ages: *8-12*

Materials: *Crayons or markers; drawing paper*

Procedure: First, have each child draw what he/she feels power means. Most likely men with muscles or superheroes will be drawn. Have the children explain what power means to them.

Discussion: Help children differentiate "outside" power from "inside" power, in other words, brains versus muscles. You might make an analogy, such as asking, "Who has more power: King Kong or the President? Why?" Stress the point that there are many different kinds of power, and that it is possible to have more than one. Also discuss the concept of using "inside power" before using "outside power."

Activity: *A Matter of Control* 📖

Ages: *5-11*

Materials: *The coloring book* A Matter of Control *(by S. Ballester & F. Pierre; see Resources)*

Procedure: Read the coloring book to the group. Talk about sexual acting out as a "matter of control." Stop on each page and discuss how the children's process parallels that of the boy in the book, for example, attempts to "run away from his control problem." Ask the children how they attempted to run away from their touching problem.

Activity: *It Makes Me Angry*

Ages: *7-12*

Materials: *Copies of "It Makes Me Angry" worksheet (following)*

Procedure: Have each child make his/her own plan for handling anger. Have them role play various situations using their plans.

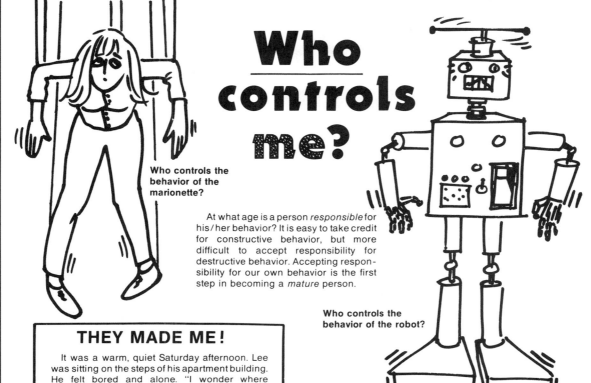

Who controls me?

Who controls the behavior of the marionette?

At what age is a person *responsible* for his/her behavior? It is easy to take credit for constructive behavior, but more difficult to accept responsibility for destructive behavior. Accepting responsibility for our own behavior is the first step in becoming a *mature* person.

Who controls the behavior of the robot?

THEY MADE ME!

It was a warm, quiet Saturday afternoon. Lee was sitting on the steps of his apartment building. He felt bored and alone. "I wonder where everyone is," he said to himself. Suddenly Bobby and Josie came around the corner.

"What 'ya doing, Lee?" asked Bobby.

"Nothing," moaned Lee. "I'm so bored. Got any ideas?"

"Let's go down by the school and see what's happening," said Josie.

They went to the school, but there was no one around.

"Let's break into the school and mess up some of the rooms," Bobby suggested.

Lee hesitated. He wasn't sure that was what he wanted to do. "I don't know," he said. "We might get caught and then we'll really be in trouble."

"No, we won't get caught," Josie said confidently. "Besides, we won't mess it up too much."

"Okay," said Lee. He didn't really like the idea, but he wanted to be with his friends.

While they were "messing up" Miss Jones' classroom, the custodian caught Lee, Bobby, and Josie and called the police. Their parents were called and told to pick them up at the police station. When Lee's parents asked him why he did it, Lee said, "*They* made me do it."

PUTTING IT TOGETHER

1. Do you agree with Lee? Can someone else *make* you do something you think is wrong?

2. How do you think Miss Jones and her class will feel when they discover the mess?

3. How do you think Lee, Bobby and Josie should "make right" the wrong they have done?

4. What does it mean to "take responsibility" for your behavior?

5. Have you ever stood up against your friends for something you believed was right? Tell about it.

★★★★★★★★★★★★★★★★★★★★★★★★★★★★★

YOUR CHALLENGE:

There may be times when someone tries to control your behavior by influencing you to do something you know is wrong. In small groups, brainstorm ways to deal with these situations.

★★★★★★★★★★★★★★★★★★★★★★★★★★★★★

Reprinted with permission from *Creative Conflict Solving for Kids,* by Fran Schmidt and Alice Friedman (Grace Contrino Abrams Peace Education Foundation, Inc., 3550 Biscayne Boulevard, Suite 400, Miami, FL 33137, 1985).

IT MAKES ME ANGRY

Have you ever felt the way the kids in the cartoon do? Draw a cartoon showing what makes YOU really angry.

When frustration is not resolved, we often become angry. Anger is a natural emotion that all people feel. Anger does not have to end in violence. Sometimes we get so angry that we feel like a "bomb ready to explode." Nature has given our bodies a lot of energy so that we may act quickly when we are in danger. What do our bodies want to do with this energy? Is it possible to *defuse* this energy without hurting ourselves and others?

Some students your age have suggested techniques for defusing anger. In small groups, discuss them and add some of your own.

Anger is the letting off of steam,
the punching at your pillow
to cool off . . .
The gritting of your teeth,
and biting your lip
to control yourself.
Mark, age 12

Remember to rip it into 1,000,000 little pieces after you write it.

YOUR CHALLENGE!

Practice one of these techniques and use it the next time you find yourself reacting in an angry way. Tell about it.

Used with permission from *Creative Conflict Solving for Kids,* by Fran Schmidt and Alice Friedman (Grace Contrino Abrams Peace Education Foundation, Inc., 3550 Biscayne Boulevard, Suite 400, Miami, FL 33137, 1985).

Discussion: This exercise needs to be repeated over and over in order for children to internalize these techniques. Note: exercises such as punching pillows are not very effective with abuse-reactive children. They have trouble differentiating when to act out their aggression, and they need to learn to *internalize* rather than *externalize* their anger.

Activity: *My Special Room*

Ages: *7-12*

Materials: *None; drawing paper may be used as a follow-up*

Procedure: This relaxation and visualization exercise begins by doing basic muscle relaxation. Then have the children imagine that they are sitting in a special room just for them:

"In your very special room are your favorite stuffed animal and other favorite things. You can color your room in any one of your favorite colors. Feel the thick soft carpet. Look at the wall and see your favorite posters of a special hero, or music group, etc. Put anything you want in your special room to make it feel safe and secure. Anytime you feel angry and out of control, you can come into your safe and special room to gain control of yourself. Your special room can handle all of your angry or out-of-control feelings. Think of somebody or something you're really angry about. Imagine that you're in your special room decorated in the way you like, and that you're getting control of your anger. Feel yourself calming down and relaxing. You feel better now, and you are ready to leave your room, knowing that anytime you feel out of control, you can come back into this room and it will help you get control of your anger. You can leave all of your angry thoughts back in the room."

As a followup, have the children draw pictures of their special rooms.

Discussion: This guided imagery gives children a sense of control. The room is a metaphor for containment. Other emotions such as fear and sadness can also be introduced in the same type of imagery. After the imagery exercise, have the children draw or discuss what their imaginary room is like and what angry thoughts or feelings they had while they were in their room. It is important for the children to learn that they can handle having these feelings without totally losing control (their ultimate fear).

Activity: *Ring Around of Temper*

Ages: *8-12*

Materials: *Copies of "Ring Around of Temper" (following); drawing paper; crayons or markers*

Procedure: Read the story and discuss the questions under "What Do You Think?" Have the children make a drawing for the "Your Challenge" section, then draw alternate solutions.

Discussion: Discuss with the group how Clem was hurt and how he reacted in an angry way (much like they have reacted to their emotional, physical, or sexual victimization). Brainstorm the different ways

A RING-AROUND OF TEMPER

1

Once upon a time, there was a man by the name of Chem. He was standing by his hut on the bank of a river, sharpening his ax, when a little shrimp crawled up on his foot and bit him. Chem became so angry that he lifted his ax and cut a nearby tree with a fierce blow.

The tree became so angry that it shook a coconut from one of its branches, and the coconut fell on the back of a rooster. The rooster became so angry that he scratched up a big ant hill full of ants.

The ants became so angry that they bit the tail of a snake.

The snake became so angry that he stung an elephant in the leg.

2

The elephant became so angry that he knocked over a big hollow stone which an old woman used to pound her rice. The stone rolled down the hill and hit the old woman's house and knocked it down.

"Stone! Stone!" called the old woman angrily. "You must pay me for my house."

"I won't! I won't!" shouted the stone. "It was the elephant who made me roll down the hill."

The old woman went to the elephant and said angrily, "Elephant, you must pay for my house."

"No, I won't!" said the elephant. "It was the snake's fault. He stung me in the leg."

The old woman went to the snake and said angrily, "Snake, you must pay me for my house."

3

"No, I won't!" said the snake. "It was the fault of the ants."

The old woman went to the ants and said angrily, "Ants, you must pay me for my house."

"No, we won't!" said the ants. "It was the rooster's fault. He scratched up our hill and spoiled our house."

The old woman went to the rooster and said angrily, "Rooster, you must pay for my house."

"No, I won't!" said the rooster. "It was the tree's fault. It dropped a coconut on my back."

The old woman went to the coconut tree, and said angrily, "Tree, you must pay for my house."

4

"No, I won't!" said the tree. "It was Chem who struck me with his ax."

The old woman went to Chem and said angrily, "Chem, you must pay me for my house."

"No, I won't!" said Chem. "It's the fault of the shrimp . He bit my foot."

The old woman went to the shrimp and said, "Shrimp, you must pay me for my house."

Now the shrimp could not blame anyone else. Nor could he build the old woman a new house.

While she was scolding him, the shrimp hopped into a pool, dived to the bottom, and no one has ever been able to find him since.

Copyright © 1948 by Sophia Lyon Fahs
Reprinted by permission of Beacon Press

WHAT DO YOU THINK?

1. What was the conflict?
2. How did each character perceive the conflict?
3. How do you think the characters felt?

YOUR CHALLENGE!

Draw a cartoon showing the chain of events in the story.

4. How did the shrimp deal with the problem?
5. Why do you think the characters blamed each other?
6. Do you sometimes blame others for your actions?

that Clem could have dealt with his sore foot other than by chopping down a tree. Also discuss the issues of blaming and running away from your problems as the shrimp did at the end of the story.[21]

Activity: **_The Angry Envelope_**

Ages: *5-11*

Materials: *A large envelope for each child; paper; pencil*

Procedure: Have each child write down all of the things, people, or events that make him/her angry. Next have the child tear up the list so each item is on one piece and put all the pieces into the envelope. Every week take out the envelope and have the child reach in and get one of the pieces of paper. Ask the child to talk about why he/she is angry about what is written on that piece of paper. After the discussion is complete, have the child throw the piece of paper in the trash; OR save the pieces in a separate envelope in case the feelings come back.

Discussion: The envelope is symbolic of containment. Essentially the therapeutic process holds the child together while he/she works through his/her anger, just as the envelope keeps all the scraps of paper together until all issues are dealt with.

Activity: **_Fight Form_**

Ages: *7-12*

Materials: *Pencils; copies of the "Fight Form" (following)*

Procedure: Go over the Fight Form with the parents. This can be a homework assignment for the children to fill out when they get into a fight during the week. Have the children bring back the completed form to the group the following week.

Discussion: Have the children discuss their completed worksheet with the rest of the group. Explore with the children other ways to deal with their anger rather than fighting; they could make a list of good and bad ways of showing anger.

Activity: **_Responding to Aggressive Behavior_**

Ages: *10-12*

Materials: *Pencils; copies of the "Responding to Aggressive Behavior" worksheet (following)*

Procedure: Do the worksheet together. Introduce the idea of short-term and long-term consequences to behaviors. Add this example to the list: An older boy wants to touch you in a way that you don't like. He threatens to beat you up if you tell. What might be the short-term effect? What might be the long-term effect?

---

[21] For similar exercises, consult the Grace Contrino Abrams Peace Foundation, 3550 Biscayne Boulevard, Suite 400, Miami, FL 33137.

Name _____

Fight Form

With whom did you fight? _____

What was the problem? _____
_____

Why did you start fighting? (Give two reasons.) _____
_____
_____

Why did the other person fight with you? _____
_____
_____

Did fighting solve the problem? _____

What are three things you might try if this happens again?

1. _____

2. _____

3. _____

Is there anything you would like to say to the person you fought with? _____
_____
_____

Name

Responding to Aggressive Behavior

1. John just took something of yours. What could you do?_____
   _____

   What might be the short-term effect of that?_____
   What might be the long-range effect of that?_____

2. Angela just pushed you hard in the hall. What could you do?_____
   _____

   What might be the short-term effect?_____
   What might be the long-range effect?_____

3. Darryl just asked to copy your homework. What could you do?_____
   _____

   What might be the short-term effect?_____
   What might be the long-range effect?_____

4. Gino is telling lies about you. What could you do?_____
   _____

   What might be the short-term effect?_____
   What might be the long-range effect?_____

5. Francine is calling you names. What could you do?_____
   _____

   What might be the short-term effect?_____
   What might be the long-range effect?_____

Discussion: Understanding that there are long-term consequences to behaviors is an important concept for abuse-reactive children to be constantly aware of; this awareness can act as a deterrent to future inappropriate behaviors. Introduce self-talk to help them stop and think about long-term consequences as a means of preventing themselves from further acting out.

Activity: *The Angry Monster Machine*

Ages: *6-11*

Materials: *The game entitled The Angry Monster Machine. (Available from Childswork/Childsplay; see Resources.)*

Procedure: This game is a terrific game using clay as a medium of expression. Use with two or more children. After the game it might be helpful to follow with the Angry Animal Book.

Discussion: Anger management is a crucial therapeutic goal for abusive children. This game allows acceptance of anger, but offers alternatives using every sensory modality.

Activity: *My Angry Animal Workbook[22]*

Ages: *5-8*

Materials: *Crayons or markers; a copy of the booklet pages (following) for each child in the group*

Procedure: The workbook is designed to be used in small segments—a page or two at a time—with discussion. If the child cannot think of an animal or a monster, some other image can be substituted. After the children have completed the booklet, discuss it as a group and with the parents' group.

Discussion: Imagery is helpful for young children. Focusing on an animal or a monster, such as Frankenstein, makes the issue of being out of control more concrete so that young children can grasp it. By using animals as imagery, the workbook helps young children to obtain a visual, concrete picture of their anger so they can learn to control it.

Anger management is an essential part of any offender-treatment program. In order for the abuse-reactive child to gain a sense of mastery and control over his/her life, specific cognitive/ behavioral approaches must be taught to each child. Therapists often feel that, if given time, children will work through their anger at their own pace. Research has shown that the aggressive, out-of-control child needs specific didactic instruction in addition to other therapeutic modalities.

---

[22] A similar approach utilizing the metaphor of monsters to represent impulse-control problems with abuse-reactive children has been developed by Ballester and Pierre (1989).

My Angry Animal Workbook

When I get angry I act like a _____ .

(name an animal)

Here is a picture of the animal that I am most like when I'm angry.

When my angry _____ comes out,
                            (name an animal)

I act like this.

(Draw a picture of when you are acting angry.)

The first time my _____ came
(name of your animal)

out, I was _____ years old.

This is what happened to make him/her come out.

(Draw or write what happened)

Here is a picture of my angry animal when he/she was the angriest he/she has ever been.

Write or draw what made your angry animal (you) so angry.

These are things I could say to my angry animal to calm it down.

(Make a list.)

These are things that I could do to make my angry

_____ stop acting badly.
(name of your animal)

(Make a list.)

Sometimes my _____ protects
(name of your animal)
me from certain feelings.

(List the feelings.)

He does this by _____

(Draw a picture or write about how your animal protects you.)

Is there another way to let your feelings out without having to use your angry animal so much?

Sometimes my angry animal gets me into trouble. When does

this happen? _____

_____

Here is a picture of how that happens.

I know that my angry animal is just a part of me.

Here is a picture of me taking charge of my angry animal.

CHAPTER SEVEN

Teaching Problem-solving Skills

Many victims of sexual abuse tend to see things in terms of black-and-white, win-or-lose, all-or-nothing relationships, a thought process that negatively affects their problem-solving and negotiating skills. Abuse-reactive children's anger and lack of impulse control also contribute to their tendency to react physically or aggressively to problems rather than thinking things through. Therefore, an important aspect of the therapeutic process is to teach children the skills of problem-solving, options identification, and negotiation. For abuse-reactive children, learning these skills will reduce their aggressive behavior, raise their level of impulse control, and increase their social skills and self-esteem. This chapter offers sources and activities that promote negotiation and problem-solving.

In her book *Kids Can Cooperate* (1984; see Resources) and in her collection of children's problem-solving books, Elizabeth Crary offers the following steps for problem-solving:

Step One: Stop and stay calm. Crary emphasizes the importance of being aware of feelings and identifying the physical signs of being upset. Suggested ways that children can practice calming themselves include: counting to 10; "draining" the anger out of their feet; taking deep breaths; creating an imaginary "protective shield" that keeps them calm on the inside.

Step Two: Identify the problem. A series of questions is offered to aid the child in problem identification. These include identifying what the child and other people feel and/or want; who else considers the situation a problem; and what occurred just before the problem.

Step Three: Generate ideas to solve the problem. Questions for the child to ask are used to identify solutions. For example, who can help the child, how can he/she negotiate for assistance, and will a different order of things or a different physical setting solve the child's problem.

Step Four: Evaluate. This step focuses on thinking of alternative plans for solving the problem, recognizing their consequences, and choosing the best one.

Step Five: Make a plan. The actual plan also is presented as a series of steps that must be identified before they are carried out. Crary reminds children in the last step to congratulate themselves on a job well done.

At the end of her book, Crary has illustrated the problem-solving approach with short scripts therapists can role play with clients. This chapter includes role plays that illustrate Crary's technique.

In their cognitive problem-solving program *Think Aloud,* Camp and Bash (1981; Bash & Camp 1985) introduced to young children a very simple four-step process in problem-solving. The child thinks and answers the following questions out loud: "1) What is my problem? 2) How can I do it or solve it? 3) Am I using my plan? 4) How did I do?" (Camp & Bash, 1981, pp. 43-46; Bash & Camp, 1985, p. 55).

Student Gus the Dragon Cue Pictures

1

WHAT IS MY PROBLEM?

2

HOW CAN I SOLVE IT?

3

AM I USING THE BEST PLAN?

4

HOW DID I DO?

Various role plays, motor and auditory tasks, and interpersonal games require children to develop a plan verbally and to follow through with it. For abuse-reactive children, thinking out loud helps them think through things slowly, rather than simply reacting. In addition, Camp and Bash (1981) have developed social *cue cards* which can be presented to children as alternative ways to negotiate, compromise, or share in order to get their needs met (see following pages). The group therapist can cut out the cards and use them during the group process to promote negotiation, compromise, and sharing.

The following activity uses role plays to illustrate one way cue cards could be used.

Activity: *Jumpin Jake Settles Down/Look Before You Leap*

Ages: *6-10*

Materials: *Workbook entitled,* **Jumpin Jake Settles Down** *and/or the game entitled* **Look Before You Leap** *(available from Childswork/Childsplay; see Resources section.)*

Procedure: Use workbook and game in a group situation. The game and workbook focus on thinking before you act and the consequences that happen when one thinks impulsively.

Discussion: Children who abuse are by nature impulsive and unable to tolerate frustration. These games teach children to stop and think before they act. This game and workbook is an excellent tool for abusive children.

Activity: *Learning How to Negotiate*

Ages: *6-12*

Materials: *Role plays (below); social cue cards (followimg)*

Procedure: Below are three examples of role plays encouraging negotiation. Use the social cue cards or other methods to help the children find ways to negotiate solutions.

1. It's your mother's birthday. You and your sister combined your money and bought a present for her together. Now, each of you wants to give her the present yourself. How will you negotiate what to do?

2. Your two best friends frequently trade basball cards with each other. They have just found out that one card is very valuable. They are fighting as to who it really belongs to. They have come to you to settle the problem. How can you help them?

3. You're having a family meeting to decide where to go on vacation. Your dad wants to go camping. Your mom wants to go to the beach. You want to go to Disneyland. Your brother wants to play baseball. Role play how your family can work it out.

After the children complete the role plays using negotiating skills, have them repeat the role plays *without* using compromises.

FAVOR

GIVE

HURT

Reprinted with permission from *Think Aloud Primary Level* by Bonnie W. Camp & Mary Ann Bash (1981). © 1981 by Bonnie W. Camp & Mary Ann Bash. Champaign, IL: Research Press.

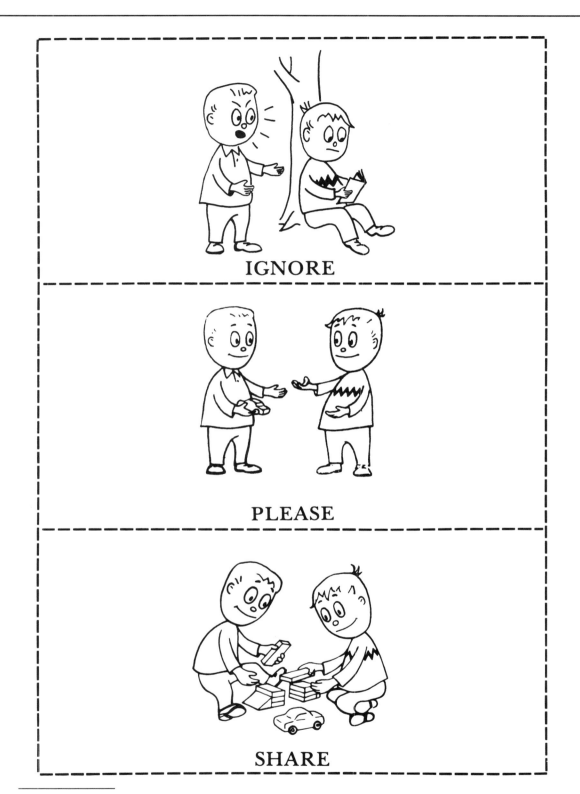

IGNORE

PLEASE

SHARE

Reprinted with permission from *Think Aloud Primary Level* by Bonnie W. Camp & Mary Ann Bash (1981). © 1981 by Bonnie W. Camp & Mary Ann Bash. Champaign, IL: Research Press.

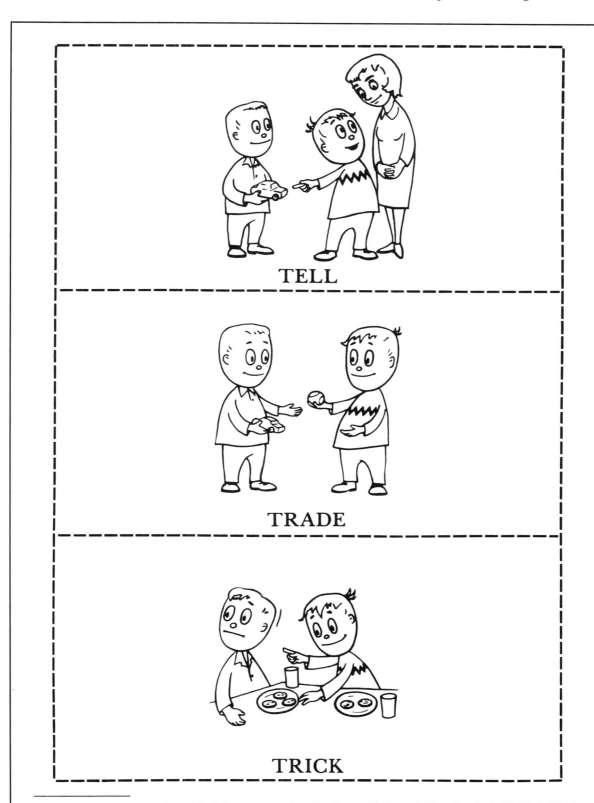

TELL

TRADE

TRICK

Reprinted with permission from *Think Aloud Primary Level* by Bonnie W. Camp & Mary Ann Bash (1981). © 1981 by
Bonnie W. Camp & Mary Ann Bash. Champaign, IL: Research Press.

Discussion: It's important to remember that experience in role play varies at different age levels. The young child may focus on only one portion of the role at a time, reflecting the egocentricity that occurs at the pre-school age. The older child will be able to internalize several dimensions of his/her experience and will be able to identify with the other characters in the role play. Whatever the age, role play is an important tool for mastering concepts, beginning the process of empathy and moral development, and learning problem-solving skills. It promotes cooperation and, although pre-school or young latency-age children may not internalize as much, they will begin to learn to cooperate and will be able to master a portion of the concepts of negotiation and problem-solving.

As the children complete each role play, ask each child how he/she felt about what happened, and ask how it feels when you can't always get your way.

After they complete the second part of the role-playing activity, ask the children to compare their feelings when they use negotiation to when they refuse to compromise. By taking part in both role plays, they can actually experience the importance of negotiation.

Activity: *The Eency Weency Spider*

Ages: *4-7*

Materials: *"The Eency Weency Spider" song sheet and worksheets (following)*

Procedure: Sing "The Eency Weency Spider" song together. Take the children through the various steps in problem-solving, figuring out what the spider's problem is. What will happen when he goes up the spout again? How does the spider feel when he keeps getting washed out of the water spout? How can the spider solve this problem? How does the spider feel when he finally solves the problem?

Discussion: You can also teach the concept of self-talk by asking the children what the spider can say to himself to reduce the spider's anger and frustration when he repeatedly gets washed down from the spout. The spider can say to himself, "Don't give up. You'll find an answer to the problem." Or he may say to himself, "I can stay calm." If he feels scared and powerless when he is being washed down from the water spout, he may choose to say to himself, "Stay calm, you will survive."

Try to come up with a group consensus on the best way to solve the spider's problem. Use negotiating skills and encourage compromising. The following worksheets may be helpful.

Activity: *Role Plays for Abuse-reactive Children*

Ages: *All ages*

Materials: *Situations listed on page 117*

Procedure: Using role plays appropriate to their age levels, have the children act out the various situations using alternative ways to solve the problem. You may choose to read the problem rather than having the children act it out. However, role playing elicits greater participation and can break through the denial that is particularly characteristic of these children.

Eency Weency Spider

– The eency weency spider went up the water spout.

– Down came the rain and washed the spider out.

– Out came the sun and dried up all the rain . . .

– So the eency weency spider went up the spout again.

Reprinted from *Creative Problem Solving for an Eency Weency Spider* by Gretchen A. Duling, © 1983, with permission from DOK Publications, Buffalo, NY.

Think and Remember...

What is the problem
for this spider?

(Write down what you feel is his problem or talk about it
as a group.)

_____

_____

_____

_____

_____

Solution Finding

Choose two (2) ideas you like

write in the two ideas	Will it make the spider happy?	Will it work?	Will it	(YOU CHOOSE 1)
①				
②				

Use faces in the boxes below the "will its" and judge the two (2) ideas against each other

GOOD   MAYBE   NO

Count the smiles to see which idea seems best. Make a check (✓) in the thin last box to show the best idea.

Situations

1. You haven't told anybody about molesting a little child. You're afraid because, even though you made the child promise not to tell, you're not sure if he/she will keep the promise. What's the problem? How are you going to solve it?

2. Some kids in school are walking down the street and when they pass you, they call you "queer," "faggot," and "gay." What is the problem? How do you feel? What are your thoughts? What are you going to do?

3. The big sister of the person you touched is in one of your classes at school. The situation has been reported and she knows what happened. What is the problem? How do you feel? What are your thoughts? What are you going to do?

4. You have been masturbating (touching your private places) a lot. You can't get your mind off it and you can't concentrate at school. What is the problem? What are you going to do? How can you stop the problem?

5. The person who molested you is the same sex as you. You are worried about being gay. What's the problem? How can you solve it? How can you deal with your anxiety?

6. You begin to think a lot about having sex with somebody younger. What's the problem? What are you going to do?

Discussion: Encourage self-talk, and explore alternatives when coming up with solutions. Ask the children if the role plays are anything like experiences they have had. Go slowly and remember that children's acting-out behavior may escalate when material resembling their own processes is discussed. It is important to predict the anxiety prior to beginning the role play and to give children specific coping mechanisms (i.e., relaxation, self-talk, etc.) to relieve anxiety when it occurs. At the end of the activity, positively reinforce the children for being able to deal with their anxiety.

Activity: *Around the World*

Ages: *5-9*

Materials: *Peanuts from "What Might Happen Next Game" (following); tagboard; glue; scissors*

Procedure: Ahead of time, trace peanut patterns on tagboard, cut the shapes out, and copy the situations onto the fronts; copy the consequences on the backs. Discuss the word "consequences" with the children. Have the children sit in a semi-circle. Have one child become "it" and stand behind one of the seated children. The therapist shows the peanuts that tell the event to both children. Whoever calls out the consequence first wins the round. If the person standing calls out the consequence first, he/she proceeds to the next seated player and another peanut card is shown. The object of the game is to be the first player to go around the world, i.e., the first player who can remain standing. If the player sitting calls the card first, he/she takes the place of the person standing and is the new "it."

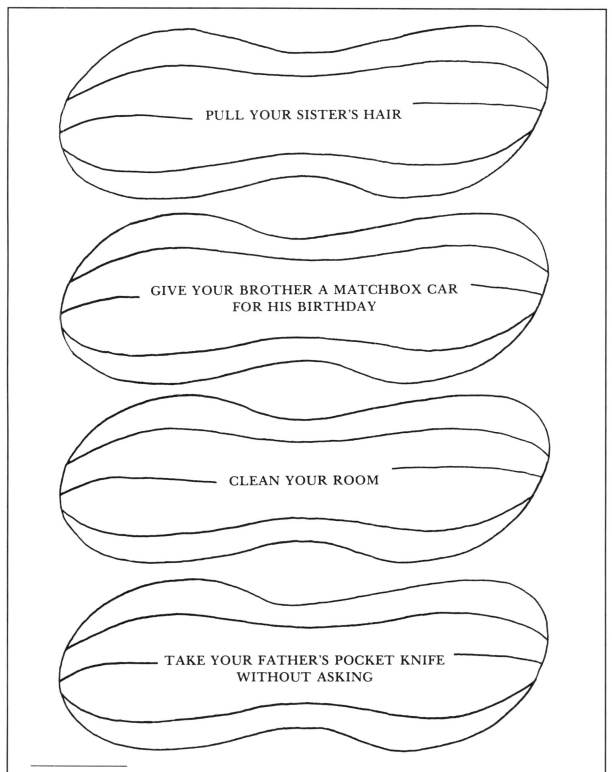

PULL YOUR SISTER'S HAIR

GIVE YOUR BROTHER A MATCHBOX CAR
FOR HIS BIRTHDAY

CLEAN YOUR ROOM

TAKE YOUR FATHER'S POCKET KNIFE
WITHOUT ASKING

Reprinted with permission from *Think Aloud Primary Level* by Bonnie Camp & Mary Ann Bash. © 1981 by Bonnie W. Camp & Mary Ann Bash. Champaign, IL: Research Press. Specific acts and consequences related to sexual abuse have been added.

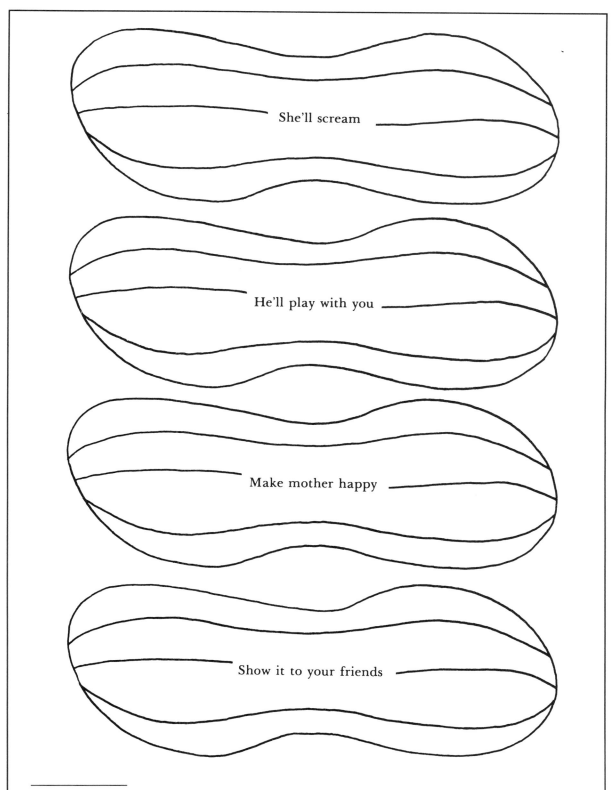

She'll scream _____

He'll play with you _____

Make mother happy _____

Show it to your friends _____

Reprinted with permission from *Think Aloud Primary Level* by Bonnie Camp & Mary Ann Bash. © 1981 by Bonnie W. Camp & Mary Ann Bash. Champaign, IL: Research Press.

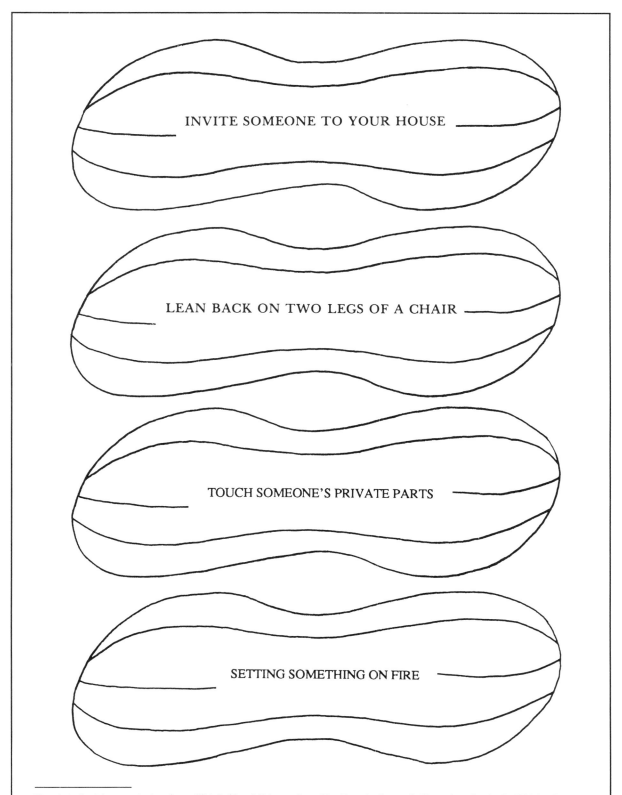

INVITE SOMEONE TO YOUR HOUSE

LEAN BACK ON TWO LEGS OF A CHAIR

TOUCH SOMEONE'S PRIVATE PARTS

SETTING SOMETHING ON FIRE

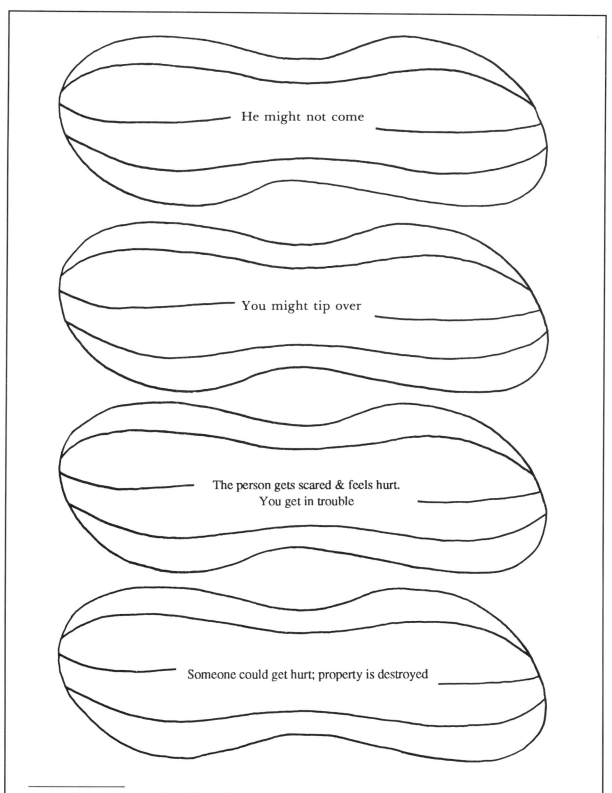

He might not come

You might tip over

The person gets scared & feels hurt.
You get in trouble

Someone could get hurt; property is destroyed

Roadblocks to Resolving Conflict

Prickler
Gets angry easily. Yells and calls names.

Hider
Refuses to talk about a conflict. Hides wants and feelings.

Blabber
Complains about a conflict to someone else instead of facing the problem and solving it with the persons involved.

Wormer
Blames others. Worms out of taking responsibility.

Pleaser
Doesn't really try to find an acceptable solution. Instead, settles for any solution—as long as it pleases the other person.

Pocketer
Saves up past conflicts, grudges, or hurt feelings and brings them up even though they have nothing to do with the current problem.

Excerpted from *Teaching Peace* by Ruth Fletcher. Copyright © 1987 by Ruth Fletcher. Reprinted by permission of HarperCollins Publishers.

Discussion: Talk about the importance of stopping and thinking about consequences before one acts. Reminding abuse-reactive children of consequences in their daily lives will help them think about the consequence that will occur if they re-molest or act aggressively. This game is enjoyable and demands quick thinking and recall.

Activity: *Roadblocks to Resolving Conflict*

Ages: *6-12*

Materials: *Copies of "Roadblocks to Resolving Conflict" worksheet (page 124); animal puppets (optional) or animal toys*

Procedure: Talk about different types of communication that make it impossible to negotiate or find solutions. Pass out a copy of the worksheet for each child or draw pictures of each animal and present the animals one at a time. Talk about how each animal's behavior blocks communication. Ask the children which animal they most resemble. Talk about how this method of responding to conflict might set them up for failure and not getting what they want. The therapist may also have the children assume these roles in a role play and/or make up metaphorical stories about each animal, asking each child if he/she has ever felt that way.

Below are two stories illustrating the use of metaphors:

Once upon a time, there was a porcupine named Prickler. When he was little, his father hurt him a lot. When his father got mad, he would hit or kick Prickler. Prickler got very scared inside. He could not trust anyone. He was afraid that if anyone got close to him they might kick him or hurt him. Prickler didn't want anyone to know that he was scared inside. When any other animals got near him or threatened him in any way, he'd yell or call them names. He'd also raise the prickles on his back so if anyone got too close he'd hurt them with his sharp prickly hairs. The problem was that no one wanted to be Prickler's friend because they did not want to get hurt by his prickly hairs. They also didn't know how scared and lonely Prickler really felt. Have you ever felt like Prickler? When have you acted like Prickler? What are the consequences if you act like Prickler?

Pocketer the kangaroo is afraid to let people know when he is angry. He is afraid that they wouldn't like him anymore if he lets them know what he wants and how he feels. Whenever someone hurts his feelings or makes him mad, he stuffs his feelings in his pouch. The problem is that Pocketer's pouch gets overstuffed. He gets uncomfortable when his pouch is stuffed with angry and hurt feelings. Sometimes his pouch gets overstuffed, then angry and hurt feelings begin to come out of his pouch and fly all over the place. Pocketer has no control when his pouch gets so overstuffed. He doesn't know how many angry and hurt feelings are going to come out of his pouch at one time. Other people don't like to be around Pocketer because when his pouch gets overstuffed, the angry and hurt feelings fly right at them. What can Pocketer do to keep his pouch from becoming "overstuffed?" How can he talk about his anger without worrying about people rejecting him? What positive self-talk sentences could he say to himself to make himself feel better?

Tom and Bill Solve a Problem

Tom was Bill's best friend in first grade. When Bill brought Tom home, he showed him his older brother's shiny model airplanes. As they were playing with one of the airplanes, they broke a wing. They tried and tried to fix it, but it would not stay on. Bill knew his older brother would blame him. He just didn't know what to do because his older brother loved that airplane very much. He was starting to cry when Tom said that he had an idea. . . .

Reprinted from *That's Not Fair* by Larry Jensen, © 1977. Used by permission of Brigham Young University Press, Provo, UT.

Draw a Solution for Tom

Tom's idea worked. His older brother was not even mad. He even put his arm around him and smiled. They certainly did the right thing.

George Feels Better

One day George was standing around with the other kids. Suddenly Bob said something bad about George. It wasn't true, and you could tell that George did not like to hear it. George decided to. . . .

Draw a Solution for George

George was happy now. He still remembered the nasty, unkind lie that Bob had said about him, but he wasn't sad or mad anymore.

Discussion: These stories use imaging to create metaphors that children can relate to. Abuse-reactive children have all six roadblocks at various times. Throughout the therapy go over these roadblocks many times, pointing out to children when they are incorporating them.

Activity: ***Problem-solving Stories***

Ages: *5-8*

Materials: *Copies of "Tom and Bill Solve a Problem" and "George Feels Better" (pages 126-129); crayons or markers*

Procedure: Read the stories with the children; have them use the problem-solving steps to find solutions. Have the children make pictures of the solutions and color them in.

Discussion: Compare different solutions to the problems. Talk about the concept that there are many different ways to solve problems. Ask the children how they think George feels and how Tom and Bill feel. Ask the children to give examples of situations where they have had similar feelings.

Decision-making skills and problem-solving abilities are ongoing necessities for children to be able to function in society. Abuse-reactive children often lack these skills and act impulsively rather than logically or in an organized fashion. Teaching these skills is time consuming and requires patience. It helps to remember that as children begin to master these skills, they move a step closer to gaining impulse control. Without such mastery, their progress toward healing will be frustrated and the risk of their continued sexual impulsiveness will remain high. It is worthwhile to go over and over activities like those in this chapter until the process of problem-solving becomes thoroughly familiar, even automatic. The *process*, rather than the *outcome*, should be emphasized and rewarded. Outside the group the children will anticipate success and associate accomplishment with how they arrive at solutions to problems, rather than merely with the results of their efforts.

Therapy Tools for Treating Victimization

CHAPTER EIGHT-A

The Use of Sandtray in Individual Therapy

While this manual has been developed as a tool for *group* therapy with children who are molesting other children, some forms of play therapy are most effective when used in *individual* sessions. One particularly successful method we've used to uncover previously undisclosed victimization, assess fears, identify hidden feelings, and metaphorically create safety around disclosure issues is Sandtray Therapy.

Sandtray therapy was first developed for use with children by British psychoanalyst Margaret Lowenfeld. It was later adapted to the Jungian point of view for both children and adults by Dora Kalff, a Jungian analyist from Switzerland (Dr. Margaret Kestly, personal communication, October 17, 1995). Jung's archetypal model and concepts are woven into the sandtray process. Many of the pioneers in sandtray work have specific methodology and symbolism they believe are crucial when working with the sandtray.[23]

The practical strategies that we have developed for sexually abused and abuse-reactive children differ specifically from the traditional Jungian methodology in that the sandtray is used as a *corrective, interactive process* rather than as a purely analytical, interpretive tool. Traditionalists may caution against "interfering" with the child's process via interactions or interpretation of the content material. But young, abused children often don't have the cognitive or emotional tools to repair, reframe, or master their early experiences on their own. If we don't find ways to interpret children's signals and help them master their traumas, we leave them stuck in time with their traumas as extra baggage.

This chapter describes a "corrective" approach to sandtray work and its use as an adjunctive tool for communicating with the abuse-reactive child. It also provides the reader with the nuts and bolts of how to set up a sandtray and offers practical strategies that work well with abuse-reactive children.

Nuts and Bolts of Setting Up the Sandtray

The Sandtray is a small wood or plastic tray measuring approximately 10 inches wide by 20 inches long and approximately 2 to 3 inches deep, preferably made of wood (a plastic dishpan, a Rubbermaid storage box, or a new photographic developing tray will do). Whenever possible, the sandtray figures should be displayed on shelves within easy view (and reach) of the child (see photo). These figures need not be elaborate or expensive; most can be purchased from dimestores, drug stores, train stores, etc.

---

[23] See Allen (1988), Kahn (1989), and Kalff (1980).

Shelves of toys displayed in the sandtray room

The basic objects and figures needed to begin a sandtray collection are *animals* (wild and domestic), *structures* (such as houses, churches, hospitals), *vehicles* (such as cars, ambulances, buses, and trucks), and *outdoor objects* (such as trees, bridges, plenty of fences, etc.). *"Scary" figures,* such as snakes, spiders, monsters, etc., are good to have. *Types of people* might include: male and female adults and children, cowboys, Indians, a bride and groom, a fairy godmother, a witch, army men, superheroes, ghosts, and space people (see photos).[24] Assembling this collection may sound like a large and costly endeavor; however, the collection can be added to gradually. If shelving is not available, plastic tubs can hold the various objects. The sand for the tray should not be beach sand or sand with gravel in it, but the specialized fine-grained sand that can be purchased at a toy store.

Before beginning sandtray work, it is crucial to take a family history (review Chapter Two for more detail); otherwise, you may make interpretations that are not applicable to the child's issues.

Therapeutic Strategies in Sandtray Work

Prior to discussing various treatment strategies, it is useful to address the significance of the *types* of toys chosen by children. Some of the toys abused children frequently select include: snakes, bride and groom set, a witch, wild and domestic animals, and various superheroes. Rather than attempting to interpret what *each object* may symbolize (an approach entirely based on opinion at this point in time), we look at *where the toy is placed* in the tray or how it might be understood *metaphorically*.

---

[24] All photographs are of the Sandtray Room at the Sandtray Training Center of New Mexico, in Corrales, New Mexico. The publishers thank director Theresa Kestly, Ph.D. for her assistance with these photographs.

Cars and trucks; candles and lanterns; kitchen ware

Army men; lock boxes; and trees

For example, if a snake is buried in sand, the burial may be a metaphor for the secrecy still surrounding the child's unresolved sexual issues. If a wild animal is fenced in, the child may not have dealt with his/her anger about being abused, and the fenced beast becomes a metaphor for containment or control over feelings. When a child selects the same toy repeatedly, it is important to take note of it. That toy or group of toys may be the child's chosen way or vehicle for mastering his/her trauma.

While observing the child making a sandtray, keep a record of the toys the child selects, the number of the sandtray (first or second, etc.), and the overall character of the tray (i.e., does it look somewhat organized; is it violent or chaotic; or is it characterized by more healing themes). In addition, it is important to note clinical impressions or significant details, e.g., does the tray look empty and depressed? Does it have people in it? Are objects buried?

Dinosaurs; horses; and farm animals

Religious figures; native American objects; women and men

A tray configuration that appears depressed may be an outward display of what the child feels inside. When objects such as snakes are buried, the child may still have sexual abuse to disclose. When the tray configuration appears violent, the child often has anger and power issues, particularly significant with young offenders or with children who live in violent environments.

In other words, the *feeling of the tray as a whole* is a map of the child's inner world. Some of the most depressed children we have seen made extremely violent trays, alerting us to the presence of explosive anger that had been turned inward and could result in self-mutilation or suicide. The *metaphor or theme of the sandtray* is where the therapeutic work begins. Most latency-age children are eager to tell a story or describe to you what is in their sandtray, what is occurring between the figures, or even who they represent.

After the story is told, the therapist attempts to correct or repair any trauma that is observed in the sandtray. For example, one boy who is a sexual assault victim repeatedly depicts people

An example of a sandtray

trapped in quicksand. Following are the steps that might be taken to do reparative work around the theme of quicksand, this boy's particular metaphor of entrapment.

Step One: Ask the child to verbalize feelings, e.g., ask how it feels to be trapped in quicksand. Spend some time empathizing with how scary it must be to be trapped in quicksand and not be able to move.

Step Two: Ask or assist the child to resolve dilemmas, e.g., help the child find a way to get the people out of the quicksand. Some object in the tray may be used to pull the people out. Often the child may not be able to figure out or problem-solve how to resolve the dilemma. Then the therapist can introduce a new figure from the shelf or with the child find some way to help the people out of the quicksand. This portion of the sandtray therapy is important: if we don't assist the child in finding a way out of the metaphorical dilemma in which he/she is "stuck," the child continues to feel trapped and we are not helping him/her to move past the trauma.

Step Three: Ask the child to project feelings onto the tray: e.g., applying the metaphor to life, ask if he/she has ever felt trapped like the people in the quicksand. If the child denies feelings that seem very apparent, sometimes it is best to leave it alone and come back to the theme another time, or to confront the child gently and say something like, "Lots of kids who are molested feel trapped. Do you feel trapped because of what happened to you?"

In another example where reparative metaphors were used to help resolve a dilemma, a child client set up a sandtray in which snakes were buried under a bride and groom, a house, and several children. The child talked about the snakes being so dangerous that they would kill the bride and groom and family if they came out from hiding. We have observed that many children who have been sexually abused use snakes in their sandtrays. The therapist suspected that this child had not yet disclosed his history as a victim, despite physical evidence of sexual abuse and behavioral evidence that the child was molesting other children. He appeared to be terrified of disclosing the abuse, and his sandtray indicated that his ultimate fear was that his buried secret would break up the family should it "get out." Therapeutic steps with a client creating trays like this might include:

Step One: Ask the child to describe what would happen to the family and how each member would feel if the snakes came out of hiding. Empathize with the fear and pain that the family might experience if the snakes came out of hiding. It is important to address the feelings of the characters in the metaphor *before* providing the corrective metaphor. By verbalizing your empathy and understanding of how the objects or characters in the metaphor must feel, you are sending a message to the child that you understand his/her own fears and pain.

Step Two: In this particular sandtray, the reparative metaphor involved finding a way of keeping the family safe (with fences, etc.), so that when the snakes came out (a little at a time), the family was not killed by them. Individually and together they were able to handle the snakes, even though it was hard for them at first.

Step Three: In an effort to apply the metaphor to the child's life, the therapist told him that sometimes kids have scary secrets they are afraid to tell because they're scared that the truth will destroy them or other family members. The therapist finally asked the child directly whether he had a scary secret that he was afraid to tell. He acknowledged that he did, but he was still too afraid to tell the therapist. However, during the next session, he was able to disclose that he had been sexually molested. In numerous cases like this one, the sandtray has shown itself to be a powerful tool that assists the therapist in eliciting disclosures or bringing buried problems to the surface.

To summarize, the four main steps in using reparative metaphors in the sandtray are:

Step One: *Ask the child to create and describe a sandtray picture.* Engage the child in placing objects and figures in the sandtray. Encourage him/her to tell a story or describe what's happening in the tray. *At this point do not participate or contribute anything yourself.*

Step Two: *When the sandtray is finished, ask the child to verbalize feelings.* Attempt to find out how the characters in the story are feeling. Spend time empathizing with or acknowledging the characters' feelings.

Step Three: *Ask or assist the child to resolve dilemmas.* Begin to help the child deal with the issues brought up in the sandtray by helping him/her find solutions or ways to work out problems presented in the sandtray. You can either participate with the child in that process or you can tell a story to the child that presents a solution, a positive ending to the story, or a corrective experience.

Step Four: *Use projection to apply the metaphor to life.* Ask the child if he/she ever identifies with (feels like) the characters in the sandtray. Ask the child to project his/her own feelings onto what is occurring in the tray.

At the end of this section is a record-keeping sheet to use every time a child uses the sandtray. It is also helpful for keeping track of repetitive themes that occur in therapy.

Some children have difficulty telling a story or even describing what they have placed in the sandtray. With these children, the following questions may be helpful in encouraging them to talk about their sandtrays:

1. If you could be anything or anybody in this sandtray, what would you be?

2. What is your favorite object in the sandtray?

3. Suppose this gorilla is a person that you know. Who would it be?

4. Is there anything in this tray that reminds you of your mom? your dad? your sister? your brother? *yourself?*

Young children under the age of five often want to use the sandtray as a sandbox, and may have diffculty setting up the objects and telling a story. As long as children use the sandtray as a communication aid or as a way to work through issues, there is nothing wrong with using it in whatever way works best with very young children.

In conclusion, the sandtray is an effective communication tool for individual therapy with children and adolescents. It can provide the therapist with a metaphorical map of the child's inner world, one that many times is not revealed in traditional verbal therapy methods.

Sandtray Worksheet

1. Name of Client _____

2. Age _____   Sex   M   F   Date _____

3. Victim   Abuse-reactive _____   Offender _____

4. Reason for referral _____
   _____
   _____
   _____
   _____

5. Number of Sandtray _____

6. Pre-disclosure _____   Post-disclosure _____

Sandtray Description

7. Organized _____   Depressed/empty _____   Chaotic _____

   Violent _____   Secretive/buried _____   Healing/hopeful _____

8. Description of Toys Chosen

1. _____	7. _____	14. _____
2. _____	8. _____	15. _____
3. _____	9. _____	16. _____
4. _____	10. _____	17. _____
5. _____	11. _____	18. _____
6. _____	12. _____	19. _____
	13. _____	20. _____

9a. Describe metaphor or theme of sandtray

   _____   _____
   _____   _____
   _____   _____
   _____   _____

b. Traumagenic themes:

   Attachment Disorder_____   Betrayal_____   Destructiveness _____

   Dissociative Disorder_____   Eroticization_____   Powerlessness _____

   Self Blame_____   Stimatization_____   Traumatization of
                                              body experience _____

_____

Form developed by Carolyn Cunningham, Ph.D., © 1991. Updated, © 1995 by Carolyn Cunningham and Kimberly Fill.

9c. Significant aspect of story:

_____

_____

_____

d. Conflict management within the story:

Conflict not present_____   Conflict present without resolution_____
Conflict present with resolution_____

10. Describe clinician's corrective/reparative metaphor or story.

_____   _____

_____   _____

_____   _____

11. Describe client's reaction to clinician's reparative interpretation

_____   _____

_____   _____

_____   _____

_____   _____

_____

Form developed by Carolyn Cunningham, Ph.D., © 1991. Updated, © 1995 by Carolyn Cunningham and Kimberly Fill.

CHAPTER EIGHT-B

Group Therapy in Victimization Recovery

Issues concerning victimization and perpetration have been addressed in a general way throughout this book. However, it is essential that both of these areas be covered in a very specific and thorough manner since they are usually at the very heart of the reason the abuse-reactive child is in treatment. This chapter discusses victimization; perpetration issues are discussed in detail in Chapter Nine.

Abuse-reactive children usually have been victimized either physically, sexually, or emotionally prior to abusing another child. As mentioned earlier in this text, the abuse-reactive child has buried the pain, isolation, and vulnerability that accompanies abuse and later re-enacts the same abuse or commits different abusive acts on someone else.

Roland Summit, child-victim specialist, notes that the "male victim of sexual abuse is more likely to turn his rage outward in aggressive and antisocial behavior. He is even more intolerant of his helplessness than the female victim. ... Child molestation and rape seem to be part of the legacy of rage endowed in the sexually abused boy" (Summit, 1983, p. 185, quoted in Porter, 1986, p. 14). Similarly, Nancy Biele has stated, "The longer you carry around a victimization, the more likely you are to develop negative coping skills, which include everything from chemical dependency to battering, from lighting fires to offending against other children or adults, even to injuring yourself, sometimes fatally" (Biele & Plotkin, 1985, quoted in Porter, 1986, p. 22).

When treatment focuses only on the act of sexual *perpetration* without helping the abuse-reactive child understand his/her own victimization and its relationship to his/her abusiveness, the child will remain at risk of reoffending. Sexual acting out may be a way for abuse-reactive children to cope with the anxiety produced by feelings of powerlessness and helplessness attached to their victimization.

On the other hand, if a child's *victimization* is treated while his/her acts of perpetration are ignored, the therapist may inadvertently collude with the child's maladaptive coping mechanisms. This is not uncommon since most clinicians are more familiar and comfortable treating child victims. Therefore, it is crucial for therapists to understand that these particular children have crossed over the line and are victimizing others. Their behavior is likely to continue unless they also receive therapeutic intervention specifically addressing the perpetration.[25]

The long-term effects of physical, sexual, and emotional abuse can be dramatic. In all forms of abuse, victims generally experience some degree of anger, depression, aggression, and helplessness. However, because of the strong link between sexual victimization and sexually abusive behavior, this chapter focuses on the long-term effects of *sexual* abuse, and offers structured techniques to help young victims work through their victimization.

Finkelhor and Browne (1986) identify four *traumagenic* dynamics—or trauma-causing factors—that result in long-term psychological consequences: 1) *traumatic sexualization*, resulting in

---

[25] For more information on the victim-to-victimizer process, see Ryan (1989).

sexual identity problems and aversion to sexual intimacy; 2) *betrayal,* creating lack of trust, fear of intimacy, dependency, anger, and hostility; 3) *powerlessness,* prompting children to dissociate, see themselves as victims in other areas of their lives, identify with the aggressor, and have difficulties with issues of power and control; and 4) *stigmatization,* the source of the child's feelings of isolation, guilt, shame, depression, and lowered self-esteem.[26]

Lynne Namka, in her 1994 publication "Shame Busting: Incorporating Group Social Skill Training, Shame Release, and Play Therapy with a Child Who Was Sexually Abused" writes, "Children may absorb some of the shameful energy of the adult who committed the offense. Sexual abuse typically causes the child to feel dirty and damaged" (p.2). As she also points out, "The denial of shame and dysfunctional behavior acts to prevent feelings and beliefs of unworthiness from surfacing by separating the self from the negative feelings" (p. 7).

Children who have been victimized and are acting out their victimization by hurting others often are defending against an internal core of shame and self-hate. Victim therapy must deal with these unexpressed feelings.

In addition, a wide range of behavioral symptoms occur in latency-age victims, including: hostile-aggressive behavior, antisocial behavior, stealing, tantrums, and substance abuse (Lusk & Waterman, 1986). Salter (1988) indicates that sexually abused children exhibit sexual symptomology, including: compulsive masturbation, sexual acting out with animals, inappropriate seductiveness, sexual acting out with younger children, attempted sexual seductiveness with adults, and fear or aversion to situations where a child's genitalia may be exposed or touched (e.g., bathing and medical exams). Post Traumatic Stress Disorder—including such symptoms as nightmares, flashbacks, severe anxiety, and phobias—is also common among sexually victimized children.

When helping abuse-reactive children work through their victimization, the following treatment goals are helpful guidelines for the therapist:

1. The child can acknowledge that the abuse occurred.

2. The child can discuss specific incidents both individually and in the group.

3. The child can verbalize anger and/or ambivalence toward the offender.

4. The child can verbalize feelings of guilt and/or self-blame.

5. The child can explore confusion about experiencing physical pleasure while disliking the behavior.

6. The child recognizes that the abuse he/she experienced was not his/her fault.

7. The child has developed sexual abuse prevention skills.

8. The child has developed appropriate physical boundaries with others.

---

[26] In girls, stigmatization tends to focus on victimization and fears of loss of virginity; in boys it centers on victimization and fears of homosexuality. See the discussion of sexuality and sex-role stereotyping in Chapter 11 (Bear, 1990).

9.   The child understands that there is a relationship between victimization and perpetration.

10.   The child has learned positive stress-reduction techniques.

Play therapy activities and structured group techniques that specifically address Finkelhor and Browne's four traumagenic dynamics, as well as issues related to loss, enable children to work through their feelings. Issues related to loss may include loss of control, loss of a parent, and loss of trust.

Resolving victimization issues takes time; the activities in this chapter may need to be repeated frequently.

Activity: *I'm the Best*[27]

Ages: *5-12*

Materials: *The book,* I'm the Best *(by Marjorie Weinman Sharmet; see Resources)*

Procedure: Read the book I'm the Best to the group. In this book, a dog, who is the narrator, describes his frustration over having lots of different owners and not feeling loved and accepted. Finally, he finds an owner who loves him and is going to keep him, despite his testing (eating plants) of the relationship.

Discussion: This is a wonderful book for children in foster placements and children with attachment difficulties. The children can readily identify with the dog in this humorous and engaging story. Discuss the dog's loneliness and need for unconditional love. Discuss why the dog needs to test his new owners by eating the plant. Talk about the children's issues of loneliness and feelings of rejection. The book ends in a hopeful, positive way. Emphasize the positive: There are always people that one can attach to. In addition, discuss how children can create their own "families" consisting of people who care about them.

Activity: *Mandy*

Ages: *8-12*

Materials: *The book,* Mandy *(by Julie Andrews Edwards; see Resources)*

Procedure: This is an excellent book for individual therapy, reading a chapter every week, and an especially good resource for female clients. Mandy is the story of a child from an orphanage who is lonely and feels empty. She finds a cottage with a garden that she spends time nourishing and keeping alive. Mandy, the main character in the story, finds that the cottage and garden take away some of the emptiness, pain and loneliness that she feels.

Discussion: This unique book provides children with a way to nurture themselves. Often we talk about self-nurturing, but for children this concept is a very difficult one to understand and internalize. Mandy gives a concrete illustration of "self-nurturing," a concept that may be introduced ahead of time. Talk

---

[27] From *I Stop My Bully Behavior Kit* by Lynne Namka (Talk, Trust, Feel Therapeutics). Reproduced with permission from the author.

about various ways children can find to get rid of the emptiness or "hole in the stomach" feeling. It may be useful to help each child come up with a concrete plan. Some ideas may be: raising a pet, planting a garden (with adult assistance), collecting something you like, developing a hobby, etc. It is important to work with caregivers so that the plan is realistic and there is follow-through.

Activity: *My Book About Feelings*[28] 📖

Ages: *6-10*

Materials: *Handout of "My Book About Feelings," from I Stop My Bully Behavior Kit, by Lynne Namka (see Resources).*

Procedure: Cut out numbers 1-6 to make one booklet. Then, cut out 7-12 to make another booklet. When you cut out squares 1-6, make sure shame is at the bottom.

Discussion: Begin to discuss the different feelings that kids have about their victimization. Discuss how anger may cover up other feelings that are more difficult to express, such as confusion, fear, hurt and shame. Talk about each feeling and have the children talk about a time in their lives (or during their victimization) when they felt that feeling.

After you complete each feeling, have each child complete the second portion of the booklet that identifies ways to let go of the stuck and bad feelings.

Activity: *The Shame Game*

Ages: *7 and up*

Materials: *Nerf ball (or ball of yarn, balled up paper)*

Procedure: This game has three steps:

Step One: Begin by playing hot potato (tossing the ball rapidly from person to person as if it were burning hot to touch). Tell children that the Nerf ball is hot and engage them for several minutes in the game.

Step Two: Continue playing hot potato. This time explain to the group that the hot potato represents "feeling ashamed." The person who victimized them didn't want to feel ashamed so he gave it to them. While you are explaining this, throw the Nerf ball to one of the group members. Ask him what he is going to do with it. Remember that it is hot.

Step Three: Most children will pass the "shame" to someone else. Stop them and ask, "What happens when you pass your ashamed feelings on to someone else?" Ask the group members if they have any other options, for example, throwing it on the floor and stomping it out, or perhaps, throwing cold water on it and looking at it saying, "You don't have that much power."

---

[28] From *I Stop My Bully Behavior Kit* by Lynne Namka (Talk, Trust, Feel Therapeutics). Reproduced with permission from the author.

3

Confusion

4

Shame is at the bottom of it all!

2

What lies under the anger?

5

Hurt

1

My Book About Feelings

by

_____

6

Fear

From *I Stop My Bully Behavior Kit* by Lynne Namka (Talk, Trust, Feel Therapeutics). Reproduced with permission from the author.

9

How it feels when
you talk about
the bad feelings.

12

Draw how you feel
when you let go of
the bad feelings.
FANTASTIC!

8   Yucky!

Draw how you feel when
bad feelingds are stuck inside.

11

Happy!

7

How it feels to have
stuck feelings.

10

Hopeful

From *I Stop My Bully Behavior Kit* by Lynne Namka (Talk, Trust, Feel Therapeutics). Reproduced with permission from the author.

Discussion: This is a wonderful way to explain projection to children. Notice, we used the word "ashamed" rather than the word shame, because shame is a difficult concept for young children. However, "ashamed" is easily understood by all. Shame is often the underlying feeling that children are defending against when they act out. After the exercise, talk about shame and how uncomfortable it is to carry around. Discuss ways to deal with shame other than projecting it onto others.

Activity: *Catch That Secret!*[29] 📄

Ages: *9 and up*

Materials: *A piece of paper with the word "secret" written on it.*

Procedure: Ask for volunteers or select three or four people to hold hands standing in a circle. Tape the paper with the word "secret" on it to the back of one of the children in the circle. Have those in the circle count to nine with one person saying "one," the next person saying "two," the next "three," and so on, until you reach nine (each person will say more than one number).

Now, have one child (not one of those in the circle) stand outside the circle opposite the child with the "secret" paper. The "outside" child's job is to try to get the "secret" paper off the back of the child wearing it. The job of the participants holding hands is to keep the "outside" child from being able to get the sign (one strategy to get them started is for the circle to spin, always keeping the outside person away from the secret person; another might be for the circlers to put the secret-bearer in the middle) while, at the same time, counting to nine as a group.

Discussion: The objectives of this activity are to help the children understand that it takes more than just one to keep a secret and to explore how keeping secrets can keep us from doing other things. Keeping a secret takes a lot of energy. Often, it is difficult to do a simple task while using so much energy in keeping the secret. Frequently more than one person is responsible for keeping a secret, just as in the activity that took all the people in the circle to keep the "secret" from being caught. An abused child may feel that s/he is the only one involved in keeping the secret. Suggested processing questions:

- What was that like for you?

- Was it easier to count to nine the first time or the second time? Why?

- What would have happened if one person wanted the secret to get caught?

- Did everyone have to be involved to keep the secret from getting caught?

- How does it affect you when you keep secrets?

- What is the difference between secrets, surprises, and private?

- If you have a secret that you need to tell, what do you do?

---

[29] With permission from Dolphin Books/Doubleday & Company, Inc., this game was adapted by Tim Boatmun, M.A., The University of Oklahoma National Resource Center for Youth Services, from "Triangle Tag," a game found in The New Games Book, New Games Foundation, edited by Andrew Fleugelman.

Activity: *Face Space*[30]

Materials: *A ball of yarn; a pair of scissors*

Ages: *7-up*

Procedure: Have your group get into pairs. Give one piece of yarn (about three feet long) to each pair. Have all participants wrap one end of the piece of yarn around their index fingers and then place their fingers on their own stomachs. Have the partners walk slowly backward away from each other until their piece of yarn is tight. Tell the group members that their job is to find their "face space." Face space is the distance between you and the person to whom you are talking. If the other person is too close while having a conversation the child may feel uncomfortable or intimidated. If the other person is too far away, the child may feel as though the partner doesn't really want to talk or be close to him or her.

Without talking, the pairs are to start moving towards each other, wrapping the yarn around their index fingers in order to keep it tight. Once they find the place where both people are comfortable, they should stop.

Now that they are comfortable with their "face space," have them take one step in and freeze. Ask them to think about how that makes them feel and where they feel it in their bodies. Then have them step back out. Ask them to think about how it feels to be back in their comfortable space. Repeat this step.

Discussion: The objectives of this activity are to he1p the children identify their boundaries, to notice what it feels like when their boundaries are crossed, and to learn ways to respect others' boundaries.

Oftentimes, when children have been abused and their physical boundaries have been disregarded, they have had to learn to ignore that internal feeling that their boundaries are being violated in order to survive emotionally. Thus, it is difficult for them to set safe boundaries for themselves or to respect the boundaries of others. With this activity, children and adults can learn to identify where their boundaries are and what it feels like when those boundaries are being invaded. They can understand that all people have different boundaries. They can also learn ways to respect their own inner feelings and other individuals' boundaries. Suggested processing questions for the group:

What did it feel like when you took a step in?

Where did you feel it in your body?

If that feeling had a color, what would it be?

Was everyone' face space the same? Another word for "face space" is boundaries. What are boundaries? (If participants have difficulty answering this question, ask them why houses have fences in backyards, or why apartments have doors and walls.)

Why would one person's boundaries be different from another's?

What are other ways in which one person can invade another person's boundaries?

What can we do when people invade our boundaries?

What signal did we send or receive that showed us it was time to stop?

---

[30] This is an original game by Tim Boatmun, M.A., National Resource Center for Youth Services, The University of Oklahoma. Reprinted with the permission of the author.

Activity: ***The Fishing Box***

Ages: *6 and up*

Materials: *A tackle box and various types of "bait" or "lures" (rubber worms and insects make good representations of "bait"). Another option is a picture of a fishing box. In some cases a verbal explanation of a fishing box will do. However, the more concrete the imagery is, the more likely the metaphor will stay.*

Procedure: Discuss with children the concept of lures and baits that fisherman use to trick fish into thinking that they are going to get food, when in reality they are going to caught. Explain how people who molest kids trick them in ways that are similar to the ways fishermen trick fish. Ask if they believe it is ever the fish's fault for getting caught. The perpetrator decides what trick or lure will work and uses it on the child. For example, a child may come from a poor family and not have many toys. A perpetrator may know this and offer the child toys if he/she participates in sexual activities. Another child may not have a father. The perpetrator may know this and befriend him like a father. Have the children talk about the ways they can be tricked. After that give them alternatives to get what they need.

For children who have been victimized and are victimizing others, ask them how they tricked the person they molested.

Discussion: It is crucial for children who have been victimized to know what their risk factors are. It is not enough for children to say no and go tell. Children who have been victimized more than once are often vulnerable, and in order to empower them it is important for them to know other ways to get what they need.

The child who lacks positive attachments may be attended to only when he/she participates in sexual acts. Thus, seduction may be the only way he/she knows to gain attention. Helping the child to understand this in an empathetic way and find alternatives is one of the greatest gifts one can give a child who feels powerless.

Activity: ***The Hurt***

Ages: *6-12*

Materials: *The book* The Hurt *(by Teddi Doleski; see Resources)*

Procedure: Read *The Hurt* to the group. In this story, a young boy experiences rejection by a friend. He doesn't tell anyone about it and "the Hurt" (which is in the shape of a big round stone) gets bigger and bigger. Eventually it takes up his entire room and keeps him from enjoying his life. As the young boy verbalizes his hurt and confronts his friend about the way he was treated, he feels better. Although hurts occasionally come back, he now knows how to handle them.

Discussion: This story (available in an inexpensive paperback) is a wonderful metaphor for any type of victimization that a child has experienced. After completing the story, discuss rejection with the children and how they feel when people whom they care about reject them. Discuss how much better the young boy felt when he began to talk about his feelings and assert himself by letting others know when he was feeling hurt. Gently bring up the issue of victimization. Discuss the issues of bad secrets, and how keeping the pain inside prevents people from enjoying life. Talk about the issue of parental rejection and the hurt that some of the members of the group feel if they have experienced rejection as a result of their victimization or perpetration. In addition, attempt to help the abuse-reactive children understand how keeping hurts inside could put them at risk to reoffend.

Activity: *It Happens to Boys Too* 📖

Ages: *7-12*

Materials: *The book* It Happens to Boys Too *(by J. Satullo, R. Russell, & P. Bradway; see Resources)*

Procedure: Read the book *It Happens to Boys Too* to the group. It is best to read this book during three or four group sessions, as it covers several issues.

Discussion: This is a particularly good book if you are leading a group of abuse-reactive boys, although it is an excellent book for individual therapy also.

Activity: *Secret Feelings and Thoughts* 📖

Ages: *7-12 (boys)*

Materials: *The book Secret Feelings and Thoughts (by Rosemary Narimanian; see Resources)*

Procedure: Read the book aloud slowly (8 to 10 pages at a time, followed by discussion of issues raised). Encourage participation by inviting group members to project how they think the characters in the story are feeling. Have the children write, draw, or tell the group which part of the story most reminds them of what happened to them and why. If some children are having trouble (perhaps because the gender of the abuser is different), ask them to write, draw, or tell the group how the story is different from what happened to them.

Discussion: This is a good book for boys who have been molested and feel a lot of shame about it or who are very curious about sex but reluctant to ask questions. Issues raised in this story include guilt, shame, homophobia, fear of AIDS, and physiological reactions to sexual stimulation. It also prompts discussion about secrecy, including when secrets should be kept (as in good surprises) and when they shouldn't.

Activity: *Working Together/Getting Together* 📖

Ages: *7-14*

Materials: *Copies of the pamphlets* Working Together *and* Getting Together *(by E. Drake & Anne Gilroy Nelson; see Resources)*

Procedure: Read *Working Together* (for male victims) or *Getting Together* (for female victims) to the group or individual client.

Discussion: These excellent pamphlets address gender-specific issues for males and females who have been sexually molested and include discussions of sexual, legal, and family issues. Because each pamphlet addresses many separate issues, take your time and spend several sessions discussing them. You may want to spend the first 15 minutes of the group, individual, or family session reading a portion of the pamphlet.

Activity: *Tell My Story Chart*

Ages: *6-12*

Materials: *Newsprint or kraft paper; marker; stickers*

Procedure: Copy the chart—using the names of children in your group—on newsprint or kraft paper to hang up in the group room. Each week have the group members answer one of the questions in round-robin fashion. Place a sticker on the chart each time a group member answers one of the questions. When all of the group members have answered all the questions on the chart, provide positive reinforcement such as a special group field trip or a party.

Discussion: Children usually disclose their own victimization in stages. This exercise is a good way to allow for that process and to gently use group pressure to encourage disclosure. Children who have *not* been sexually molested can be encouraged to talk about a time when they felt victimized or were taken advantage of in some other way.

Tell My Story Chart[31]

Question Name or Initials →								
Who molested you?								
How old were you?								
Did it happen once or many times?								
How many times?								
Where did it happen?								
Describe what happened.								
How did you feel?								
Who else knew about it?								
How did it stop?								
What was it like to tell?								

---

[31] Adapted from *Treating the Young Male Victim of Sexual Assault* by Eugene Porter, 1986. Permission given by The Safer Society Press, Orwell, VT.

Activity: *My Own Set of Armor*[32]

Ages: *5-7*

Materials: *A set of armor, including a helmet, shield, and sword (can be purchased cheaply at toy stores or made out of cardboard or paper spray-painted silver)*

Procedure: Explain to the children in the group or to your individual client how knights used armor to protect themselves from people who might harm them. Let the children in the group take turns trying on the armor. Explain how each piece of armor can protect them, i.e., the helmet from people who say bad things to them (threaten them, try to talk them into things, etc.). The shield protects their bodies from other people, and the sword helps keep people from coming too close to them, i.e., getting in their space.

After the children have had some time to play with the armor, discuss the concept of having their own *imaginary* set of armor. Start with the helmet. For example, "Telling people how you feel about what they are doing to you is one way to use your imaginary helmet. Your imaginary shield is the word, 'no,' especially when someone is trying to touch you in your private parts or in a way that you don't like. Practice yelling 'No!' Your imaginary sword lets people know when they are in your space and are getting too close. You can practice using your sword by backing away when people get too close or letting people know when you don't want to be touched."

Discussion: Young children enjoy trying on the armor. Using the metaphor of the armor helps children gain personal power as well as anti-victimization skills. This exercise should be used in conjunction with a sexual abuse awareness program.

Activity: *Stages of Loss*

Ages: *8-12*

Materials: *Paper; pencil; blackboard*

Procedure: On a blackboard write Elizabeth Kubler-Ross' (1969) stages of loss: anger, denial, bargaining, depression, and acceptance. It is important to describe each stage in ways young children can understand. Explain to the children that when you lose someone or something important to you, you go through certain feelings and stages. Talk about each step beginning with denial. Describe denial as not wanting to admit that something happened. Discuss denial in a general way, and then discuss the specifics of denial in relationship to loss. Continue with anger, bargaining, depression, and acceptance in the same way. Have each child identify what stages he/she has felt. Older children should be guided not only to identify *people or pets* they have lost, but what other kinds of loss they have suffered as a result of being molested.

Discussion: Often therapists overlook the issue of loss when working with children who have been victimized. Many children who have been molested experience numerous losses. The disclosure process itself often produces parental and sibling loss when a child is placed out of the home. In addition, the less obvious losses include the loss of innocence, loss of trust, and the loss of privacy. It is

---

[32] A similar technique utilizing the concept of armor to promote empowerment and mastery has been developed by Ballester & Pierre (1989).

imperative in any abuse program that loss issues be addressed several times. After completing the activity, it is helpful to map out for children a plan to advance to the next stage of the loss process. For example, if a child is locked into "anger," help him/her make a plan to work through anger.

Activity: **The Loss Timeline**

Ages: *8-12*

Materials: *Paper; crayons*

Procedure: Explain to the children the concept of a timeline (see example following). Have the children construct a timeline of losses they have experienced throughout their lives from the time they were very young to the present. Explain that a loss might be a long separation, a death, moving away, or (for older children) the loss of trust or of privacy from being molested. After completion, discuss as a group.

Discussion: This can be an intense experience for the children as well as the therapist. It is extremely informative, as children may come up with incidents the therapist had no idea happened. It also can be useful to share the child's timeline with parents in a family session. While the children are making their timelines, you might have the parents do a similar activity in the parents' group.

Activity: **All Kinds of Separation**

Ages: *5-8*

Materials: *The book All Kinds of Separation (by Carolyn Cunningham; see Resources)*

Procedure: Read out loud the treatment workbook *All Kinds of Separation.* Have the children do the activities in each section. Help the children to differentiate short and long separations, and coping mechanisms to be able to handle loss and separation.

Discussion: This workbook for young children helps them identify and work through many types of separation and loss. It also can be used as a coloring book that children can take home and read with their parents.

Activity: **The Bind**

Ages: *7-12*

Materials: *"The Bind" (following)*

Procedure: Read "The Bind" aloud in group. After reading the story, discuss how Scott could take care of himself, including different ways he could talk to his father. Then brainstorm with the group what Scott should do tomorrow. Also discuss ways that Scott can get his power back. Have the children role-play the solutions.

Loss Timeline Examples

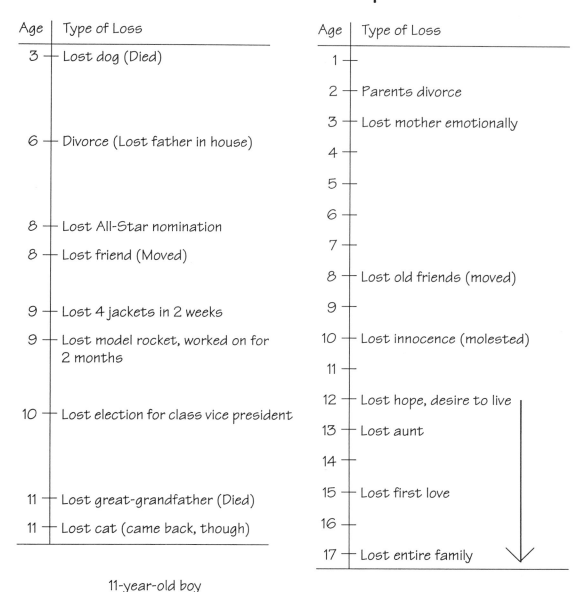

Age	Type of Loss
3	Lost dog (Died)
6	Divorce (Lost father in house)
8	Lost All-Star nomination
8	Lost friend (Moved)
9	Lost 4 jackets in 2 weeks
9	Lost model rocket, worked on for 2 months
10	Lost election for class vice president
11	Lost great-grandfather (Died)
11	Lost cat (came back, though)

11-year-old boy

Age	Type of Loss
1	
2	Parents divorce
3	Lost mother emotionally
4	
5	
6	
7	
8	Lost old friends (moved)
9	
10	Lost innocence (molested)
11	
12	Lost hope, desire to live
13	Lost aunt
14	
15	Lost first love
16	
17	Lost entire family

Adolescent girl

Thanks to Bram Elias (who assisted in developing this technique) and to the adolescent female client at Glendale Family Services Program for constructing and contributing these timelines.

Name _____

Date _____

My Loss Timeline

Age	Type of Loss

The Bind

Scott is a fourth-grader at Cypress School. He gets picked on a lot because he's short for his age. This year there's a new kid at school. His name is Jim and everyone is afraid of him. He's a sixth-grader, and is he ever huge! The kids call him "King Kong" because he's a bully. He beats up on smaller kids a lot. Scott is really afraid of Jim because he lives right up the street.

Last month, on a Monday, Jim cornered Scott on the way to school and said, "Give me your lunch money, you stupid punk." Scott felt terrified inside, but managed to say, "I don't have any. See, I brought my lunch."

Jim said, "Tomorrow, punk, I want all of your lunch money on the way home or I'm going to beat you up." Scott stared at the ground and mumbled, "Okay."

Just to be on the safe side, Scott decided to buy only a carton of milk Tuesday. Sure enough, Jim grabbed Scott on the way home from school. "Hand it over, punk." Scott reluctantly gave him his lunch money. This went on for three more days.

By the next Monday, Scott was feeling mad inside. He also was getting very hungry. He thought to himself, "I'm not going to let stupid King Kong take advantage of me. I'm going to show him." So he decided to buy lunch. It was pizza that day and it tasted so good that Scott forgot about Jim for awhile—until after school when he started to walk home.

Jim stomped over and growled, "Give me your lunch money." Scott told Jim he didn't have any. Jim answered in a heavy, accusing voice, "I thought I told you to save your lunch money every day and give it to me." Scott's legs began to wobble and his stomach felt like a piece of rope with a huge knot in it. Then, all of a sudden Scott's face felt as if a ton of bricks had been dropped on it. Jim screamed, "You're going to have a big shiner like this one every day that you don't bring me your lunch money!" Scott couldn't even answer, he was in so much pain. When he got home he looked in the mirror. His eye was swollen and purple. He thought to himself, "What am I going to tell my dad?" He decided to lie.

When Scott's father came home, he asked Scott, "What happened to your eye, son?" Scott said, "Oh, I hurt it in a tackle football game after school." Scott's father said, "I'm glad to hear it wasn't some other kid taking advantage of you. No kid of mine will ever be a sissy or let other kids push him around."

Scott felt sick inside. What will happen if his Dad finds out about King Kong? What if he really is a sissy...?

What should Scott do tomorrow?

Discussion: Ask the children the following questions: 1) How can Scott handle King Kong? 2) What should Scott tell his father? 3) What is a sissy? Is Scott really a sissy? 4) How can Scott have as much power as King Kong without hitting him back? 5) Why did Scott lie to his father? 6) How do you feel about Scott's father? 7) How do you feel about Scott?

Activity: *Signs of Stress*

Ages: *9-12*

Materials: *"Signs of Stress" checklist (following)*

Procedure: Pass out copies of the checklist or read it together. Have the children fill out the chart or verbally acknowledge if they have experienced particular signs of stress. Add the following items to the list:

1. Hurting animals

2. Setting fires

3. Hurting other children

4. Unable to stop masturbating

5. Thinking about molesting other children

6. Thinking about violent things

7. Being sexual with other children or touching their private parts

Discussion: Talk with the children about what they can do when they recognize these signs of stress. Introduce relaxation exercises, self-talk, leisure time activities, and physical exercise as positive ways to alleviate stress. Practice these techniques with the group. Also help the children to identify the original trauma that created the stress, i.e., feeling powerless, molestation, family problems, etc.

Activity: *Desensitization*

Ages: *All ages*

Materials: *"Desensitization" (following)*

Procedure: Desensitization is a well-known way to relieve anxiety. Begin by talking to children about fear. Help them to identify common fears. For older children, read together the information on page 160 on desensitization. For younger children talk about the concept of desensitization in children's terms. Initially, encourage children to pick their own fear to deal with. They can make their own desensitization charts or even choose a cartoon format. *Eventually* the goal is to use desensitization techniques to deal with the childrens' fears from the original trauma and on-going fears, including the fear of being remolested, physically abused, etc. The process of desensitization to talking about prior abuse might go as follows:

1. Relax. Picture the room or the place where it happened; what it looked like, felt like, the sounds, smells, etc.

2. Think about what he or she said, looked like, acted like, etc.

3. Think about the feelings that you are having.

4. Think about the abuse itself, being touched in your private parts, having to touch someone else's private parts. Being hit or grabbed; being hurt or threatened not to tell, etc.

5. Think about what you did afterwards and how you felt.

Name _____

Date _____

Signs of Stress

DIRECTIONS: Look at the following symptoms of stress. Place a checkmark in the column marked "R" if you experience this symptom rarely. Place a checkmark in the column marked "O" if you experience it often. Fill in the symptoms for a relative, too.

Me			My Relative	
R	O		R	O
		1. Headaches		
		2. Stomach problems—diarrhea, constipation, nausea, heartburn, urinating often		
		3. High blood pressure or heart pounding		
		4. Pain in neck, lower back, shoulders, jaw		
		5. Muscle jerks or tics		
		6. Eating problems—no appetite, constant eating, full feeling without eating		
		7. Sleeping problems—unable to fall asleep, wake up in middle of the night, nightmares		
		8. Fainting		
		9. General feeling of tiredness		
		10. Shortness of breath		
		11. Dry throat or mouth		
		12. Unable to sit still—extra energy		
		13. Teeth grinding		
		14. Stuttering		
		15. Uncontrollable crying or not being able to cry		
		16. Smoking		
		17. Use excessive alcohol		
		18. Use drugs		
		19. Increased use of medication—aspirin, tranquilizers, etc.		
		20. General anxiety, nervous feelings, or tenseness		
		21. Dizziness and weakness		
		22. Irritable and easily set off		
		23. Depressed		

(continued on page 158)

Signs of Stress

(continued from page 157)

Me			My Relative	
R	O		R	O
		24. Accident prone		
		25. Feeling angry in general		
		26. Feeling overwhelmed and unable to cope—want to run away, cry, or end it all		
		27. Doing weird things without thinking		
		28. Nervous laughter, easily startled, jumpy		
		29. Always concerned about disease and death		
		30. Bored with life		
		31. Always worried about money		
		32. Afraid of weekends or vacations		
		33. Feeling that you can't discuss problems with anyone else		
		34. Afraid of heights or closed spaces		
		35. Feeling rejected all the time, especially by your family		
		36. Unable to concentrate or finish things you start		
		37. Never laugh		
		38. Allergies		
		39. Always in a hurry		
		40. Don't have friends and may not care about being with other people		
		41. Don't do your assignments		
		42. Can do one thing well and most of your time is spent on it		
		43. Joining a cult group		

From the book, *Coping for Kids* by Gerald Herzfeld, Ph.D. & Robin Powell, Ph.D., © 1986. Used by permission of the publisher, The Center for Applied Research in Education, West Nyack, NY.

A variety of visual aids can be employed in this process. You might consider any of the following materials (some of which must be obtained from parents, relatives, or guardians of the child):

1. Anatomically detailed drawings to mark parts of the body that were traumatized, touched, or associated with abuse or that the child still feels bad about.

2. Family photographs

   – of the child at the age that he or she was abused

   – of the perpetrator

   – of the location of the abuse

   – of family members whom the child told about the abuse and who knew/should have known/failed to protect, etc.

3. Lists of words which may trigger associations to the abuse, i.e., names of body parts, names for abuse, threats, and names of feelings.

4. Pictures from magazines

   – of children the same age as the child when victimized

   – of young children in little or no clothing

   – of adults who resemble the perpetrator

   – of beds, bathtubs, the park, or other places and things approximating the surroundings of the abuse.

5. Anatomically detailed dolls used for the same purposes and/or to recreate the actual acts or interactions.

6. Police or social services reports (or portions thereof) of the child's victimization (if available, and if appropriate for the child's age and comprehension level) to help the child to acccept the reality of the event and the fact that other adults believed it.

7. Newspaper clippings describing abuse cases similar to the child's situation.

8. Drawings or cards (used in projective techniques) that trigger associations to physical, sexual, or emotional abuse.[33]

Discussion: Recreating the original trauma can be therapeutic and cathartic. However, prior to attempting this exercise, trust in the therapist is essential. The child should be able to talk about the abuse and should complete many of the other activities first. By following this activity with positive imagery, such as taking the child through the steps of saying no and getting help, you can help the child to leave the session with a positive sense of mastery.

---

[33]One source for such cards, available in minority and nonminority sets, is Northwest Psychological Publishers, Inc., PO Box 494958, Redding, CA 96049-4958 / phone (916) 223-4735 (see Caruso & Pulini in Resources).

Desensitization

DIRECTIONS: Read the following information, then complete the worksheet.

This technique can be tried at any time, but it is even more powerful once relaxation techniques are learned. It is helpful to be adept enough to truly relax when you attempt to relax. The reason is that you are going to be trying to learn to relax while you are in contact with an unpleasant or stressful situation.

Take the example of Peter, who is afraid of snakes. The desensitization procedure may be something like this:

First, Peter does the relaxation exercises and gets into a relaxed state. Then he has contact with something related to snakes. This contact must start out as something very far removed from actual contact with snakes. He might simply hear the word "snakes" or see it written on a piece of paper. He must try to continue to relax. If Peter can't, he stops looking at the word and relaxes again. After a number of trials (or even sessions) Peter should be able to relax in the presence of this, as it is very far removed from the actual object of his fear.

The next step is for Peter to try to relax in the presence of something a little more closely related to the real object of fear, such as a magazine article about snakes. After learning to relax in the presence of this, a still more threatening stimulus is used, such as a picture of a snake. Each step may take some time before it can be successfully dealt with. The idea is for Peter to get closer and closer to the real thing in small steps that are easily handled. For Peter, future steps might be relaxing in the vicinity of the reptile house at the zoo, in the reptile house itself, in front of a snake display, and even possibly holding a harmless snake. Again, realize that this may take a long time.

The priniciple is, then, that you are relaxing in situations that start off far removed, but then get closer and closer to the real thing on which the fear is based. The technique can be used on other, less dramatic fears also. Overcoming the fear of speaking in front of a group, another person, taking tests, and so on, is possible. By learning to relax in situations approximating the feared one, you may be able to relax in the situation itself.

Desensitization Worksheet

Name _____

Date _____

Desensitizing My Fear of _____

DIRECTIONS: After your teacher has explained how desensitization works, plan out your own sequence. Choose a fear you have or a situation that upsets you. Decide on at least five steps that would get you closer to the real situation.

EXAMPLE: If you said you were afraid to fly in an airplane, you might do the following:

1. Learn to relax while looking at a picture of an airplane.
2. Learn to relax while talking to someone else about flying in an airplane.
3. Learn to relax while sitting in an airplane simulator.
4. Learn to relax while in an airport.
5. Learn to relax in a plane on the ground (knowing that it will not take off).
6. Learn to relax on a plane actually flying somewhere.

DIRECTIONS: Write your fear here:

My fear is _____.

On the back of this sheet, write what steps you would take to desensitize yourself of this fear.

Activity: *The Knight Who Was Afraid of the Dark*

Ages: *5-11*

Materials: *The book,* **The Knight Who Was Afraid of the Dark** *(by B. Hazen; see Resources); blackboard or flipchart; markers or pens*

Procedure: This book is about a bold and much-loved knight who is terrified of the dark and doesn't want anyone to know. He meets a princess and, while struggling to tell her his secret, he learns that she is equally terrified of bugs. This story is a wonderful metaphor for the therapeutic process of telling "yucky secrets." It also provides a nonthreatening example of the struggle that male victims go through when admitting vulnerability and victimization.

Discussion: After reading the story, make a "fear chart" of all the things that the children in the group are afraid of. Also spend some time talking about how much better the knight felt when he talked about his fear. If the group members don't identify any fears relating to their victimization, gently bring them up. These fears may include: fear of the perpetrator, fear that the molestation may happen again, etc. Discuss the concept that the knight was strong even though he was afraid of the dark. Relate that to the young male's feelings that if he was victimized he is a "sissy." This may also be a good time to bring up the issue of males' fears of homosexuality.

This wonderful story can serve as a catalyst for a multitude of therapeutic issues.

Activity: *Children Do, Grownups Don't*

Ages: *5-9*

Materials: *The book,* **Children Do, Grownups Don't** *(by Norma Simon; see Resources)*

Procedure: Read the book *Children Do, Grownups Don't* to the group. Discuss how important it is for kids to be kids and adults to act like adults. After reading the story make a group list of the things that kids do in each of their families versus what adults do.

Discussion: Many times in families where abuse has occurred, children become parentified at an early age and take on an enormous amount of responsiblity.[34] Helping to clarify family roles is crucial in the dysfunctional family. After completing the activity, it is important for the therapist to explain to the parentified child that in this group, he/she can be the kid—freeing the child of the enormous burden of taking the adult role. This book can also be used in a family session or in a family group.

---

[34] The therapist should be aware that "appropriate" family roles are culturally determined. In some cultures, children have a great deal of responsibility at a fairly young age. This is not necessarily a sign of poor boundaries or parentification; cultural factors must also be evaluated.

Activity: ***PTSD Workbook***

Ages: *7-12*

Materials: ***PTSD Workbook*** [35] ***(photocopies of the following pages); crayons or markers***

Procedure: Read through the PTSD workbook with the children. Go slowly—this can be used over several weeks or sessions.

Discussion: This workbook explains the symptomology of Post Traumatic Stress Disorder in younger children's terminology. Since each child reacts differently, it is written for various types of traumas that the child might be exposed to. It is important to explain to the child's parents the symptomology of PTSD while you are working with the child.

---

[35] Developed in 1988 and © 1991 by Carolyn Cunningham and Kee MacFarlane. Permission given to photocopy only for group members' use.

My PTSD Workbook

This workbook will help you to understand PTSD, what it is, how it got there, and how to control it.

The letters PTSD really stand for Post Traumatic Stress Disorder, fancy words for something lots of kids get when something scary or bad happens to them or to someone close to them.

PTSD is the way some people think, feel, or act after something really awful has happened. An easier way to think about these letters and the feelings that go with them is:

P. T. S. D. =

Pretty Tough Stuff, Dude!

When something bad or scary happens to somebody, it is called a trauma. Some examples of traumas are getting hurt badly and going to the hospital, being physically or sexually abused, losing someone that you love because of divorce or because they moved away or died, or seeing a parent or a pet or somebody that you love get hurt.

Traumas are stuff that gets you upset!

Draw a picture of a **trauma** that you have had or seen:

When people have traumas they react in certain ways.
Sometimes they worry a lot or get really nervous. Sometimes
they get nightmares or "flashbacks." A "flashback" is a strong
memory or picture in your mind, a smell, or physical feeling
about something in the past that makes you feel like it's
happening right now.

Sometimes people who have had traumas are scared of loud noises, or sometimes they feel numb or "spaced out." These feelings are your body's way of letting you know that **something is wrong**. That is what PTSD is—a memory of a trauma. Sometimes the memory lasts for a long time.

Sometimes kids get nightmares after they have had a trauma. Do you have nightmares? If you do, draw one of your scariest nightmares:

Even though nightmares can be very scary, there are things you can do to feel better about them. One thing you can do is make up a good ending for your nightmare or draw your nightmare in a way that makes it less scary. For example, if a monster is chasing you, you can draw the monster in a cage. If someone is hurting you, imagine somebody else who is keeping you safe. Now draw or retell your nightmare with a good ending.

My Picture:

When some people who have had traumas get **flashbacks**, they feel that the trauma is happening all over again. Flashbacks can be caused by things that remind you of the first time the trauma happened. For example, you might feel scared around a person you're meeting for the first time because he reminds you of someone else who hurt or abused you. A loud noise might make someone who was in an earthquake react as if the earthquake is happening all over again.

Flashbacks are scary, but you can get help in dealing with them. One way is to talk to someone about what happened to you. Another way is to use "self-talk" by telling yourself, "What happened to me is over and this is just a flashback." Another way is to tell an adult who cares about you, "I am having a flashback about _____ and I'm feeling _____ . Can you help me deal with it?"

On this page write the scariest things about your trauma or draw the answers to these questions.

The worst part about my trauma was_____

_____.

When it was happening, I felt _____.

Right after it was over I felt _____.

Sometimes I still feel _____.

_____ probably could have
(friend, relative, superhero, police officer)

rescued me by _____

_____

Draw a picture of that person helping you.

If it happened again, I would _____

_____

_____

_____

Write or draw a picture of what you could do if it happened again.

With your therapist make a plan of ways to control your flashback and write it on this page. Write down the things you can say to yourself that can help you make the flashback go away. This is called "self-talk." Then list the adults who understand what happened to you, or on the back of this page, draw pictures of them helping you.

My Plan Is:

My self-talk will be:

People who understand:

_____

_____

_____

_____

_____

_____

_____

_____

_____

_____

_____

_____

_____

_____

_____

_____

_____

_____

_____

_____

_____

_____

Sometimes after a trauma people feel "spacey." They have trouble concentrating, and may feel "numb"—like your hand or foot feels after it's fallen asleep, or like your mouth feels after you get a shot from the dentist. But this type of numb is about your happy, sad, mad **feelings**. Sometimes people stop feeling happy, sad, or mad and they start feeling ... well ... nothing. If you feel numb, it is really important that you talk with your therapist or someone important to you about what has happened to you. The more you talk about what happened to you and about your feelings, the less "numb" you'll feel.

Remember, lots of people who have had a **trauma**, have **PTSD**. Even though you may feel like you're going crazy at times, it's just your body's way of trying to help you deal with Tough Stuff. Trauma is **Pretty Tough Stuff, Dude.** It takes time to get over painful experiences. Now that you understand what Post Traumatic Stress Disorder is, you'll be able to find new ways to deal with it. Draw a picture of yourself feeling a lot better.

CHAPTER NINE

Treating Perpetration

Before addressing the perpetration issues of the abuse-reactive child, it is helpful for clinicians to become familiar with four related theories of human behavior: 1) Post Traumatic Stress theory; 2) the addiction model; 3) the sexual abuse cycle;[36] and 4) the "Four Preconditions of Abuse" model (Finkelhor, 1984).

Early perpetration may be conceptualized as a combination of elements contained in these theoretical formulations (among others). For example, an abuse-reactive child victim initially may react to feelings of powerlessness from a stressor by identifying with his/her abuser (Post Traumatic Stress theory). Later, when the child experiences a powerful negative emotion (such as feeling betrayed or criticized), he/she may re-enact the original sexual abuse. This impulse or behavior may be fostered by a family environment that lacks the boundaries and controls which otherwise might compensate for the child's own lack of control ("Four Preconditions" model). Finally the behavior becomes repetitive due to the reinforcer of sexual arousal and/or the achievement of temporary relief from feelings of powerlessness or anxiety.

In his "Four Preconditions of Abuse" model, Finkelhor (1984) describes factors that influence adult family members of either gender to cross sexual boundaries. We have applied them to the abuse-reactive child in the following ways:

1. *Motivation to Sexually Abuse.* With abuse-reactive children, this motivation may take the form of an initial reaction to their own abuse. This reaction may be reinforced sexually during a critical time of sexual development. In addition, the abusive child usually feels powerful and in control over the victim. Thus, the behavior may satisfy a deep emotional need to alleviate the child's feelings of vulnerability.

2. *Overcoming Internal Inhibitors.* Most children do not sexually victimize others, even when they have been victims of sexual abuse. However, abuse-reactive children may develop aggressive, sexual, and self-destructive thinking. In addition, many of these children come from families where there are few role models of internal control. Thus, they lack empathy and their development of appropriate moral values is impaired.

3. *Overcoming External Inhibitors.* Frequently, the family of the abuse-reactive child lacks clearly defined boundaries and the external controls that otherwise might compensate for the child's lack of internal inhibitors. Sometimes they unconsciously place the abuse-reactive child in situations that encourage sexual acting out or they fail to provide adequate protection for young child victims. These acts of commission and omission and other behaviors that can sabotage treatment may occur because many family members have been victims themselves and need the child to become the "identified patient" for the whole family.

---

[36] Brief summaries of these three theories (with reference citations) are provided in the Introduction.

4. *Overcoming the Victim's Resistance.* Abuse-reactive children generally pick victims who are younger, smaller, or less powerful than they are. They then use coercion, bribery, or threats to break down the victim's resistance.

Therapists can choose to address the issues of perpetration separately or simultaneously while the child is working through his/her victimization issues. There are no set rules; some therapists prefer to address perpetration issues first, while others begin with victimization. Some therapists make the choice depending on the dynamics of a particular group, or allow older children to make the choice. The most important thing is that *both* issues are addressed. ,

It is also important for therapists to recognize that there are cases where the child perpetrator either does not have a history as a victim of sexual abuse, or will not acknowledge that any abuse has taken place. Some of the children who have not been sexually abused may come from environments that are sexually over-stimulating; others have families who enforce exceptionally strong sexual taboos. As a result, the child may act out the family's sexual issues. In these cases, it is especially helpful for the child and family to receive family therapy in conjunction with the structured group and individual treatment program.

Cognitive behavioral interventions appear to work best in relation to issues of perpetration. Even very young children can and must come to understand the feelings, thoughts, and events that precede or promote their sexually abusive acting out, as well as any sexual fantasies associated with their acts of perpetration. These issues are very difficult for an adult to recognize, let alone for an impulsive young child. However, if taken slowly and addressed repeatedly, it can be done. With children, these issues must be presented in a nonthreatening activity format, and progress should be positively reinforced throughout the process.[37]

Perhaps one of the most debatable issues in treating perpetration by children is whether—and how far—treatment modalities that appear effective with adult and adolescent offenders can be adapted and applied effectively in treatment with these youngest abusers. While it is important and possible for even very young children to identify and disclose some of the cognitive, emotional, and behavioral *precursors* to their abusive behavior, it is unclear whether *all* of these precursors can be identified in young children. While anger and revenge scenarios ("getting even") are identified by adult, adolescent, and some child offenders, there is no scientific evidence on whether young children have identifiable, conscious sexual fantasies or how much of a role they play in children's abusive behavior. Similarly, our own experience has not shown that younger children's abusive behavior involves a conscious arousal response to a particular sexual stimulus. On one hand, some clinicians never address issues of sexual arousal with younger children; on the other hand, treatment methods that assume the presence of a sexual arousal pattern in all child offenders are equally likely to miss the mark. Obviously there is much research to be done in this area. Therapists must be very careful not to treat abuse-reactive children as if the dynamics of adolescent offending automatically apply; doing so may set up expectations for behavior and for treatment that are beyond their developmental capacity.

---

[37] In addition to these activities, see *Steps to Healthy Touching* by Kee MacFarlane and Carolyn Cunningham (1988; see Resources), a companion workbook developed to help abuse-reactive children take responsibility for their sexually abusive acts. *Pathways: A Guided Workbook for Youth Beginning Treatment* by Timothy J. Kahn (1990; see Resources) contains a cognitive behavioral application of Finkelhor's "Four Preconditions to Abuse" in treatment with adolescent sexual abuse perpetrators.

Although the entire text addresses the issue of abusiveness, the activities in this chapter specifically address perpetration.

As we are aware from adult abusers, narcissistic behavior is a common dynamic that begins in early childhood. Children who abuse others often feel that their behaviors are justified and that the world owes them for what they haven't received in life.

Lynne Namka has written about "Children of Entitlement" (1994) and suggests cues to interpret behavior that appears demanding and narcissistic; while it is written using the generic male pronoun, these insights apply to both girls and boys.

"You Owe Me"— Children of Entitlement [38]

"I want_____ , Give_____ to me, Buy me_____" seem to be the constant demand of some children. Some children feel owed or entitled to get their way. While it is normal for a child to ask for what he [or she] wants, some children are overly demanding and needy. They have not learned to balance taking from others with giving; they view other people as existing merely to give to them.

For some children, this behavior may be a stage that they go through and grow out of. For example, two-year-olds constantly seek and explore the environment. Demanding that their needs be met is one of the ways that two-year-olds develop independence. Another phase comes up during adolescence. Teenagers are notoriously known for requiring the best of everything. Rampant materialism appears to be the middle name for some young people during the teen years— it is a stage that some young people go through. However, if the child does not grow out of his selfish behavior, there may be a serious problem.

Some children have a lifelong pattern of selfishness and feeling owed. The demanding child often focuses on issues of "It's not fair." He feels on an unconscious level that what happened to him was not fair. And in a sense, he is "owed" because he missed out on basic nurturing, love, and structure. When early dependency needs were not provided, the child feels a sense of loss and shame that manifests itself in being angry. This child may go through life angrily trying to get others to make up for what his parents did not provide.

This type of child may react continuously to perceived small injustices in daily life. In effect, he is saying to other people, "You owe me. Pay up." He can't get what he wants from his parents, so he tries to get it from other people. Symbolically, continual anger can be a covert statement to his parents, "It is not fair. Give me my basic needs. Pay attention to me or I will blow up." Yet the sad part is that no matter how much is given to him it is as if he has a hole inside that can never be filled.

The child who feels owed often has limited skills and tools to interact with people and sets up demands that cause others to distance themselves from him. His defenses prevent him from gaining acceptance and friendships from others in acceptabole ways. He learns to substitute anger, cruelty to others, addictive substances, workaholic behavior or material objects to fill his neediness. Behavior that focuses primarily [on] negative ways of getting the needs of the self met without regard to others is called narcissistic.

---

[38] Excerpted from Namka, L. (1994). Children of Entitlement. I Stop My Bully Behavior Kit. Tucson, AZ: Talk, Trust & Feel Therapeutics. By permission of the author.

Causes of Narcissistic Behavior

The roots of this problem may be due to a conbination of stresses of nature and nurture. There may be neurological involvement. Faulty brain wiring may be due to genetics or there could have been an injury to the brain.

How the child is raised makes a difference in how he views himself and others. This type of child may not have had his basic needs met when he was young. The mother may not have had the capacity to support the ego-emerging aspects of the child. She may not have been available either emotionally or physically during this important developmental period of his life. Around the age of two, children learn to separate from their mother and develop an independent sense of self. Deprivation of the child's needs during the period of his life can result in ego fixation and developmental arrest.

Selfish behavior can be learned. The child may have witnessed one of his parents displaying a pattern of domination and selfishness while the other parent gave in much of the time. The child learns to expect others to meet his needs as modeled by the dominant parent whom he perceives as powerful. Children who have experienced early physical and sexual trauma, including neglect and rejection, may develop narcissistic defenses to deal with their early pain. Spoiled and overindulged children sometimes are at risk for the narcissistic behavior pattern of wanting to control others. Children who are required to live up to high parental expectation of being charming, talented, intelligent, beautiful so that the parent's self esteem can be enhanced are also at risk. This is particularly true when the parents are disappointed and rejecting when the child does not live up to their expectations.

Children whose parents are getting divorced may react to the stress by becoming more demanding. The child may feel pulled between the two parents and play one against the other to gain presents and special privileges. Sometimes one parent unwittingly plays into the child's materialism by "buying" the child's favor through giving gifts or exciting outings.

Defenses Against Shame

Narcissistic behavior is a defense against internal negative feelings. The original self has become fractured. The result of the fractured self is a way of interacting to keep himself from feeling. The real self of the child was shut down in early life due to trauma or parents' over-involvement with their own needs. The child forms a false sense of self to help avoid depression, abandonment and the all-encompassing shame. His defenses of neediness and selfishness keep the child from feeling vulnerable and unworthy. The entitlement defense helps keep the child from his internal global belief of "I'm bad" that may have developed when he felt parental rejection and feared abandonment early in life. His secret belief is that "I must be really bad or my parents would have loved me." He avoids remembering early painful experiences of hurt and shame.

Masterson describes the narcissistic wound as being so great that the individual cannot even consider the balm to provide the healing. This form of denial and rigid thinking is one of the hardest defenses to break into. The child continually seeks self-gratification to pursue relief from shame. These unquenchable demands are the result of arrested growth. The depth of these defenses is the depth of the trauma. When the child is stressed or threatened, he engages in more self-serving behavior. ...

Cues to Break Into Statements of "You Owe Me!"

You feel that your needs aren't being met. I wonder why you need to get angry when that doesn't get you what you want? Does going into time out make you happy? What is another choice you could make instead of insisting that you get your way?

Maybe you get angry to avoid feeling bad feelings inside. You could make a different choice.

What is our rule about buying you things every time? You can learn to feel good inside without having to have new toys all the time. Really feeling good is about learning to talk about your scary feelings.

This is not a big deal. Big deals are parents screaming at you or hitting you, leaving you or your becoming anxious when parents fight. Little deals are not getting your own way. You don't have to get angry over little deals. What could you tell yourself to let this go so you could feel happy?

It is sad to see a smart person like you making yourself so angry all the time. Some people talk about feelings so they don't have to get angry so much. Hmmm. I wonder if you could do that?

You get angry when I don't give you what you want. How does not getting your way hurt you? That's life. Tell yourself, "I don't always get my way. That's how it is. I don't have to get mad."

It is so painful for you to look at yourself. You keep insisting that I buy you things. I wonder why you want to argue instead of doing things that would make you happy?

Yes it is hard to talk about feelings at first. It does feel uncomfortable inside at first. Then you get used to it just like riding a bicycle is hard at first. The uncomfortable feelings go away and you feel good. When you learn to talk about your feelings, you won't have to get angry all the time.

You used to take care of the bad feelings inside by insisting that you get your own way. That doesn't work any more. What else can you do instead of blowing up?

I'm curious why you think it must go your way. Let's find the hurt underneath the anger. Look for the hurt feelings. Tell me about a time when someone hurt you.

Maybe someone hurt you a long time ago when you were little. Maybe you could start to talk about the old hurts. Then you could feel good inside again. I really want you to feel good inside. The only way to feel good inside is to talk about the hurt and go through it.

You can learn to handle those bad feelings inside. I know they make you nervous, but you can do it. I believe in you!

References:

Kernberg, O. (1975). *Borderline conditions and pathological narcissism.* New York: J. Aronson.
Kernberg, P. (1989). Narcissistic personality disorder in childhood. In Otto Kernberg (Ed.), *The Psychiatric Clinics of North America,* 12(3).
Masterson, J. (1988). *The search for the real self: Unmasking personality disorders of our age.* New York: Macmillan Free Press.

CHILDREN WHO SET FIRES

Many clinicians and an increasing number of authors have noted the similarities and observed the relationship between the behaviors of individuals who sexually abuse others and some who set fires. Certainly both behaviors may be secretive, compulsive, and fantasy-bound, often cloaked in denial (to others and to self). This denial is usually maintained by an assortment of thinking errors (cognitive distortions). A child's firesetting problem may be easily minimized or denied because many children are interested in fire and will try to play with it given the opportunity.

More significantly for the clinician, since sexual abusiveness and fire setting usually occur in secret and have few, if any, witnesses, we often don't know about them unless the victim or perpetrator tells us. (Of course, victims of arson usually know only about the effects of the behavior, not the perpetrator.) This secrecy argues most powerfully for the need for direct inquiry about both behaviors. Children need a safe place and permission to freely discuss these activities which are often shame-based and hidden. However, even among experienced clinicians who work with sexual abuse victims and perpetrators, it is surprising how few ever directly inquire about the possibility that their clients are acting out their feelings with fire.

As awareness increases and as clinicians begin to explore children's feelings and behavior concerning fire, we may be surprised at just how strong the relationship is. In at least one treatment program for abuse-reactive children, approximately eighty percent of the treatment population are also fire starters (Cunningham, personal communication, 1993). As with the problems of sexual acting-out, cruelty, and aggression, the sooner we can intervene in a child's life, the better. And, of course, the sooner we identify the issues, behaviors and underlying feelings, the sooner we can begin to intervene.

This section has been added to provide a few rudimentary tools to help the clinician evaluate and/or treat problems involving fire setting by young children. There appears to be very little existing information and few practical tools available in this subject area. This section consists primarily of materials developed by Alison Stickrod Gray, M.S., one of the most innovative therapists in the field, who has worked with both abuse-reactive children and young fire setters. Additional contributors to this section are: Connie Isaac, Sandy Lane, and Fire Marshall Charles Campbell of Eugene, Oregon. These materials are for use with children under the age of twelve. We hope that they will provide a framework for thinking about and working with children who abuse fire. As always, we encourage those who encounter these children to use their creativity and experience to expand upon what is offered here to help children address the underlying feelings and hurt that is all too often masked by their behavior.

Kee MacFarlane
Carolyn Cunningham

Introduction to Fire Setter Decision Criteria*

Assessment tools for use with juvenile firestarters in the mid-1980s omitted exploring any history of abuse by fire; nor did they provide a method for evaluating family fire-related risk factors which often play an interactive role in pertetuating a child's fire misbehavior. To address these concerns, Gray and Campbell collaborated from their work in fire evaluation, fire education, and treatment interventions with high-risk youth and families. Inspired by the Wenet and Clark Juvenile Sexual Offender Decision Criteria (first published in the *Oregon Report on Juvenile Sexual Offenders*, 1986, pp. 59-61) as a model for structuring interview data, the assessment tool that follows was designed for use with juvenile firesetters and was pilot-tested by the authors with children ages 8 to 18 at the Lane County (Oregon) Juvenile Department and the Eugene (Oregon) Fire Department in 1987. In collaboration with MacFarland and Cunningham, this model was modified with language better suited for use with young children in 1994.

Include the criteria as part of a clinical interview process which obtains additional information from psychometric testing, children's drawimgs, child protective service abuse reports, police and fire reports on the child or family members, any available juvenile records, psychological evaluations, medical information, school reports or teacher report forms, and released information from therapists who may already be involved with the child and family.

Taking time to prepare is key to effective interviewing and evaluation. The criteria are designed specifically for the evaluator to use before interviewing a child or caregiver in order to prompt the notation of known and unknown information. While a structure for interview topics is represented in the criteria format, the evaluator's opinions should be recorded after the interviews are completed. The criteria document is not intended to be used as a checklist during the interview. Opinions are reflected in the criteria after all records are considered.

For each item where data or observations exist to support the evaluator's opinion, a selection is made, with "1" representing yes, "0" representing no, and "dn" for don't know. Tally the scores for section one separately: a higher number of factors present suggests that there can be a lower level of professional concern. Then tally sections two and three. The presence of a higher number of factors in each of these sections suggests reason for a higher level of professional concern. For the evaluator to differentiate an opinion overall of moderate or high concern, he or she must consider the weight of entries in section one as positive factors against the negative weight of factors in the following sections. Keep this in mind as a guide to aid in analyzing total known factors: numbers or scores in any single section in themselves do not represent a scientific indication of outcome or prediction of risk. Finally, enter your selected opinion at the bottom of the scale which recommends one of the following responses: 1) speciallized plan; 2) community-based treatment; 3) residential treatment; or 4) secure treatment.

It is expected that a report of professional recommendations summarizing the notations made on the criteria should in each case describe the interviewer's supporting observations. The criteria itself should be considered work product and not a report in itself.

---

*All original materials by Gray in this section should be cited as "Gray, A.S. (1996). Introduction to juvenile firesetting. In C. Cunningham and K. MacFarlane, *When children abuse: Group treatment strategies for children with impulse control problems* (pp. 183-192)."

Evaluators often feel pressure to diagnose a child's risk for reoffending, and that pressure may tempt an evaluator to use the criteria as if it suggested scientific validity, when such is not the case. In order to guard against creating any faulty impressions that this criteria has the capability of predicting future behavior, evaluators should emphasize the level of professional concern for the child's behavior rather than any supposed level of risk to reoffend.

FIRE SETTER DECISION CRITERIA[39]

The following criteria are guidelines for evaluating young fire setters. The clusters of characteristics suggest the level of concern for a child's dangerousness, strengths, deficits, and amenability to specialized treatment. This is a decision-making aid which has not been empirically validated as a predictor of behavior. It should be used with additional assessment tools.

Indicate your observations by assigning numbers to each item: 1 indicates a "yes"; 0 indicates "no"; "dn" represents "don't know."

Low Concern: Child

1. _____ Acknowledges and understands the negative impact of the behavior on others.

2. _____ Accepts responsibility for committing the behavior without blaming others or circumstances.

3. _____ Shows regret (very young children) or remorse (older children) and awareness of the danger of fire setting.

4. _____ Volunteers additional, previously unknown information regarding fire setting history.

5. _____ Has a history of adequate school behavior.

6. _____ Shows no initial signs of depression, behavior disorder, suicidal thinking.

7. _____ Shows a history of appropriate fear of fire.

8. _____ After thorough examination, the fire set behavior appears clear and limited to curiosity.

9. _____ Once the fire is started, the child attempts to put the fire out.

10. _____ Child's problem-solving following the fire start appears reasonable, and non-attention getting or revenge seeking.

Low Concern: Family

1. _____ The parents acknowledge that the child has committed the behavior for which he/she is referred.

---

[39]Firesetter Decision Criteria by Alison Stickrod Gray, M.S., Center for Prevention Services, Underhill Center, Vermont and Charles Campbell, Fire Marshall, Eugene, Oregon Dept. of Public Safety. Reprinted with permission of Alison Stickrod Gray. These criteria are a modification of the Adolescent Firesetter Decision Criteria, ©1987 by Gray & Campbell. The original authors express their appreciation to Drs. Gary Wenet and Toni Clark who permitted modification of the Juvenile Sexual Offender Decision Criteria. Thanks also to Joseph Richardson of the Providence (RI) Fire Department and Thor Steen of the Lane County Juvenile Department, Eugene, Oregon.

2. _____ The parents hold the child responsible for the behavior without blaming others or circumstances.

3. _____ The parents acknowledge and understand the negative impact of the behavior on victims and community.

4. _____ The family is supportive of treatment and agrees to become involved in specialized education and counseling.

5. _____ The parents have a history of:
   a) giving clear messages of the harmfulness of fire
   b) providing carefully supervised fire safety practices
   c) teaching fire is a tool not a toy

6. _____ The parents have consistently supervised use of fire in the home.

7. _____ Parents identify problems within the family unit which are separate from the child's fire setting behavior.

Moderate Concern: Child

1. _____ Resists discussing the fire setting behavior.

2. _____ Minimizes own involvement or the negative impact of the behavior on others.

3. _____ Expresses little or no guilt or remorse.

4. _____ Blames others or circumstances for the fire.

5. _____ Depression symptoms, negative self esteem.

6. _____ Shows risk attitudes, feelings, or behaviors about fire safety in the past (careless, reckless, secretive).

7. _____ History of sexual, physical, or emotional abuse.

8. _____ The fire set was motivated by a desire for attention, power, or revenge.

9. _____ Victim of fire abuse (teasing, burning, scaring, or intimidation by fire or threat of fire).

10. _____ Anger is:
    a) never expressed, denied, or chronically suppressed
    b) chronically constant
    c) indiscriminate, generalized at the whole world
    d) inflated far more than situations warrant

11. _____ Previous fire setting behaviors.

12. _____ Preplanned the physical target, place, or person.

Moderate Concern: Family

1. _____ Mother, father, or siblings indicate unresolved issues from sexual, physical, or emotional abuse (circle member and type of abuse) and resist education or counseling.

2. _____ Family member has been victim of abuse by fire (teasing, burning, scaring, or intimidation by fire or threat of fire) but the family is open to help.

3. _____ The family has difficulty identifying problems, (other than the child's fire setting behavior) within the family unit.

4. _____ The parents are resistive to participation in the evaluation without refusing altogether.

5. _____ Family members are smokers.

6. _____ Family members model occasional fire as play - smoke rings, entertainment with fire, recreationalize fire, but acknowledge its harmfulness.

7. _____ Family member has caused fire trauma to the child or other siblings in the family.

8. _____ Mother or father exhibit problems of denial about addictive behaviors (the use of drugs, alcohol) and have negative attitudes about seeking outside help.

9. _____ There is a history of fire starts in the household (reported or unreported).

10. _____ Parents acknowledge fire start behavior but redefine or minimize dangerousness, risk, or extent of child's involvement.

11. _____ Family interaction is frequently coercive.

12. _____ Family inappropriately defends child from outside attention while neglecting the child inside the family.

High Concern: Child

1. _____ History of repeated fire setting behavior despite intervention by others and/or prior treatment.

2. _____ Fire setting behavior is sophisticated, precocious, or shows extensive pre-planning.

3. _____ The child formed knowledgeable intent to physically injure persons, animals, property,(applies to older children; very young children form intent without knowledge of consequences).

4. _____ There is evidence of a progressive increase in the fire setting with regard to: substances lit or frequency of behavior.

5. _____ Motive is revenge seeking, attention getting or power seeking.

6. _____ The child completely denies the referral behavior and blames others for victimizing him/her.

7. _____ Shows animal abuse history.

8. _____ Fire setting is all-consuming to the child, a driving force, and obsessional.

9. _____ The child has been a frequent victim of physical, sexual, or extreme emotional abuse.

10. _____ The child engages in frequent fantasies involving fire setting behavior.

11. _____ The child engages in fire setting fantasies and experiences sexual arousal with them.

12. _____ The child has history of self-abuse behavior (hair pulling, head or body bashing, accident prone, plays chicken, dangerous dares).

13. _____ The child has been abused by fire and has not received appropriate help.

High Concern: Family

1. _____ The parents refuse to participate in evaluation.

2. _____ The parents deny that the child committed any part of the fire setting and blame others for victimizing their child.

3. _____ The parents deny that the child has any psycho-social problems.

4. _____ The parents refuse to participate in any recommended treatment for the child and family.

5. _____ Family obtains control of the child through coercive means by frequent threat of violence or threat of abandonment or neglect.

6. _____ Anger is chronically suppressed in the family.

7. _____ Parent/child relationship is highly dysfunctional, parent uses the child to fulfill the parent's emotional and/or physical needs.

8. _____ The child's family unit is chronically dysfunctional, chaotic, disengaged or addicted.

9. _____ Family is passive-aggressive with outside systems by appearing cooperative and supportive and chronically fails to fulfill their obligations.

QUESTIONS/TOPICS FOR EXPLORATION ABOUT FIRE SETTING[40]

1. Describe latest fire setting incident

   What happened?

   Who was involved besides you?

   What methods were used?

   Why did it happen? What were your reasons?

2. List the feelings you had: before, during and after.

---

[40] ©1987 by Alison Stickrod, M.S. Reprinted by permission of Alison Stickrod Gray, M.S., Center for Prevention Services, Underhill Ctr., Vermont.

3. How do you feel now? Why?

4. How do you think your parents feel about it? What have they said/done? Do they know about other incidents in the past?

5. How do/would your friends feel about what you did?

6. How old were you when you first began this behavior? What did you do? What happened as a result? How did you feel?

7. Describe all earlier fire setting, fire tricks, fire playing.

8. What age were you when you were first fascinated/scared by fire? What happened?

9. Have you reported fires/pulled fire alarms? How many were false?

10. Do you feel scared before/during/after starting a fire? How can you tell? How do you act when you feel scared or trapped?

11. What kinds of daydreams/fantasies do you have about fire?

12. Have others taught you about fire safety? Who? When? What methods did they use? How did it make you feel?

13. In what ways have others scared you or joked with you about fire? Do you know anyone else who starts fires?

14. Have you ever felt tricked or punished by fire? In what way?

Treatment Goals and Objectives for Addressing Fire Setting Behavior in Children[41]

Treatment Goals

1. To increase the child's sense of personal responsibility for past fire setting behavior.

2. To increase the child's understanding of the impact of fire setting on its victims, on the community, on animals and property, and on the fire setter and his/her family.

3. To increase the child's awareness of his/her thinking, feelings, and actions which led to the fire setting.

4. To increase the child's understanding of ways to meet his/her emotional/social needs without starting fires, and without hurting him/herself or others.

5. To increase the child's repertoire of feelings, skills and behaviors which can substitute for fire setting behavior.

6. To increase the child's sense of responsibility for preventing his/her fire setting behavior, for getting help during times of high risk, and for providing some type of restitution.

---

[41] ©1987 by Alison Stickrod, M.S. Reprinted by permission of Alison Stickrod Gray, M.S., Center for Prevention Services, Underhill Ctr., Vermont.

Treatment Objectives

1. Child will acknowledge responsibility for the fire setting behavior which brought him or her into treatment.

2. Child will openly and honestly discuss his/her fire setting history.

3. Child will not minimize, blame others or excuse his/her choice to play with and/or set fires.

4. Child will be able to recognize and articulate the risks and harmfulness (to self and others) of fire setting behavior.

5. Child will be able to identify the likely feelings of the victims (or potential victims) of his/her fires.

6. Child will be able to identify and discuss his/her cycle of thinking, feelings and actions which preceded the fire setting behavior.

7. Child will be able to understand and acknowledge the kinds of needs he/she was attempting to meet by setting fires.

8. Child is willing and able to learn methods of breaking the cycle of fire setting, and shows willingness to seek help.

FIRE SETTING FANTASY SURVEY: INTRODUCTION FOR CLINICIANS

It is important for the interviewing clinician to approach the topic of fire setting thoughts and fantasies from a position of open acceptance, encouragement for disclosure and suspended judgement. Children rarely have opportunities to discuss these issues and, when they do, they are surrounded by secrecy and a sense of shame. Gathering detailed information about fire setting thinking is essential to gaining an understanding of the needs which the child is attempting to meet through his/her fire setting behavior.

It is important to remember that thoughts about fire setting may not be perceived as dangerous by the child. He or she may employ fire setting planning, beliefs, or labels for the behavior which involve redefining and minimizing. One goal of fire setting fantasy exploration is to understand the child's beliefs and labels for fire fantasy based upon his/her perspectives.

A second goal of the fantasy assessment process is screening for additional and previously unreported fire setting behaviors. The clinician looks for offense *patterns* that reappear in reported fire thoughts. Fantasy content may include: offense location, victim age, methods of fire start, variety of fire setting behavior and type. All are clues to additional offenses. Careful listening often leads to discovery of previously undisclosed offenses. Oftentimes clients redefine their behavior as non-fire oriented, as recreational behavior, or as non-harmful. Disclosure of other deviant behaviors and deviant thinking is aided by fire setting fantasy exploration and is essential for effective and lasting intervention.

A third goal of such an inquiry is to determine how fire fantasy may be reinforced. Detailed exploration of the feelings the child has experienced, before, during, and after fire setting fantasy is often a source of important information.

By definition, fire setting activity is a form of behavior and, at some level, volitional in nature, no matter how compulsive or impulsive it may appear. Overt behavior is clearly modifiable. One theory, based on cognitive behavioral theory, suggests that fire setting behavior is preceded by thought. This thought is defined as covert behavior. Modification of these preceding covert thoughts and the correction of thinking errors that support them can assist in modification of a child's behavior.

Fire setting fantasies, once acted upon, essentially take the form of behavioral planning and may be woven into the reinforcement chain which continues deviant behavior. Understanding a child's fire setting thinking and fantasies provides the clinician with information needed to establish effective covert behavioral modification strategies, an important avenue of intervention in the treatment of these troubled children.

Alison Stickrod Gray, M.S.
Center for Prevention Services
Underhill Center, VT

Activity: *Fire Setting Fantasy Survey*

Ages: *7-12*

Materials: *A copy of the Fantasy Survey List by Alison Stickrod Gray (following) for each child.*

Procedure: Explain the concept of fantasies. Give an example of a fantasy (not fire-related). Then introduce the exercise in the following way:

"All of us have daydreams, thoughts, fantasies, and private ideas. I want to learn more about your daydreams that have any fire ideas in them. I want to help you talk about what comes to mind when you have thoughts about fire. When you have thoughts about fire do they include any of the things on this list?"

You can either read the list aloud to younger children (omitting words that are beyond their comprehension) or give them the list with instructions to circle any words that describe what they think or feel or daydream about when they think about fire. Discussion: This activity can provide insight into the child's perspective and underlying issues regarding fire, its meaning and associations to the child, and what it reinforces. After going through the list, children should be encouraged to think about and add their own private thoughts and fantasies which they associate with fire.

FANTASY SURVEY LIST[42]

When you have fire setting thoughts do they include any of the following:

secrets	burn self	jumping	thrilled
helper	breathers	neighbors	watching
approval	fire engine	money	staring
cloth	police	animals	audience
cheering	hose	rubbing	explode
gasoline	lighter	aroused	put down
hugging	matches lit	warm	scaring
fireman	torch	smoking	burn
kissing	ash pile	name calling	feel numb
smiling	waste basket	hitting	feel weird
pinching	comforting	peeking	escape
sticks	shouting	comfort	scared
chasing	sneaking	running	adults
teasing	snuggling	looking	mean
pushing	holding	risky	masturbating
stroking	pushing down	controlling	movie stars
yelling	excited	mad	get back
laughing	scaring	frustrated	gifts
giggling	loving	crouching	hidden
whispering	talking	helpless	singed
trash	joking	despairing	girls
dangerous	tricking	bushes	rush
games	forcing	scars	smokebomb
bribes	threatening	death	aerosol
boys	sex	rescue	buddies
parents	scorch	glue	burn pile
trapped	match book	friends	boss
rags	hero	hurting	commando
get help	funny	telephone	showing off
watching	girls	betting	bucket

Add your own thoughts and words here:

_____

_____

_____

FIRE SETTING CYCLE FOR KIDS

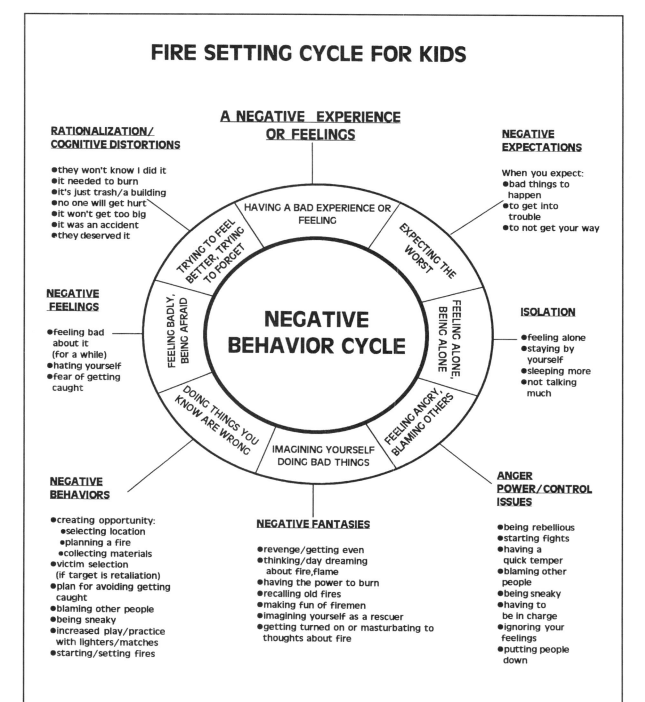

**RATIONALIZATION/
COGNITIVE DISTORTIONS**

- they won't know I did it
- it needed to burn
- it's just trash/a building
- no one will get hurt
- it won't get too big
- it was an accident
- they deserved it

**NEGATIVE
FEELINGS**

- feeling bad
  about it
  (for a while)
- hating yourself
- fear of getting
  caught

**NEGATIVE
BEHAVIORS**

- creating opportunity:
  - selecting location
  - planning a fire
  - collecting materials
- victim selection
  (if target is retaliation)
- plan for avoiding getting
  caught
- blaming other people
- being sneaky
- increased play/practice
  with lighters/matches
- starting/setting fires

**A NEGATIVE EXPERIENCE
OR FEELINGS**

**NEGATIVE
EXPECTATIONS**

When you expect:
- bad things to
  happen
- to get into
  trouble
- to not get your way

ISOLATION

- feeling alone
- staying by
  yourself
- sleeping more
- not talking
  much

**ANGER
POWER/CONTROL
ISSUES**

- being rebellious
- starting fights
- having a
  quick temper
- blaming other
  people
- being sneaky
- having to
  be in charge
- ignoring your
  feelings
- putting people
  down

NEGATIVE FANTASIES

- revenge/getting even
- thinking/day dreaming
  about fire,flame
- having the power to burn
- recalling old fires
- making fun of firemen
- imagining yourself as a rescuer
- getting turned on or masturbating to
  thoughts about fire

Inner ring labels:
- HAVING A BAD EXPERIENCE OR FEELING
- TRYING TO FEEL BETTER, TRYING TO FORGET
- FEELING BADLY, BEING AFRAID
- DOING THINGS YOU KNOW ARE WRONG
- IMAGINING YOURSELF DOING BAD THINGS
- FEELING ANGRY, BLAMING OTHERS
- FEELING ALONE, BEING ALONE
- EXPECTING THE WORST

Center: **NEGATIVE BEHAVIOR CYCLE**

Adapted with permission from *The Sexual Abuse Cycle in the Treatment of Adolescent Sexual Abusers* by Connie Issac and Sandy Lane (©1990, The Safer Society Press). The juvenile firesetter cycle was first presented by Alison Stickrod Gray at a 1988 training entitled, *Juvenile Firesetter: Applications of Juvenile Sex Offender Treatment*, Columbus, Ohio.

Activity: *The Victim Chart*

Ages: *8-12*

Materials: *Paper; markers, pens, pencils, or crayons*

Procedure: Divide a piece of paper into two columns. Label one column "People I Victimized This Week." Label the other "How I Victimized Them." Make enough copies for each group member to have one. At the beginning of group talk to the children about what a victim is.[43] After you and the children have defined what a victim is, ask them if they victimized anyone *in any way* during the week. This might include: bullying someone, blaming someone else for something the group member did, hitting or teasing somebody, etc. Positively reinforce the group for honesty. As a homework assignment, give each group member a copy of the victim chart to be brought back completed and signed by their parents.

Discussion: It is essential for children to understand how they are victimizing other children and how they can get their needs met without being hurtful to others. Most likely, abuse-reactive children have not only victimized others sexually, but physically as well. Perpetration may be in the form of hitting, fire-setting, verbal abuse, threats, etc. Begin with less threatening material, then as the children feel more comfortable, proceed to the sexual victimizing. Discuss the purpose of this exercise with parents before handing it out as a homework assignment. For younger children it might be helpful to give a name to the aspect of themselves that hurts others. It could be a person's name or an animal name, etc. Have the children keep track of when their hurtful part comes out and whom it hurts. Work with younger children on a plan for how to shrink the part of them that hurts others.

Activity: *Thoughts Before Touching Trouble*

Ages: *all ages*

Materials: *"What Was Going On Inside of Me Before I Was Hurtful"* work**sheet (following)

Procedure: In this exercise, assist the child in remembering the last time he/she molested another child. Have each child talk about what he/she was thinking, feeling, saying, or doing prior to the touching. Make copies of the worksheet for older children to fill out. With younger children spread the exercise over several sessions and make a mural each week: the first week's mural on thinking, the next week's on feelings, etc.

Discussion: This exercise and the one following lead right into presenting the Sexual Abuse Cycle (Isaac & Lane, 1990, see below). In order to stop the abuse cycle, it is crucial that children be aware of their thinking prior to their sexually abusive touching. While this process is more difficult for children to articulate than for adolescents, children do have "preoffense thinking." This "preoffense thinking" may involve sexual fantasies (particularly for older children) or fantasies of revenge, power, or control.

---

[43] It might be helpful to refer to "What is a Victim?" on page 64 in *Steps to Healthy Touching* (MacFarlane & Cunningham, 1988; see Resources).

WHAT WAS GOING ON INSIDE OF ME BEFORE I WAS HURTFUL

Now it's time to remember and write down what you said and what you thought about just *before* you touched someone else in a way that was wrong.

Before I Touched:

1. I was thinking . . . _____

_____

_____

2. I was feeling . . . _____

_____

_____

3. I said . . . _____

_____

_____

4. I was doing . . . _____

_____

_____

DANGER SIGN THOUGHTS

There are times when you might start thinking about what you did or what you might do again if you have the chance. Picturing it in your mind might even get you turned on or excited. Those kinds of thoughts (which some people call "fantasies") are "Danger Sign" thoughts and they should tell you that you need to talk to someone and ask for help right away.

Danger Sign thoughts can lead to bad messages you say to yourself. Picture them as a vulture who sits on your shoulder and criticizes you. This vulture in your head says negative things about your touching problem. Things like: "I don't care if I get in trouble or hurt someone else, I want to do it anyway." Write down some dangerous things that you or your vulture might say to you when you're having these kinds of thoughts.

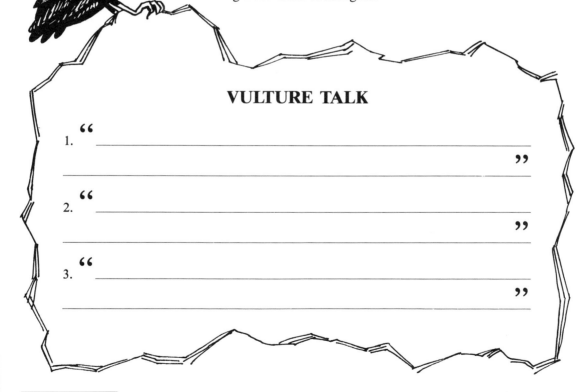

VULTURE TALK

1. " _____
   _____ "

2. " _____
   _____ "

3. " _____
   _____ "

You know how to talk back to that vulture.
You can tell him to stop, you can tell him he's wrong, and you can
make those bad thoughts and messages
go away. Write down the things you will
say to that vulture and to yourself that will
help the Danger Sign thoughts disappear.

VULTURE BACK-TALK

1. "_____
_____
_____"

2. "_____
_____
_____"

3. "_____
_____
_____"

4. "_____
_____
_____"

Activity: *Danger Sign Thoughts/Vulture Back-talk*

Ages: *all ages*

Materials: *"Danger Sign Thoughts" and "Vulture Back-talk" worksheets (previous pages)*

Procedure: Discuss with the children the concept of negative or "dangerous" thoughts that can get them angry or wanting to touch somebody in a hurtful way again. Use the metaphor of a vulture who sits on their shoulders and says negative things about them ("you're stupid") or about their touching problem ("go ahead, who cares"). Have the children write down or discuss what their vultures say that can get them upset or into trouble. After the children are able to articulate their "vulture thoughts," have them plan ways to talk back to the vulture.

Discussion: Younger children may not be able developmentally to understand the concept of sexual fantasies, but they can understand the idea of having angry thoughts and thoughts about touching another little boy or girl. Older children can be introduced to the concept of *inappropriate sexual fantasies* as involving bribery, tricks, unequal power, coercion, threats, or force. The concept of "thought-stopping" (talking back to the vulture) is a crucial part of therapy for children with sexual behavior problems.[44]

Activity: *The Sexual Abuse Cycle (or the Sexual Abuse Steps)*

Ages: *8-12*

Materials: *The Sexual Abuse Cycle and the Sexual Abuse Steps (see diagrams following)*

Procedure: Draw the Sexual Abuse Cycle either on a flipchart or on a chalkboard. Explain each part of the cycle.[45] Encourage the group to suggest additional examples for each step. You might also have the children stand or sit in a circle, with each child representing one or more of the stages of the cycle. Go around the circle and have each child explain, give examples, and/or act out the stage he/she represents. After the group has gone through the cycle once, see how fast they can do it a second or third time (the kids usually find it fun to go faster and faster; the second and third rounds emphasize the repetitive quality of the cycle).

Because the Sexual Abuse Cycle Diagram may be too difficult for young children to understand, the "Steps to Getting In Trouble" diagram (following) can also be used to explain the Sexual Abuse Cycle concept. We wrote "The Angry Baseball Player" as a metaphor to make the theoretical concepts more concrete and easier to translate into real life.

---

[44] For more information and in some cases additional activities dealing with thought-stopping, see Bash & Camp, 1985; Bays & Freeman-Longo, 1989 (pp. 73-74); Bays, Freeman-Longo & Hildebran, 1990 (pp. 27-30); Committee for Children, 1988; Hoghughi, 1988; MacFarlane & Cunningham, 1988; Vernon, 1989; and Wolpe & Lazarus, 1966.

[45] This activity requires that therapists fully understand the dynamics of the Sexual Abuse Cycle. Isaac and Lane have made an excellent training videotape or audio cassette: *The Sexual Abuse Cycle in the Treatment of Adolescent Sexual Abusers*, available from The Safer Society Press, RR #1 Box 24-B, Orwell, VT 05760-9756. For a detailed explanation of the Sexual Abuse Cycle, see Lane (1991).

SEXUAL ABUSE CYCLE FOR KIDS

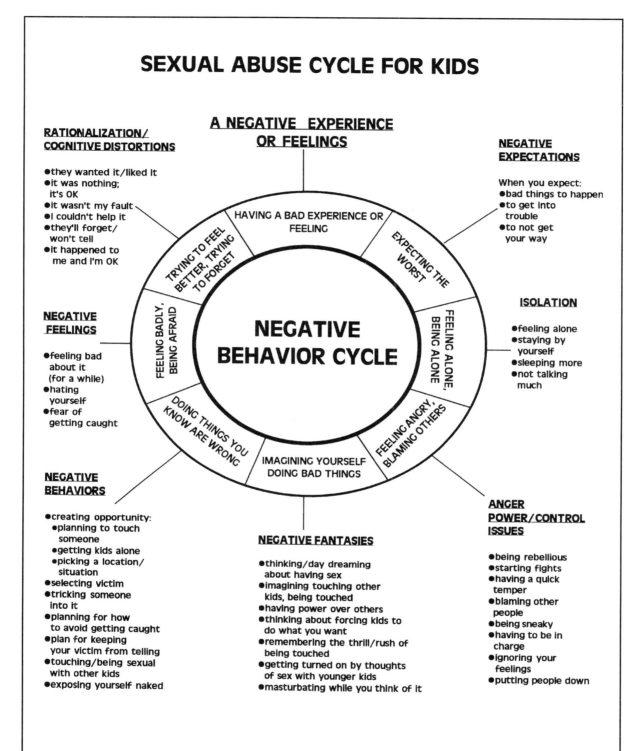

A NEGATIVE EXPERIENCE OR FEELINGS

RATIONALIZATION/ COGNITIVE DISTORTIONS

- they wanted it/liked it
- it was nothing; it's OK
- it wasn't my fault
- I couldn't help it
- they'll forget/ won't tell
- it happened to me and I'm OK

NEGATIVE FEELINGS

- feeling bad about it (for a while)
- hating yourself
- fear of getting caught

NEGATIVE BEHAVIORS

- creating opportunity:
  - planning to touch someone
  - getting kids alone
  - picking a location/ situation
- selecting victim
- tricking someone into it
- planning for how to avoid getting caught
- plan for keeping your victim from telling
- touching/being sexual with other kids
- exposing yourself naked

NEGATIVE FANTASIES

- thinking/day dreaming about having sex
- imagining touching other kids, being touched
- having power over others
- thinking about forcing kids to do what you want
- remembering the thrill/rush of being touched
- getting turned on by thoughts of sex with younger kids
- masturbating while you think of it

NEGATIVE EXPECTATIONS

When you expect:
- bad things to happen
- to get into trouble
- to not get your way

ISOLATION

- feeling alone
- staying by yourself
- sleeping more
- not talking much

ANGER POWER/CONTROL ISSUES

- being rebellious
- starting fights
- having a quick temper
- blaming other people
- being sneaky
- having to be in charge
- ignoring your feelings
- putting people down

Adapted with permission from *The Sexual Abuse Cycle in the Treatment of Adolescent Sexual Abusers* by Connie Issac and Sandy Lane (©1990 The Safer Society Press).

VIOLENCE CYCLE FOR KIDS

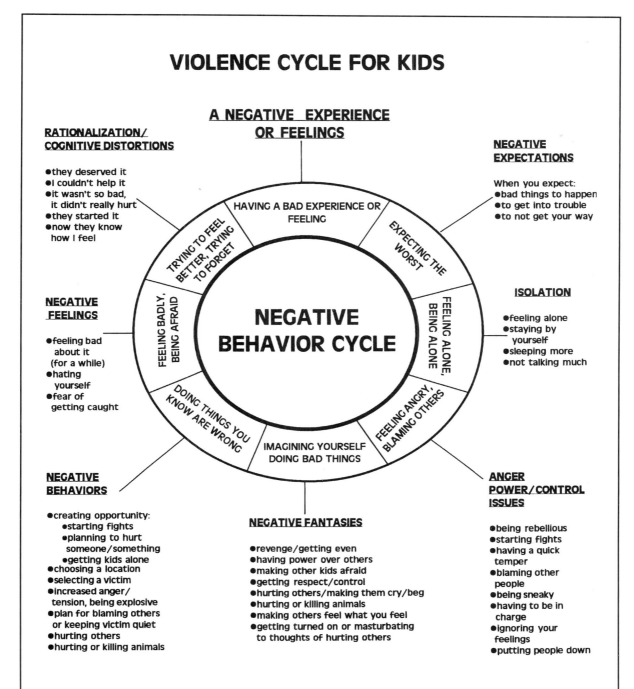

A NEGATIVE EXPERIENCE OR FEELINGS

RATIONALIZATION/ COGNITIVE DISTORTIONS

- they deserved it
- I couldn't help it
- it wasn't so bad, it didn't really hurt
- they started it
- now they know how I feel

NEGATIVE EXPECTATIONS

When you expect:
- bad things to happen
- to get into trouble
- to not get your way

ISOLATION

- feeling alone
- staying by yourself
- sleeping more
- not talking much

NEGATIVE FEELINGS

- feeling bad about it (for a while)
- hating yourself
- fear of getting caught

ANGER POWER/CONTROL ISSUES

- being rebellious
- starting fights
- having a quick temper
- blaming other people
- being sneaky
- having to be in charge
- ignoring your feelings
- putting people down

NEGATIVE BEHAVIORS

- creating opportunity:
  - starting fights
  - planning to hurt someone/something
  - getting kids alone
- choosing a location
- selecting a victim
- increased anger/ tension, being explosive
- plan for blaming others or keeping victim quiet
- hurting others
- hurting or killing animals

NEGATIVE FANTASIES

- revenge/getting even
- having power over others
- making other kids afraid
- getting respect/control
- hurting others/making them cry/beg
- hurting or killing animals
- making others feel what you feel
- getting turned on or masturbating to thoughts of hurting others

Inner cycle (NEGATIVE BEHAVIOR CYCLE):

- HAVING A BAD EXPERIENCE OR FEELING
- EXPECTING THE WORST
- FEELING ALONE, BEING ALONE
- FEELING ANGRY, BLAMING OTHERS
- IMAGINING YOURSELF DOING BAD THINGS
- DOING THINGS YOU KNOW ARE WRONG
- FEELING BADLY, BEING AFRAID
- TRYING TO FEEL BETTER, TRYING TO FORGET

NEGATIVE BEHAVIOR CYCLE

Sexual Abuse Cycle/Steps to Getting In Trouble

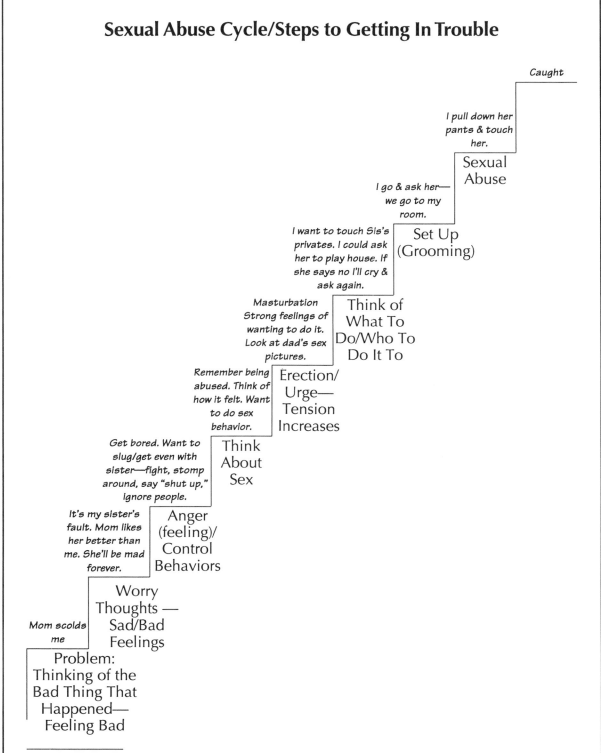

Adapted with permission from *The Sexual Abuse Cycle in the Treatment of Adolescent Sexual Abusers* (Videotape & audio cassette reference materials), by Connie Isaac and Sandy Lane (1990). © The Safer Society Press. The case example was furnished by a 9-year-old offender.

The Angry Baseball Player

There was a boy named Andy who didn't feel very good about himself. The only thing Andy thought he was good at was baseball. Andy *was* an excellent hitter. One day, Andy had a bad game. He struck out every time he was at bat. He said to himself, "I can't do anything right. I can't even hit anymore." He figured that everyone watching thought he was a lousy hitter (even though he didn't ask them what they thought). He felt so bad about himself that he kept away from the other team members and didn't talk to anyone when he got home.

After a while, Andy began to blame Sam, the pitcher for the other team, for his strike outs. He thought about it all the time. He started to think about how much bigger and stronger he was than Sam. Then Andy started to think about hurting Sam for making him look bad. In fact, that's *all* he thought about.

One day Andy made a plan to get even. He decided to beat Sam up before the next baseball game. He knew where the team was playing, so he rode his bike over there early and started a fight with Sam. Andy gave Sam a black eye. As Andy was riding away, he began to worry that his coach would find out about what he did and kick him off the team.

The coach *did* find out and suspended Andy for one game. Andy felt bad about it—but only for a little while. Then he started to think to himself, "Sam really deserved it; what I did was okay." As time went on, he forgot all about it.

Discussion: As you can see, the story follows the sexual abuse cycle. Some questions for discussion include:

1. What could Andy have done or said to himself to keep from feeling so bad?

2. What could Andy's parents or team members have done to help Andy when he started to keep away from other people?

3. Why did Andy start to blame Sam?

4. How could Andy stop himself from thinking about hurting Sam and getting even? (thought stopping)

5. How did Andy end up victimizing someone else?

6. How do you think Sam felt?

After discussing Andy's story, have the children give examples of times that they have been on the sexual abuse cycle. Gradually bring in the issue of sexual acting out. Help the children chart their sexual acting out. The issues of fantasies and thought-stopping should also be addressed (e.g., "When you start thinking about victimizing or molesting someone, what can you do?").

Note: It is a good idea to present The Sexual Abuse Cycle to parents at the same time that you present it to the children. Parents can learn to identify when their children are on the steps or in the cycle and help them interrupt it.

Activity: *The Babysitting Disaster*

Ages: *9-12*

Materials: *Story: "The Babysitting Disaster" (following)*

Procedure: Read aloud the story below and discuss its implications.

Discussion: This true story pairs anger and aggression with sexual arousal. It is important to get the children in the group to discuss why Mark touched Jimmy. Eventually you can make the connection between the story and the children's own experiences by asking such questions as: "What were your feelings and thoughts right before you touched ____(victim's name)____. How do you think Mark felt during the touching? How did you feel while you were molesting ____(victim's name)____? How did Mark feel afterward? How did you feel afterward? What were you thinking about?"

Talk to the group about warning signals and how to get help when those feelings or thoughts come back. Asking the children to describe how Jimmy felt will provide insight into their own superego functioning. How children end the story also will give you insight into how much they fear getting caught. If children end the story with Mark getting away with it, their lack of fear is a concern. Instilling awareness of the potential consequences might be useful in these cases.

The Babysitting Disaster

Mark, who is 12 years old, was really looking forward to the senior high football game tonight. All of his friends were going, and his girl friend was going to be there, too. After the game Mark and his friends were going to a party. Mark had been looking forward to it for a long time.

He also was hoping that he'd get home before his report card did. "Please, please, please," he prayed, "let the mail be slow so my report card comes tomorrow. Let the Post Office lose my report card ..." He knew that his grades were going to be pretty bad. On his way home, Mark was thinking about all the different ways he could talk his mom into letting him go to the game even after she saw how bad his grades were.

As soon as Mark opened the front door, he saw his mom waiting for him in the front hall with his report card in her hand. "This is the worst report card you've ever gotten," she yelled.

Mark tried to calm his mother down. "I'll do better next time, I promise, Mom."

But his mother kept yelling at him. "You're right, you're going to do better—you're grounded! Starting tonight, you stay home every night and study. Wait until your father finds out about this!"

Mark felt his stomach go into a knot. "But Mom," he pleaded, "what about the game tonight—*please?*"

"No way!" she declared. Mark was really upset and really angry. He had planned to go to the game for a long time. What would his friends think? What would his girlfriend think?

When Mark's father came home, the angry shouting started all over again. Mark felt pretty bad after listening to his father yell, "You'll *never* amount to *anything!*" Then his parents decided to go out and made him stay home to babysit his 5-year-old brother Jimmy. He hated to babysit.

After his parents left, Mark thought about the game he was missing, and what a good time his friends and his girlfriend were probably having, and how they were probably thinking he was a baby who couldn't go out by himself at night. He got angrier and angrier inside. He *really* wanted to get even with his parents. "I *hate* them," he thought to himself.

Everything Jimmy said or did irritated Mark. The *last* person he wanted to be with was his brother. *Finally* it was 8 o'clock—time for Jimmy to take a bath and get ready for bed.

Mark got Jimmy's bath water ready. He thought about making it too hot, just to get even with his parents, but he decided that would get him into too much trouble. While Mark was helping his brother get undressed for the bath, he started to get a different kind of feeling inside— a warm feeling. He was still mad, but there was something else, too. Mark thought about how he usually felt better when he touched his penis, how it made him feel grown up and not like the baby his parents seemed to think he was.

After Jimmy got in the bathtub, Mark still had that funny feeling. He felt his penis getting hard. Then Mark decided he was going to touch Jimmy's penis. He pretended to help Jimmy wash himself, but after helping him wash, Mark started to touch Jimmy's penis. Jimmy yelled, "I don't like this! I'll tell Mommy!"

"Oh yeah?" Mark said. "I'll say that you *asked* me to touch you, and if you tell Mom, *you're* going to get into a lot of trouble. Mom will believe me because I'm older." Jimmy looked scared and promised that he wouldn't tell.

After Jimmy went to bed, Mark felt strange and confused inside. He was terrified that his parents would find out. What if Jimmy told? He would be in *big* trouble.

What do you think will happen next?

Activity: ***The Bobcat Story***

Ages: *5-12*

Materials: *Story: "Bruno the Bobcat" (following); character puppets (for younger children)*

Procedure: Read aloud "Bruno the Bobcat" and use puppets for dialogue.

Discussion: This metaphor is one that children really relate to. Younger children love to act the story out with puppets. Questions for discussion include:

1. Why was Bruno so angry?

2. What did he do every time he felt sad? (A: got mad instead)

3. Have you ever felt like Bruno?

4. Why do you think that Bruno picked on the monkey?

5. Why did Bruno feel better for a second after he took the monkey's home?

6. What else could Bruno have done when he felt sad and lonely?

Encourage the children to act out the various characters. Exchanging roles will give them a sense of the relationship between victimization and perpetration and encourage the development of empathy.

Bruno the Bobcat

Deep in the forest lived Bruno the bobcat. Bruno spent weeks and weeks building himself a home where he could be safe and warm. He took special pride in his sleeping place where he put straw and leaves to make his very own private spot. No one else could enter without his permission.

One day while Bruno was peacefully sleeping, a huge gorilla—twice Bruno's size—barged into Bruno's safe space without even knocking. With a loud grunt, the gorilla kicked Bruno out of bed and plopped himself down right in the middle of Bruno's special spot.

Bruno wandered around the forest, feeling like he wanted to cry. But everybody in the forest knew bobcats were strong, so Bruno was afraid to cry. He felt sad and confused and didn't know what to do. Rather than feeling sad and crying, Bruno got mad instead. Every time he thought about that gorilla taking over his special place, he got angrier and angrier and began to growl louder and louder.

One day as he was sitting alone in the forest, he spotted his friend Mickey the monkey sitting in a tree. Mickey had built his own special place, just like the one that Bruno used to have. Bruno thought to himself, "Mickey looks just like that gorilla, only he's much smaller." In a flash, Bruno growled and kicked Mickey out of his home. Bruno curled up in Mickey's nest. For a while he felt better and more powerful. He thought to himself, "At least I don't feel like a helpless wimp anymore."

But somehow, it just didn't feel right. Bruno knew exactly what it was like to have someone take advantage of him. Bruno was sure that Mickey was feeling just as sad and angry as he had felt when it happened to him.

Bruno left Mickey's tree and started walking in the forest. Once again, Bruno felt as if he wanted to cry, but he didn't want to show his feelings. A little further away, Bruno spotted Mother Monkey with her new baby. Mother Monkey asked, "Bruno, could you watch my baby monkey for a minute while I hunt for some bananas?"

It felt good for Bruno to feel important. He said, "Sure."

After just a few minutes of playing with the baby monkey, Bruno suddenly felt angry again. He began to think about hurting the baby. Suddenly, he kicked the baby monkey out of the nest. The baby fell and broke his leg. When Mother Monkey came back, she gasped and asked Bruno to tell her what happened to the baby. Bruno lied and said, "Baby monkey fell down."

Bruno felt guilty because he lied. He also felt bad because he had hurt the baby. And most of all, he felt confused and upset. He ran away, lay down in the forest, and cried and cried.

A little while later, Bruno heard a "Whoooooo" sound. It was Ozzie Owl. He asked Bruno, "Why you are so sad?" Bruno answered, "Someone took my home and now I don't know what to do."

Ozzie asked, "Do you think that kicking others out of their homes will get you your home back?" Bruno was startled. "How did you know ...?" Then Bruno hung his head and mumbled his answer. "No. ... But I just get so angry that I can't stop."

Ozzie said, "It's okay to feel sad, and it's okay to cry. It's okay to feel angry too. But hurting others isn't okay. It isn't fair to them and it makes you feel guilty."

"What should I do?" Bruno asked.

Ozzie thought a moment and then said, "Use your words, not your muscles. Talk to the other animals who are older and wiser than you about what happened to you and what you did. They will help you."

So Ozzie Owl helped Bruno tell Lennie the Lion and Terry the Tiger what happened. They went back to Bruno's home, where they were big enough, strong enough, and wise enough to get the gorilla to go with them to a place where he could get help for his problem.

Then Ozzie Owl went with Bruno to visit Mickey Monkey. "Bruno has something to say to you, Mickey," Ozzie began. "I'm sorry for taking your nest," Bruno apologized. "It was really mean. You must have felt really bad. I'd like to help you make your nest nice again, that is, if it's okay with you." Mickey said he would think about it.

Bruno and Ozzie went to see Mother Monkey, too, so Bruno could apologize for hurting Baby Monkey and then lying about it. Bruno offered to find bananas two days a week for Mother Monkey since she didn't feel that it was safe for Bruno to babysit anymore. He could understand that. It took a while for Bruno to feel safe again, too.

Apologizing was really hard, but eventually, it helped Bruno feel better about himself. He learned that it's okay to feel sad and that it's okay to cry. He learned that you can get help if you ask for it. He also learned that it's better to talk about the hurt than to hurt others, and that when you hurt others, you're also hurting yourself.

Activity: ***Goal Results***

Ages: *6-8*

Materials: *Crayons; copies of the "Goal Results" worksheet (following)*

Procedure: Follow the directions on the worksheet. Help the children set appropriate goals around touching behaviors. Have the parent assist the child in coloring the squares when his/her behavior is appropriate and respectful of other children; or use the triangles and circles as days of the week. Give a reward when all of the "I Remembered" triangles are colored in.

Discussion: Behavior modification is an excellent tool to extinguish negative behaviors. While sexual acting out is a symptom of unresolved issues, for young children, a behavior modification chart such as this can help provide external control. This assignment usually also helps the parent feel a sense of control. As the child's behavior decreases, he/she will find more appropriate ways to bind his/her anxiety, or to gain attention from others.

Name	Date

GOAL RESULTS

Today I am going to try to_____

_____

Each time I remember, I will color the △ .

Each time I forget, I will color the ○ .

I Remembered	**I Forgot**

I remembered _____ times.

I forgot _____ times.

GOAL RESULTS

Name _____

Date _____

Goal _____

Each time you are successful in your goal, put a check mark in the "I Made It" column. Each time you are unsuccessful, mark the "I Missed It" column.

	I MISSED IT					
	I MADE IT					

Activity: *Goal Wheel*

Ages: *6-10*

Materials: *Crayons; copies of the "Goal Wheel" worksheet (following)*

Procedure: Have each child make a picture of him/herself using the goal of appropriate touching in the center of the wheel (if this goal is too direct, too abstract, or too threatening, other more concrete goals can be substituted). Have the parents check each day or draw in a happy or sad face to show whether the child has reached his/her goal of touching appropriately.

Discussion: This is another example of a behavior modification chart. Having the child draw him/herself acting appropriately helps create an unconscious image that will serve as a reminder. This also is an excellent chart for inappropriate anger as well as for children who mutilate themselves.

Activity: *The Questions/Directions Game*

Ages: *8-12*

Materials: *Index cards; marking pens*

Procedure: Copy the following questions/directions onto index cards, one on each card. Have each group member pick a card, read it out loud, and then respond to it.

Questions and Directions

D: Go around the group and tell each person why you like him or her.

Q: What is the worst criticism that you have received? Ask the person across from you the same question.

Q: Is there anyone in the group you don't believe sometimes? What don't you believe?

Q: Who in the group is most scared to share his/her feelings? Why do you think he/she is so scared? How can you help him/her?

Q: How do you feel about an older kid or grownup sexually touching a younger kid who is the same sex as them? Do you think that little kid will be gay? Ask someone else in the group this question.

D: Pick out someone in the group who you think would like to tell the group something but can't. Say for him or her what you think "it" is.

Q: Who in this group do you think is most honest about telling what he/she did to get put in this group?

Q: Who in this group do you think is most honest about what happened to him/her?

D: Name one group member whom you trust. Explain why.

Q: Who in the group seems most interested in other group members? Explain why you think so.

Q: Who in the group has taught you the most? What have you learned?

Name	Date

Goal Wheel

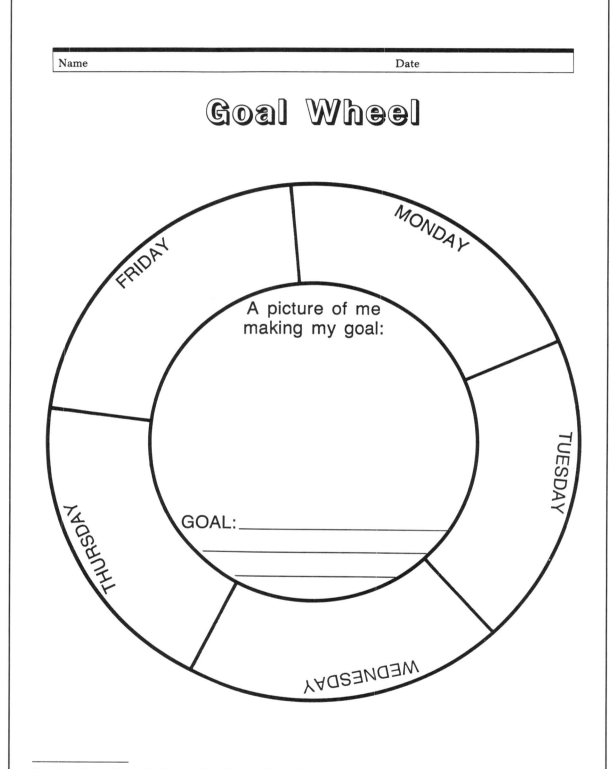

FRIDAY

MONDAY

A picture of me
making my goal:

TUESDAY

THURSDAY

GOAL:_____
_____
_____

WEDNESDAY

Q: Who in the group is having the hardest time admitting his/her touching problem? What can you say or do to help him/her?

Q: Who works hardest in the group? Why do you feel that way?

Q: Who in this group seems most angry most of the time? Do you think this group can help this person with these angry feelings? Why?

Q: Who in this group is the biggest clown? Why do you think he/she does that?

Q: Have you ever tried to hurt yourself on purpose? What was going on? What did you finally do? Ask somebody else the same question.

Discussion: This is a great game to promote group cohesion as well as a tool to help the clinician see how the group members feel about themselves, each other, and the group itself. It gently provides a space for group members to confront each other in a game format rather than directly, a difficult task for children.

Understanding the relationship between victimization and perpetration is an important way for children to link their unconscious feelings of powerlessness and anger with their conscious and (especially with older children) planned acts of perpetration. The activities in this unit should be repeated throughout the course of treatment so that the abuse-reactive child will internalize the concepts taught.

Remember, it is essential to involve former child victims in a sexual victimization awareness program that provides assertiveness training and teaches victimization awareness skills. Making amends to their own victims, practicing anger control, and taking responsibility for their actions are equally important for recovery.

While many of the sexual acts committed by these young perpetrators are as violent and as harmful as those committed by adolescents, it is important to go slowly and to use puppets, metaphors, and other communication tools. More importantly, we must positively reinforce these children for being honest and open, no matter how terrible the stories they have to tell. Latency-age children are authority conscious; if they feel negative toward the group leader or feel that the group leader disapproves of them, they will be more likely to shut down.

CHAPTER TEN

Building Empathy Skills

Empathy, the ability to feel for others and to put ourselves in another person's place, is an essential part of psychological development. The relationship between lack of empathy and aggressive antisocial behavior has been investigated and empirically supported (Feshbach & Feshbach, 1969; Feshbach, Feshbach, Fauvre, & Ballard-Campbell, 1983; Selman, 1980). Studies indicate that the development of aggressive behavior appears to be associated with empathy deficits in role-taking ability and that empathy is a learned behavior (Feshbach et al., 1983).

Abuse-reactive children tend to lack the ability to understand how their coercive behavior harms others as well as themselves. In order to stop the abuse cycle, abuse-reactive children must be able to put themselves in others' shoes and understand how their behavior hurts innocent victims. This chapter provides specific activities that foster the development of empathy in young children.

The development of empathy skills and altruistic attitudes occurs in small steps and can be a slow, methodical process. The material presented to abuse-reactive children should be repeated often; expectations of progress must be realistic. The tendency of abuse-reactive children to react in impulsive and egocentric ways makes empathizing difficult for them; therapists should not expect that these children will readily be able to understand their victims' pain.

In addition, children who themselves were victimized usually deny the impact of their abusive behavior on others. Denial (both conscious and unconscious) operates to protect them in at least three ways: 1) it protects them from having to face the pain of their own abuse, since acknowledging it in others can lead to acknowledging it in themselves; 2) it allows children to identify with the original abuser rather than with the victim—thereby replacing feelings of helplessness with feelings of power; and 3) it helps to reduce feelings of reponsibility and self-blame associated with sexual victimization.

The progress of therapy is usually enhanced if the formerly abused child has worked through his or her own victimization issues prior to concentrating on empathy development. However, beginning empathy skills can be taught to abuse-reactive children throughout the course of therapy, particularly in the context of a group setting. One way of managing the different aspects of empathy development is to divide them into categories which can then be integrated at various points in the group treatment process.

In their book *Responsibility and Morality* (1979), Jensen and Hughston identify the following process in the development of empathy skills:

1. The child must learn to identify the *needs* of others.

2. The child must be able to learn to identify the *feelings* of others.

3. The child must attempt to *put him/herself in the shoes of others*.

4. The child discovers *how he/she would feel* if the same thing happened to him/her.

5. Finally, the child must be able to *act upon his/her feelings* of empathy.

Group activities for each of the five areas suggested by Jensen are included in this chapter, along with activities that encourage sharing and kindness among group members. The last portion of the chapter provides various activities that are useful in working with previously victimized children.

Area One: Identifying the Needs of Others

Activity: *Learning to Differentiate Needs from Wants*

Ages: *6-11*

Materials: *Chalkboard, magnetic board, or flip chart; chart or marking pens*

Procedure: Have children identify their basic needs (e.g., physical needs, safety needs, love and friendship needs). Write them down in one column. In a second column, make a list of things that the children *want* to have. Talk about the difference between what one wants and needs. Discuss various ways to get what you need and what you want.

Discussion: This activity helps children conceptualize the difference between needs and wants.

Activity: *Who Needs It?*

Ages: *8-12*

Materials: *"Who Needs It" worksheet (following)*

Procedure: Talk about the Maslow pyramid of basic needs explained in the worksheet. Have children attempt to identify the needs associated with the behaviors listed at the bottom of the page. Have children attempt to figure out where their needs fit on the Maslow pyramid.

Activity: *What Would You Need If?*

Ages: *6-10*

Materials: *Magnetic board, chalkboard, or paper; writing materials*

Procedure: Write the following words on the magnetic board, chalkboard, or paper and encourage group members to complete each question. Add your own questions and encourage the children to add theirs.

What Would You Need If...

1. You were lost?

2. You were caught in an elevator?

3. You were sick with the flu?

4. You were physically abused?

5. You were molested?

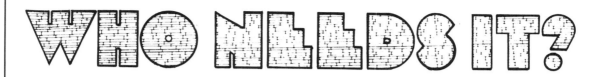

WHO NEEDS IT?

Everybody. People all over the world have the same *basic needs*. These needs must be satisfied if we want to have a good self-concept and get along well with other people. When our needs are satisfied, we feel happy and contented. When they are not satisfied, we feel frustrated, angry, sad, confused, hurt, jealous, and hateful. These feelings can cause conflict.

Dr. Abraham Maslow, *a psychologist*, believed the basic needs of people. Maslow arranged that most behavior could be explained by understanding these needs in the order of their importance to us.

SELF FULFILLMENT —
need to become everything that you are capable of becoming — a creative human being.

SELF-WORTH NEEDS —
need to feel important, capable, worthy, confident; need for recognition, attention and respect.

LOVE AND FRIENDSHIP NEEDS —
need to give and receive love; need to belong in a group.

SAFETY NEEDS —
need to be safe from threats; to be treated fairly; to be trusted and to have trust.

PHYSICAL NEEDS —
need for air, food, water, shelter, medical care, rest, recreation, sometimes called **SURVIVAL** needs.

PUTTING IT TOGETHER

Much of our behavior is a combination of needs. For example, when you eat with a friend, you are satisfying both the need for food and friendship.

Do you think that understanding basic needs will help you to understand behavior? Let's find out.

Analyze these behaviors and use Maslow's pyramid to identify the needs.

Five-year-old Mary cries and holds on to mother. It's the first day of school.

_____

You're not invited to a party. All of your friends are going. You're upset.

_____

Raymond talks loud and acts like a "bigshot."

_____

Andy's friends are pressuring him to drink beer with them.

_____

YOUR CHALLENGE!

Write down some basic needs that you had during the first two hours you were awake this morning. Were they met? How? If not, what did you do?

Used with permission from *Creative Conflict Solving for Kids*, by Fran Schmidt and Alice Friedman (Grace Contrino Abrams Peace Education Foundation, Inc., 3550 Biscayne Boulevard, Suite 400, Miami, FL 33137, 1985).

Discussion: Teaching children to become aware of their own needs as well as those of others is a crucial part of learning empathy skills. Since abuse-reactive children often are unaware of their own needs, they are prone to react impulsively.

Activity: *What Do They Need?*

Ages: *5-8*

Materials: *Magazine pictures of people in various situations*

Procedure: Show children the pictures. Ask the children to tell you, draw, or write down what the people in the pictures need.

Discussion: This process may be a slow one, and may be more difficult than expected. This activity can be repeated throughout therapy.

Activity: *What Do the People in My Group Need?*

Ages: *All ages*

Materials: *None*

Procedure: When a child in the group acts out, looks upset, or is left out of the group activities, stop the group and ask the group what they think he or she needs. This process will help foster caring and empathy.

Discussion: Teaching empathy and cooperation in the group builds a cohesive group structure of trust and commonality.

Area Two: Identifying the Feelings of Others

Activity: *Identifying the Feelings of Others*

Ages: *All ages*

Materials: *Pictures cut out from magazines that show people in various situations*

Procedure: Show children the various pictures that have been cut out. Have them verbalize the feelings they think the person in the picture has and the reasons that the person may feel that way.

Discussion: This simple but powerful exercise will help the therapist evaluate the child's ability to identify the feelings of others.

Activity: *New Crayons*

Ages: *5-8*

Materials: *Story: "New Crayons" (following)*

Procedure: Read the story "New Crayons" to the children. After reading the story, use the discussion questions as a springboard for role playing. The questions encourage children to put themselves in others' shoes.

Discussion: Ask the children how John felt. Ask them if they have ever felt like John. Encourage discussion and examples from group members' own experiences.

Activity: *Conflict Situations*

Ages: *All ages*

Materials: *Copies of "The Emotional Wheel" and "Conflict Situations" (following); game tokens*

Procedure: Construct an "Emotional Wheel" similar to the example provided. You may want to substitute "hurt" for one of the feelings on this wheel. Have the children role play various scenarios. Instruct one child to play the victim and one the victimizer. After each role play have the children switch roles, the victim becomes the victimizer and vice versa. Encourage the children to select a feeling from the wheel describing how they felt. Encourage them to talk about the different feelings in each role.

Discussion: This is an excellent activity for abuse-reactive children, as all have been abusive and many have been victimized as well. Having children put themselves in the victims' shoes is a step toward victim empathy. After each role play, encourage the children to come up with ways to help the victim in the situation. At the end of the activity, add role plays specific to abusive acts committed by members of the group. Follow the same procedure: have children switch roles from victim to victimizer. Be prepared for an increase in anxiety and acting out. Predict that this might be a hard activity and remind the children of their ability to self-talk their way through flashbacks. As always, reward participation.

Activity: *Victimizing Others*

Ages: *All ages*

Materials: *Puppets for younger children*

Procedure: Encourage children in your group to make up short scenarios related to the following topics: 1) bullying; 2) fire setting; 3) hurting an animal; 4) verbally abusing someone; 5) molesting someone else. Ask one child or group of children to be the victim, and the other, the victimizer.

Discussion: Encouraging children to create their own scenarios gives the therapist valuable insight into how they perceive their own victimization. With younger children, it is helpful first to do a role play using puppets in order to show them how to proceed. Talk about how it feels to be the victim and/or victimizer and how victimizing affects other people. Emphasize how the other person feels in each role play.

New Crayons

John was happy today. He had a new box of crayons to bring to school. John loved to color, but he didn't have very many colors in his old box. Now he had a brand new box, and he was so proud. John was looking at his crayons on the bus while he was riding to school. He was showing all the pretty colors to Shane, his best friend. "See how many colors I have in my new box of crayons, Shane," said John. "You better be careful," said Shane, "or you might drop them!"

John carefully put the crayons back in the box because it was almost time to get off the bus. The bus stopped in front of the school; Shane and John got in line. Just as John was about to step down the steps of the bus, the boy in back of him ran into him because the girl in back of him ran into him, and so on. One of the big boys in the back of the bus had pushed a child, and everybody had run into everybody else. John fell, and all his crayons fell down the steps of the bus. "Keep moving," the bus driver said.

"But my crayons," said John. "They fell all over the street. I have to pick them up. They are all new." John started to cry.

"Keep moving," said the bus driver. "I still have another load of kids to pick up."

As the children filed out of the bus, they stepped all over John's crayons until they were all broken.

"My crayons are all ruined," cried John. "I'll never have any new crayons, ever."

Shane felt very sad for his best friend, John. That night when Shane was getting ready for bed, he asked mother to get him a paper bag. "What for?" asked mother.

"I need to take some crayons to school," said Shane.

"Why?" asked mother. "Don't you already have some crayons at school?"

"Yes," said Shane, "but these are for my friend, John. His crayons are all old and broken and stepped on."

"Oh," said mother. "Well, I guess that would be okay. You have a lot of crayons anyway."

The next day Shane brought a bag of new crayons for John, and John was very happy. "Thanks, Shane," said John. "You are my very best friend."

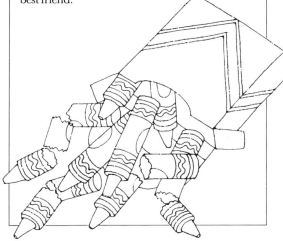

I. *Discussion Questions:*

1. Why did John feel sad when his crayons dropped?
2. Would you feel sad if you dropped your crayons?
3. What would you do if you dropped your new crayons all over the road?
4. What would you do if you were John's friend?
5. Did Shane do a good thing when he brought John some of his crayons from home?
6. If you were Shane, would you bring new crayons to your friend?

II. *Role Playing:*

Let the children select the parts they would like to play. The adult will read the story as they act it out. The second time, have the children verbalize the parts as they remember them. Children learn through repetition; therefore, the role-playing may need to be repeated several times to allow all the interested children to participate.

III. Make up stories or tell true stories that have happened to the children.

Reprinted from *Responsibility and Morality* by Larry Jensen & Karen Hughston, © 1979. Used by permission of Brigham Young University Press, Provo, UT.

The Emotional Wheel

As the sentences are read aloud, place a marker over the
word or words that best tell how the character is feeling.

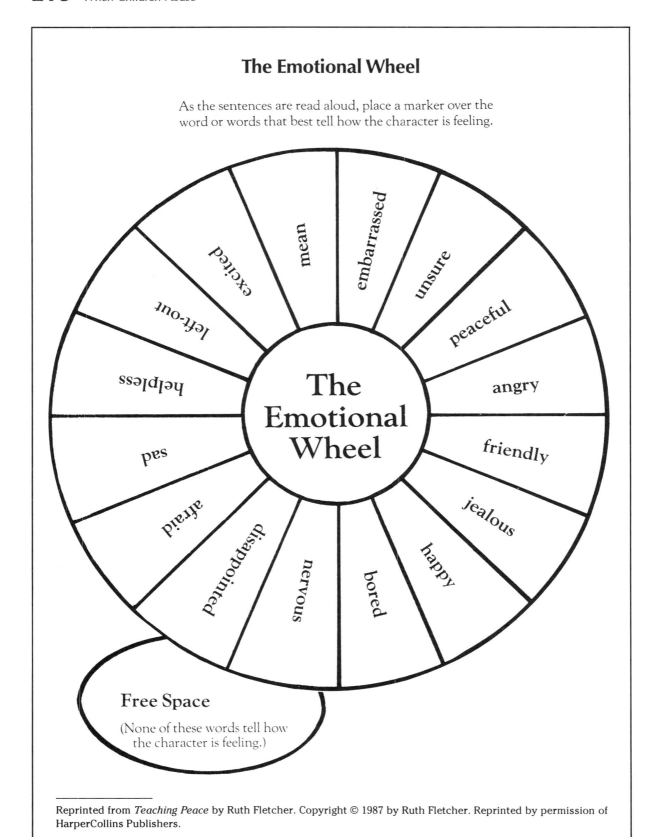

Conflict Situations

In the school hallway, a bully knocks the books out of Joshua's arms. Then the bully steps on the books and laughs. How does Joshua feel?

_____

Sue sees Brendan using her pencil. Brendan tells Sue he brought the pencil from home. How does Sue feel?

_____

In the school cafeteria, Frank returns to his seat to find that someone has poured milk on his hot dog roll. Two other students are nearby, laughing. How does Frank feel?

_____

Students returning from gym are lined up at the drinking fountain. The teacher calls Lina to get a paper from the desk. When Lina returns, the others tell her she can't have her place back. How does Lina feel?

_____

Some boys Jim knows have been making fun of his last name. Even Jim's best friend is joining the teasing. How does Jim feel?

_____

Kathy and Allie are best friends. One day Kathy passes Allie a note. The teacher takes it away from Allie and Allie gets in trouble. How does Allie feel?

_____

Raul and his two friends are playing basketball on the school grounds. Raul misses a basket because one of the boys knocks him down. He kicks the ball onto the school roof. How does Raul feel?

_____

On the way to school, Veronica is stopped by an older girl who tries to take Veronica's lunch money. How does Veronica feel?

_____

Mona is at a convenience store looking through the comic books. She has read most of each series and keeps looking to find a new one. The owner thinks Mona is reading without paying, or that she is getting ready to steal a book. He accuses her loudly. How does Mona feel?

_____

Derick is home one evening reading a magazine. His little brother comes in the room and wants the book. How does Derick feel?

_____

Sarah just returned home from school. Her mother has found cigarettes in Sarah's pocket while doing the laundry. Her mom does not approve of smoking and is upset that Sarah has been so secretive. How does Sarah feel?

_____

Area Three: Putting Oneself in Others' Shoes

Activity: *Feeling Like the Monkey*

Ages: *5-10*

Materials: *Story: "Bruno the Bobcat" (see Chapter Nine)*

Procedure: Reread "Bruno the Bobcat" and ask the children to role play the monkey's part. Then ask them how they felt when they were the monkey. Ask them for ideas about what the bobcat can do to make it up to the monkey. Ask them what the other animals in the forest could do to let the monkey know that they understand how he feels.

Discussion: This is an opportune time to introduce the concept of making amends after you do something to hurt somebody. In addition, you are encouraging empathy skills when children project themselves into another's shoes.

Activity: *What Should I Do?*

Ages: *9-12*

Materials: *Copies of the "What Should I Do?" worksheet (following); pencils or markers*

Procedure: Read the scenarios on the worksheet. Help the children identify the feelings and needs of the children in the vignettes. Help them identify how these feelings and needs lead them to inappropriate behavior. Older children can fill in the worksheets themselves.

Discussion: As discussed earlier in this chapter, figuring out ways to get their needs met appropriately is a valuable and important skill for abuse-reactive children. After finishing this activity, help the children to relate their needs and wants to their own inappropriate acting out.

Activity: *Empathy Building*

Ages: *6-13*

Materials: *Game entitled* Kids Day in Court *(available from Childswork/Childsplay; see Resources)*

Procedure: This game has two versions depending upon the age of the players. The game is self-explanatory. Discussion: This is an excellent game in relation to empathy building and value clarification. The game forces the player to put himself or herself in others' shoes and make decisions. The children love it and enjoy the court setting that the game is structured around.

WHAT SHOULD I DO?

Love and friendship are such important needs that they sometimes cause people to do foolish things. Read the stories and complete the charts.

"CAUGHT"

Joan is eleven years old and feels that no one pays attention to her. It isn't that her parents don't love her, but her Dad works long hours and the three little ones at home seem to take up most of Mom's time. Joan is the oldest and Mom expects her to come home from school and help her do the chores. Mom always seems too busy to talk to her.

It is a hot day and Joan feels restless. As she walks home from school, she decides to stop off at Woolworth's for a soda. On her way out, she stops by the cosmetics counter. She opens some of the lipstick cases and thinks how pretty they all look. Suddenly, she puts one in her purse and walks out of the store. A store security man comes up to her.

Joan's feelings	Joan's needs	Inappropriate behavior

"CHICKEN"

Richard and his friends are playing ball in the park. They are having fun when Tom suggests a better game. The boys are interested and ask, "What kind of game?" Tom says they will have to go to his building. The boys begin racing towards Tom's house. When they get there, Tom says, "Okay. See this balcony? You have to jump from here to the next building."

Some of the boys think it is a "neat" idea. Richard isn't so sure. He says, "It's stupid. I'm going home." Tom then yells, "Chicken, Chicken. . .," and the other boys join in. Richard is afraid. He knows he can't jump that distance.

Richard's feelings	Tom's feelings
Richard's needs	Tom's needs

YOUR CHALLENGE! Write an ending for one of the stories telling how Joan or Richard's need for love and friendship could be satisfied in an appropriate way.

Used with permission from *Creative Conflict Solving for Kids*, by Fran Schmidt and Alice Friedman (Grace Contrino Abrams Peace Education Foundation, Inc., 3550 Biscayne Boulevard, Suite 400, Miami, FL 33137, 1985).

Activity: *Scapegoating*

Ages: *6-13*

Materials: *Story: "Scapegoating" (below)*

Procedure: Define the word "scapegoating" and talk about what it means. Read the following story to the group.

Scapegoating

Ms. Thomas, the fifth-grade teacher at Cyprus School, is out of the room talking to another teacher. Some of the kids are throwing wads of paper in the classroom while Ms. Thomas is out of the room, but others—like Michael, who never talks and doesn't really have any friends—just sit at their desks looking embarrassed and scared. Eric, the class troublemaker, throws a baseball and it hits a glass sitting on the teacher's desk. The glass falls to the floor and shatters into dozens of pieces. Shocked silence—no one moves. Ms. Thomas walks back into the classroom just at that moment. Eric picks up the baseball and says, "Michael did it."

After reading the story, ask the children the following questions: Why do you think Eric put the blame on Michael? How did Michael feel? How would you feel? How could you help Michael if you were in the class?

Discussion: Abuse-reactive children tend to scapegoat others whom they perceive as less aggressive than they. When presenting this activity, appeal to the children's sense of fairness, since that is most likely what they can identify with developmentally. Ask them if it is fair to scapegoat others. Ask whether they blamed the person they touched in a hurtful way (or someone else) for what happened. Ask them if they have ever been scapegoated. Discuss ways to help people feel better after that happens to them.

Activity: *The Scapegoat Chart*

Ages: *7-12*

Materials: *Chalkboard or flipchart; markers; copies of the Scapegoat Chart*

Procedure: Before group, make three columns on the board or flipchart. Label the lefthand column "Who I Scapegoated," the middle column "What Happened," and the last column "How the Other Person Felt." Make a copy of the chart on notebook-sized paper for each member of the group. In group discuss the concept of scapegoating and fill out the big chart together as a group to help the children understand the concept. After a thorough discussion, pass out copies of the Scapegoat Chart to the group for a homework assignment during the week. Have the children bring the completed chart into the next group session. Be sure to let the parents know about this homework assignment.

Discussion: Helping the child to understand how scapegoating affects others is a step toward building empathy skills and addresses one of the main thinking errors that sexual offenders use in order to avoid taking responsibility for their actions.

Activity: *Sticks and Stones*

Ages: *7-12*

Materials: *Story: "Sticks and Stones" (following); discussion questions following it*

Procedure: Read the story "Sticks and Stones." Use the discussion questions at the end of the story as a springboard for role playing or talking further about victimizing.

Discussion: What is particularly significant in this story is Jeremy's statement: "I'm trying to hurt their feelings." Ask the children how many of them at times want revenge and have deliberately hurt other children (or adults) for that reason. Revenge is part of the abuse cycle. Using the abuse cycle, talk about how Jeremy could have stopped himself. In addition, have the children come up with ways that Jeremy could make amends to Ali. Ask the children how Ali felt.

Sticks and Stones[46]

Jeremy and Adam were becoming best friends. It was something Jeremy had always wished would happen. After all, Adam was good at everything he did. He received the highest grades in school, won all the races in gym, and told the funniest stories. It had been so hard getting close to Adam—he just did so many things and had so many friends. But Jeremy had done it!

Ali, another student in the class, had been friends with Jeremy for many years. They were next-door neighbors and their families spent a lot of time together. Ali was good at sports and she and Jeremy would play together almost every day—that is, until Adam entered the picture. Since Adam and Jeremy became friendly, Ali was left out of all their games. You see, Adam didn't like playing with girls. He said they weren't good enough at sports. So, Jeremy went along with him—he didn't want to make Adam mad.

One day, some boys in the class were organizing a baseball game during recess. Ali wanted to play. She liked baseball and was a terrific batter. But Adam said no—he wouldn't play if a girl played. All the boys backed Adam, even Jeremy.

Ali was very mad. She looked at Jeremy and said, "Jeremy, you know I can catch and hit the ball better than most of the boys here!"

Jeremy looked first at Ali, then back at Adam. Adam had a defiant look on his face. Jeremy knew if he disagreed with Adam, that would be the end of their friendship. So, Jeremy yelled back at Ali, "Girls are sissys. You're too little and weak to play with the boys."

Ali was furious. She stomped away and refused to speak with Jeremy for the rest of the day. Jeremy felt guilty. He didn't really mean what he had said, but he didn't want to look bad in front of the other boys, especially Adam.

That night, Jeremy was very quiet. He ate his dinner quickly, and then disappeared into his room. A short time later, his door opened and his mother walked in. "Hey buddy," she said, "is something bothering you?"

---

[46] Reprinted from *Explore* by Jay Cerio, © 1983, with permission from DOK Publications, Buffalo, NY.

Jeremy looked at his mother for a few seconds. Hesitantly, he began relating the story about the baseball game. His mother listened patiently.

When Jeremy was done, his mother said, "So you feel crummy about what you did."

"Yeah," replied Jeremy.

"How do you think Ali felt?" she asked.

"Really angry ... maybe hurt," Jeremy said.

"Why?" asked his mother.

"Well, probably because I called her some names," he said.

"When you call people names, what are you doing?" she asked.

"I'm trying to hurt their feelings. I know I can hurt their feelings by picking on something that makes them different from others." Jeremy appeared to be surprised at the words that were coming out of his mouth.

"That's right," said his mother. "We pick on people's differences or weaknesses to hurt their feelings. Now that you've succeeded in hurting Ali's feelings, what can you do about it? You know once the words come out of your mouth, you can't take them back."

Jeremy knew his mother was right but he didn't know what he could do to make things better. He sat on his bed with a blank look on his face.

After a few minutes, his mother said, "Think about it, Jeremy, and we'll talk more later." With that she walked quietly out of his room. Jeremy was left alone thinking, "Sticks and stones may break my bones, and names DO hurt me."

Discussion Questions:

1. What do you think about the way the boys tried to keep Ali out of the game?

2. What do you think about Jeremy's handling of the situation?

3. What's another way Jeremy could have solved his problem?

4. When people call other people names, what are they trying to do? (Hurt someone's feelings.) What are they calling attention to? (Weaknesses; differences in appearance, beliefs, abilities, etc.; their own prejudices.)

5. How do you feel when someone calls you a name? How do you react or behave? (Make a list of positive and negative reactions on the board.)

6. What are some positive ways to handle name calling, that is, some things you can do which will solve the problem? Let's list them.

Area Four: Developing Feelings of Empathy

The process of developing victim empathy requires that children take the risk of involving themselves in their victims' pain and hurt. Victim work is an essential part of the healing therapy for young offenders. *Steps to Healthy Touching* (by Kee MacFarlane & Carolyn Cunningham; see Resources) provides a method for younger children to make amends or apologize to their victims. For older children and pre-adolescents some of the following can be included:

Activity: *From a Victim's Point of View*

Ages: *10-13*

Materials: *Paper; pencils*

Procedure: Have the child write or describe exactly what he/she did from the victim's point of view. Tell the child to pretend that he/she is the victim. Then say, "Write or role play what happened, how it felt, and how you feel now."

Discussion: This is a difficult exercise, and may need to be repeated several times in order to break through the child's denial system.

Activity: *Letter of Apology (making amends)* [47]

Ages: *All ages*

Materials: *Paper; pencils*

Procedure: Help the children to brainstorm various ways they might make amends to the person(s) they hurt. Encourage each child to share with the group ways he/she will make amends. If writing a letter of apology doesn't come up in the discussion, suggest it. Then tell the group that they will all write a practice letter. Before handing out paper and pencils, ask the group for suggestions on what might be included in a letter of apology. This might include: how the writer feels now, mention of what happened, why it happened (including "I don't know" if applicable), whose fault it is (absolving the victim), and concern for the victim. Letters should be *very personal* in nature—a personal letter from the child perpetrator to the victim child, not a general message such as you would find in a greeting card. Younger children and those who have difficulty with this task will need individual help with this activity. When completed, ask each child to read his/her letter to the group.

Discussion: Encourage group feedback as to whether or not the individual letters or other methods of making amends seem sincere. Some children will attempt just to get by. These children should repeat the exercise until sincerity and caring are evident. Note: *In most cases, the letters should be placed in the child's file, rather than mailed to the victim.*

---

[47] For a more detailed discussion of the concepts and uses of perpetrator communication with victims (including but not limited to apology letters) see Bera (1990) and Hindman (1990).

Tribes Program Handout

Appreciating Others

Self	Best Friend

Mom/Dad	Group Member

Suggested positive statement forms

_____ I liked it when you

_____ I appreciate it when

_____ I'm glad you

_____ I want to give you a warm fuzzy because

_____ Thanks for

Area Five: Acting Upon Feelings of Empathy

Activity: *Appreciating Others*

Ages: *5-12*

Materials: *Copies of the "Appreciating Others" handout (previous page); pencils or markers*

Procedure: Talk about how positive statements can demonstrate caring and empathy. Ask the children to fill in the squares with statements that show appreciation and caring. Have the children read their statements out loud to the group.

Discussion: After completing the activity, talk about how it feels to show appreciation and caring to important people in your life.

Activity: *You Are Important, Too!*

Ages: *7-10*

Materials: *Copies of the "You Are Important, Too!" worksheet (following); pencils or markers*

Procedure: Follow the directions on the worksheet. Have the children complete the worksheet.

Discussion: Discuss with children things they can do to make other people feel important. Discuss why some of the statements on the worksheet keep one from having close relationships with other people.

Activity: *My Appreciation and Caring List*

Ages: *6-12*

Materials: *Paper; markers; pencils or crayons*

Procedure: This can be a week-long assignment. Fold a piece of paper in thirds lengthwise. Title the page "My Appreciation and Caring List." Headline one column "Who I Showed Caring For"; title the middle column "What I Said to Them." At the top of the third column, write "What I Did for Them." Make a copy for each group member (or have the group members make their own). Have the children keep a list of the ways they demonstrate caring and appreciation to friends and family. Prior to sending this home with children, be sure to tell their parents the purpose of the exercise so that they can remind their children to complete the assignment.

Discussion: Ask the children how it felt to show caring and appreciation. Discuss how people responded to their attempt to show empathy. Were the responses positive? Was it difficult to show caring and appreciation? Be sure to get their parents' feedback on how the assignment went.

11. You Are Important, Too!

Check the different things you do to show that you like a person. Circle the one thing you do most often to show someone you like him/her.

a. __ Buy the person a gift.

b. __ Tell the person you like him/her.

c. __ Hug the person.

d. __ Spend a lot of time with the person.

e. __ Do things for the person.

f. __ Give the person whatever he/she wants.

g. __ Ask the person to do things for you.

h. __ Make sure the person only associates with you.

i. __ Other _____

Reprinted with permission from *Caring*, by Mary Anne McElmurry, © 1986 (Good Apple Press, Carthage, IL).

Name	Date

Recording Friendly Deeds

MY FRIENDLY DEEDS			
	Person	My Friendly Action	Their Response
Monday			
Tuesday			
Wednesday			
Thursday			
Friday			

Activity: ***Recording Friendly Deeds***

Ages: *6-9*

Materials: *Copies of "Recording Friendly Deeds" worksheet (precedes this page)*

Procedure: First, when working with the child's parents, educate them on the importance of empathy skills. Discuss the importance of children being able to establish caring relationships early in their lives. Go over the homework assignment to be done with the children during the week. Stress the importance of bringing the completed assignment back next week. Go over the assignment with the children in group, instructing them to bring the finished sheet back the following week. Remember to give plenty of positive reinforcement when the exercise is brought back.

Discussion: Involving the children and their parents in the development of empathy is an important step in stopping abusive behavior toward others. This exercise should be repeated throughout the treatment cycle.

Activity: ***Friendship Goal***

Ages: *6-10*

Materials: *Copies of the "Friendship Goal" worksheet (following)*

Procedure: Have a group discussion about the importance of having friends and how to make friends. Have each group member do the first portion of the worksheet one week, making a plan on how to make more friends. The following week have the group or each individual fill out the bottom part of the worksheet and discuss together if the plan that they had decided on worked or not.

Discussion: Abuse-reactive children usually have problems with social skills. Isolation is not only an issue for the young child perpetrator, but adolescent and adult offenders as well. Therefore, social skills should be an important part of the therapeutic process. For many abused children, the only way that they know to make contact with others is through inappropriate sexual acting out. Thus, you actually must teach these children how to make friends. In addition to utilizing this worksheet, role playing or implementing a social skills program would be advisable.

Activity: ***What Would You Do If?***

Ages: *8-12*

Materials: *Index cards; marking pens*

Procedure: Copy the questions (below) onto index cards. Pass one card to each child. Have each child read the questions out loud to the group and answer them.

Discussion: These are thought-provoking questions that elicit children's ability to put themselves in other people's shoes, which is part of empathy building skills. Using these questions repeatedly throughout the program will reinforce these skills.

Name   Date

Friendship Goal

Something I do that makes me a good friend:

Something I'd like to improve in to be a better friend:

How I will do it:

When I will try it:

How did it work?:

What I'll try differently the next time:

What Would You Do If?

1. If you lost a game at school, what could someone say to make you feel better? What could you say to someone who has lost a game at school?

2. If you were not sharing, how would you want someone to tell you? How could you tell someone that he is not sharing?

3. If you made a mistake on your math test, what could someone say to make you feel better? What could you say to someone who has made a mistake on the math test?

4. If you got into trouble, what could someone say to make you feel better? What could you say to someone who has gotten into trouble?

5. If someone did not like what you did to him/her, how would you want that person to tell you? How could you tell someone that you don't like what he/she did to you in a way that is not hurtful but makes your feelings clear?

6. If someone did not like what you said to him/her, how would you want him/her to tell you? How could you tell someone who said something mean to you in a way that is not mean or hurtful?

7. If you were crying because your feet hurt, what could someone say to let you know they care or to make you feel better? What could you say to make someone else whose feet hurt feel better?

8. If you were afraid to go to sleep at night, what could someone say to make you feel better? What could you say to someone who is afraid of going to sleep at night?

9. If you were a victim of sexual molestation or bad touching, what could someone say to make you feel better? What could you say to someone else who has been molested?

10. If someone is angry with you, how would you want him/her to tell you? What could you say to someone with whom you are angry?

Empathy is an important skill for all children. A lack of empathy may lead to continuing abusiveness or criminal behavior. However, the process of empathy development is very slow, so it is important to use these exercises repeatedly. Single activities may not be sufficient to have any meaningful impact. Empathy toward a victim is unlikely to develop until the child perpetrator has integrated the five steps mentioned in the beginning of the chapter. By using general activities at the beginning and then gradually working up to empathy development and making amends, the therapist will be replicating the process by which such material is incorporated as part of a child's psychological development.

CHAPTER ELEVEN

Healthy Sexuality / Countering Sex-role Stereotyping

Sexuality is an integral part of life. It may be denied, repressed, or used effectively, but it is part of our selves. Sexuality is a process commencing at birth, and ending only with death (Clarity Collective, 1983).

In today's world, the area of sexuality includes sex education, values clarification, and gender identity, all important parts of every child's education. But for the child who is a victim of sexual abuse, and/or is acting out sexually, it is even more crucial that the issues concerning sexuality be thoroughly explored. A common misperception is that because children have been exposed to sex at an early age, they know more than the average child. On the contrary, the sexual abuse victim is often more confused because of this early exposure.

Children need to feel that their initial sexual experiences are "under their own control and for their own benefit." In contrast, the molested child's sexual activities "are dominated by the perpetrator's emotional needs and selfish orientation toward sexuality. Tension, fear, betrayal, pain, and mistrust color the victim's sexual awakening" (Maltz & Holman, 1987, p. 14).

For the abuse-reactive child, there is even more confusion, as sex becomes a vehicle for power and control over another human being. Therefore, in the area of sexuality, dealing with sex-role stereotyping is a crucial part of the therapeutic process for the abuse-reactive child and his/her family. Equally important is educating the parents that sexuality is a highly charged issue, and that they may see reactions in their child.

Sex Education

Many excellent sex education programs are readily available. Network Publications (ETR Associates) is one excellent resource for sex education materials for all ages. Children's Institute International has a specialized sex-education manual for abuse-reactive children and their families written by Toni Cavanaugh-Johnson. In addition, the Clarity Collective publishes an excellent sex education resource for ages 9-17 (see Resources for all three listings).

Sex Education Activities

Activity: *My Body*

Ages: *8-12*

Materials: *Copies of "My Body ... Continuums" worksheet (following); pencils or pens*

Procedure: Pass out a copy of "My body ... Continuums" to each child. Have him/her fill out the continuum. After each child fills out the continuum, discuss as a group.

My Body ... Continuums

Mark the point on the continuum which best describes your reaction, or how you feel.

How do you feel about your body?

....

totally
satisfied

totally
dissatisfied

Would you rather be?

....

very
strong

very
weak

I want my body to be

....

the thing that
people most
remember me for

the thing that
people least
remember me for

I would rather be

....

overweight
and fit

underweight
and unfit.

Discussion: Children who have been molested generally have negative feelings about their bodies. This would be an excellent time to explore these issues. For example, some children feel that their bodies are dirty, others feel that there is something wrong with their bodies, while still others have disconnected themselves from their bodies (dissociation). In addition, many molested children develop eating disorders at early ages.

Activity: *What I Do with My Body*

Ages: *8-12*

Materials: *Copies of the "Selection Ladder" worksheet (following); pencils or pens*

Procedure: Pass out the "Selection Ladder" worksheet to each child. Have the children fill in the entire page, including the sentence completion (using the words at the bottom of the page).

Discussion: If the children in your group were victims, they may become anxious as they discuss their bodies. It is important to allow the anxiety to be present, but not let the group get out of control. Rather, it is crucial to help the children bind their anxiety. Remember to reinforce positively children who can talk about difficult things.

Activity: *Relationship Collage[48]*

Ages: *10-12*

Materials: *Glue; scissors; magazines; butcher paper*

Procedure: Ask the group members to close their eyes and think about the important relationships that they have had in their lives. Ask them to create a collage that will express why those relationships are special. Discuss as a group when the collages are complete. See if the group members can come up with qualities of a good relationship.

Discussion: With abuse-reactive children, it is crucial to define good relationships versus inappropriate ones. It is also important to discuss how relationships can start out well and become inappropriate. See if they can identify what was inappropriate about the relationship they had with the child whom they molested.

Activity: *The Card Game*

Ages: *8-12*

Materials: *"Card Game" questions (following); index cards; poker chips or checkers; standard game board (optional); anatomically detailed dolls or drawings—one male, one female (optional)*

Procedure: Copy the questions onto index cards. Have the children take turns selecting a card, reading the question aloud, and answering it. Give a chip to each child when he/she answers the question. Give

---

[48] Excerpted from *Taught Not Caught* by the Clarity Collective, © 1983, by permission of Spiral Education Resources, Fitzroy, Australia.

Selection Ladder

What I need most   1 ....
     2 ....
     3 ....
     4 ....

What I need least   5 ....

sight   touch   taste   smell   hearing

What I do most with   1 ....
my body   2 ....
     3 ....
     4 ....
     5 ....
     6 ....
     7 ....
     8 ....
     9 ....
     10 ....
     11 ....

What I do least with   12 ....
my body

check it	worry about it	criticise it
enjoy it	touch it	care for it
forget about it	display it	use it
admire it	smell it	look at it

positive reinforcement or a reward to the child with the most chips. An alternative way to use the cards is to draw or use a standard game board, and move the chips progressively along the game board.

Discussion: Take time and discuss each card. Some are factual and some ask for opinions. Some of the cards ask for names of private parts. (Note: It is assumed that this information has already been presented in a sex education program.)

Card Game

How is sex different from sexual abuse?

What is an erection? How often and when do boys have them?

What is a wet dream?

How often do you masturbate?

What is a period and why do girls get them?

A boy feels embarrassed when he wakes up and realizes that he has had a wet dream. What can he do?

How do your parents feel about masturbation?

Is it normal for girls to masturbate?

Name the different body parts of the male figure (point to them in a drawing).

How does your body change when you become a teenager?

Name the different body parts of the female figure (point to them in a drawing).

Where did you get most of your information about sex?

Why do you think people have sex?

The part of my body that I feel is out of control is _____

The part of my body that I have the most control is _____

The thing that scares me about growing up is _____

How do you feel when you are touching yourself?

What do you think about when you are touching yourself?

What is a nurturing touch? Why is a nurturing touch important?

How do you think that your feelings and fantasies will change when you start liking someone your own age?

Remember your body when you were real little? How is it changing?

An 11-year-old boy molested his 5-year-old sister last year. He is beginning to have sexual feelings toward a girl in his class. He feels afraid and confused. Why?

What feelings and thoughts are warning signs that you might touch a younger child? What can you do when you get them?

Boys have sex because _____

Girls have sex because _____

Older kids have sex with younger kids because _____

Sex is safe when _____

Sex is dangerous when _____

Activity: ***I Feel*** [49]

Ages: ***9-12***

Materials: ***Copies of the handout, "I Feel" (following); pencils or pens***

Procedure: Read the following incomplete sentences aloud to the group. After each sentence, have the children circle a feeling word from the handout page that describes how they feel about the sentence you just read. Make sure all of the children understand the words on the page. After you finish each sentence, discuss how each child felt.

1. The idea of people touching their own private parts is _____.

2. Wet dreams are _____.

3. The idea of having a wet dream is _____.

4. If I woke up one morning and there was a wet patch on my sheets I would be _____.

5. Masturbation is _____.

6. Periods are _____.

7. The first time that I found out about my period was _____.

8. An 11-year-old girl has sexual feelings toward her 5-year-old neighbor. She feels _____ _____ . He feels_____.

9. When I hear the word "gay" I feel _____.

10. A 12-year-old boy who molested his 7-year-old brother is beginning to have sexual and confused feelings toward his brother again. If you were in his shoes, you would feel _____ _____.

Discussion: This can be a very informative exercise. Take your time and select the cards that are most appropriate for your group. There may be a lot of anxiety while talking about some of the above issues. It is important to address the anxiety and continue with the exercise.

_____

[49]Adapted from *Taught Not Caught*, by the Clarity Collective, © 1983, by permission of Spiral Education Resources, Fitzroy, Australia.

I Feel...

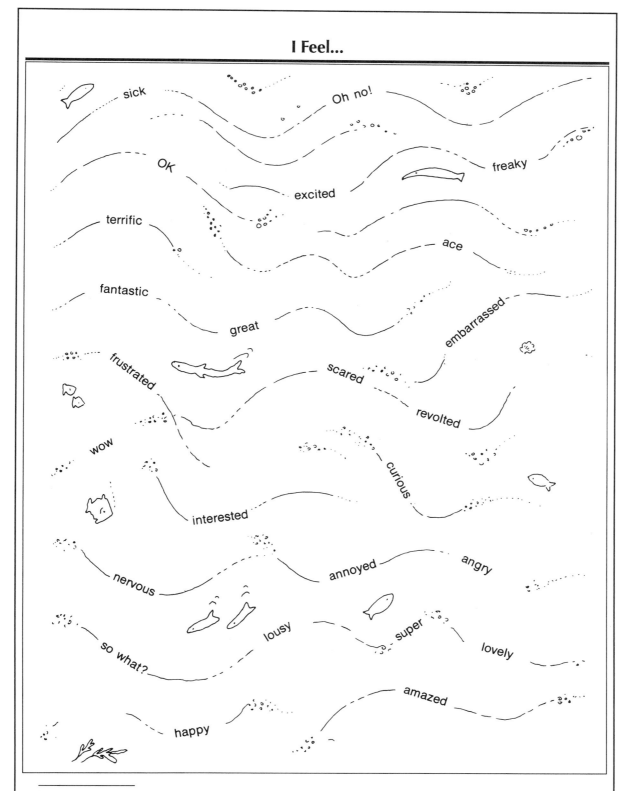

Activity: ***Discussion Sheets*[50]**

Ages: *Parents*

Materials: *Copies of the Discussion Sheets (following)*

Procedure: Hand out copies of the following pages to the parents to use as a springboard for discussion. Ask the parents to read each sheet and express their opinions regarding the various statements made on the page.

Discussion: While the children are addressing issues of sexuality, the parents also should be dealing with their own sexuality issues. Parents' values and feelings regarding sexuality are passed down to the children. It is important to understand and respect the parents' opinions and feelings around sexuality, so that the children do not receive conflicting messages from their parents and therapists.

In addition, it is crucial to explore with the parents their feelings specifically in the areas of masturbation, homosexuality, incest, and prostitution. If the therapist feels that the parents' feelings around these issues are detrimental to the child, the therapist should gently challenge the parents' belief system. For example, if a parent feels that masturbation is evil, it is important to explore this with the parent, and discuss how that attitude may affect the child. Again, the therapist should not give the child confusing messages around sexuality. To successfully conduct all the activities in this chapter, therapists should be comfortable with sexual subject matter and with their own sexuality, as well as being familiar with the material being presented.

Sex-role Stereotyping and Sexual Identity

Sexual stereotyping and the expression of sexual identity are related issues; both young people and adults encounter societal pressure about them throughout their lifetimes. They influence every area of life, including careers, relationships, and emotional expression.

Abuse-reactive children and children who have been molested are particularly affected by stereotyping and sexual identity issues. Some female victims of sexual abuse (particularly in latency and pre-adolescent stages) are afraid that their emerging sexuality and bodily changes will encourage more unwanted, abusive sexual contact. As a result, they may develop eating disorders, wear clothing that conceals their bodies, or identify with the masculine role as a way to master their fears. Other female victims may take to heart the stereotypical lesson that women's value lies solely or primarily in the sexual use of their bodies. They may unconsciously sexualize most relationships, making them vulnerable to further exploitation and victimization, including prostitution. As a result, female victims are often blamed for being "seductive" or "provocative."

Another factor in self-image and sex-role stereotyping for girls relates to attitudes about virginity. While boy victims often fear homosexuality, girls may feel damaged by their perceived loss of virginity, especially in latency and pre-pubertal stages. When virginity is considered a prime value for women, its loss (or, more realistically, its *theft*) undermines girls' reasons to say no to unwanted sexual contact, again making them vulnerable to further exploitation and victimization.

---

[50] Adapted from *Taught Not Caught*, by the Clarity Collective, © 1983, by permission of Spiral Education Resources, Fitzroy, Australia.

Discussion Sheets

Sexuality and ageing

'One of the strongest buffers against a world that looks at old people and doesn't really see them, is the intimacy of two people who have shared years, joys and sorrows. Together they continue to be themselves, instead of society's stereotype of the aged. Sharing quiet conversation, closeness and a sense of belonging is both special and fulfilling.'

'What old people want is the same as people in other life stages — privacy and the right to establish relationships if they wish. What they don't want is to be demeaned or treated as children. They know their own minds and don't need their morals policed by busybodies who regard evidence of normal sexual appetite in an older person as evidence of dementia.'

'Ageism is the idea that people become inferior, different and somehow dehumanised by virtue of having lived a specified number of years. Ageism is a prejudice like racism, which is based on fear, folklore and the hang-ups of a few people who propagate these prejudices. Like racism, it needs to be countered by information, contradiction and confrontation. The people who are the target of the prejudice have to stand up for themselves in order to put it down.'

Masturbation

'Masturbation is a common sexual activity that is usually enjoyable. The vast majority of people do it regardless of other sexual activity.'

'Many people still believe that masturbation is wrong. In the past, people believed that masturbation could cause blindness, insanity, sterility, or hairs to grow on their palms. Many church teachings still say that masturbation is a sin.'

'Many people, especially younger people, think they are the only ones who masturbate or that they masturbate too much. This can be a worrying idea.'

'For many people, masturbation is a positive way of finding out about their bodies, and what gives them pleasure.'

'Girls and women enjoy masturbating; it is not only boys and men who masturbate.'

Reproduced from *Taught Not Caught*, by the Clarity Collective, © 1983, by permission of Spiral Education Resources, Fitzroy, Australia.

Discussion Sheets

Incest

'Historically, the taboo against incest was a way of ensuring children left the family and made links with others, thus providing the security of family networks.'

'Incest is a very emotional subject. For the victims there can be feelings of shame, humiliation, guilt, anger and confusion — for others in the family, feelings of hostility and misunderstanding.'

'Most people have strong feelings for members of their families. Sexual thoughts and feelings about family members are not in themselves wrong or unnatural. Sexual feelings and love often go together.'

'Incest is not talked about. People don't want to be involved. It's hard to get someone to listen. So who can a victim turn to?'

'To some people, incest is a grave and dreaded sin that is too horrifying to talk about.'

'The most common form of incest, that between father and daughter, is now recognised as a form of child abuse.'

Rape

'Rape is not about sex. If sex is about caring for another person and about mutual pleasure, then violently attacking another person, enjoying humiliating and terrifying them or beating them up is just the opposite of sex. Rape is about power and violence.'

'All men benefit from the violent oppression of women by a few men.'

'Not all men rape women. But what happens if you are on your way home at night, and you see a man or a group of men walking towards you? What do you do? Cross the road? Walk faster and look straight ahead? Ignore them, but feel scared all the same? It doesn't really matter if they are decent men because in that kind of situation you can't tell. Every man you meet *is* someone to be scared of because he is a man. As long as some men attack women, then every woman has to be frightened of, or at least wary of every man.'

'Women have learnt to see themselves as weak and men as strong. As a result of this, women do not feel they have the power to do anything about rape.'

'Many women who are raped by their husbands do not see themselves as victims of rape.'

'Most of us believe that rapists are violent strangers. This is not always true. The vast majority of women are raped in their own homes by men they know.'

'Each time a woman is raped, society and every individual in it is responsible. We are at the same time victim and attacker. If we know about the problems and don't respond by trying to change a society that makes it possible, we are just as responsible as the rapist.'

Discussion Sheets

Pornography

'Viewing pornography can influence us in our behaviour towards each other.'

'Pornography distorts reality by showing women and men as physically stereotyped and unreal. It portrays relationships and situations that would be unacceptable and emotionally unsatisfying to most people.'

'In the past, pornography was defined as the display of naked bodies, and of people having sex. This made objects of women. A different kind of pornography is emerging now, which not only degrades women, but also involves violence and humiliation.'

'Pornography makes money for a few people at the expense of many.'

Prostitution

'Many women who become prostitutes do so to earn an income. If they could earn a similar amount in another way, they would probably give up prostitution.

'Prostitution could be viewed as a woman renting her body; marriage could be seen as a woman selling her body.'

'Our society is two-faced in its attitude to prostitution. The woman in the doorway in St Kilda, or under a lamp post in Kings Cross is regarded as offensive and socially unacceptable. It is not seen as offensive for men to hoot from a car, whistle from a building site, leer from the kerbside or jostle women in the street, and offer those women a price.'

'Men have sex with prostitutes to prove their masculinity, sexual ability, or to demonstrate their power over women.'

'The law is harsher on prostitutes than their customers. In some places it is against the law for a prostitute to solicit, or accept a customer, but it is not against the law for the customer to ask for services.'

Discussion Sheets

Lesbianism

'Many lesbians have had sexual relationships with men, and some have been, and still are, married. Being a lesbian does not necessarily mean hating men — many lesbians still have close friendships with men.'

'People sometimes ask what makes a woman a lesbian. It's as easy to ask what makes a woman a heterosexual.'

'There are no specific laws against lesbianism because the people who made the laws didn't believe that it existed. Women have been loving and caring for each other for centuries. Sometimes this is sexual, sometimes not.'

'Life is not always easy for lesbians. Often they have to hide their feelings and lie about their close relationships and social life. There are many situations in which it would be impossible to admit to being a lesbian, so they need to think about everything they say.'

'Being a lesbian means loving other women.'

'For some women, being a lesbian isn't just a personal thing, it's also a political statement. Many lesbians believe that they are stronger as women by not relating sexually with men. They feel that they can be more independent individuals.'

Male homosexuality

'Kissing is accepted between heterosexual people. It is an expression of affection between homosexual people as well. If you accept gay people, you accept their behaviour too.'

'Is it moral or immoral? I don't know. Can I judge? I do know that my son's homosexual relationship is a loving, caring, faithful one. What more could I want?'

'Men may express their homosexuality in a number of different ways, at different times and in varying degrees. As for the causes of homosexuality — why is there a need to find a cause? No-one ever asks what causes heterosexuality.'

'Public opinion polls show that more and more people approve of decriminalising sexual relations between consenting adults. However, people who make these statements publicly can still be intolerant and repressive in their treatment of lesbians and male homosexuals. To be open about sexual preference is still a difficult and courageous stand to take.'

Society's acceptance of females as victims is a complex but important message to identify, decode, and counter in all its cultural manifestations and media disguises. The findings of Mathews, Matthews, and Speltz's (1989) study suggest a connection between victimization with subsequent sex-role conformity in female sexual abusers and their perpetration as adults. By offering abuse-reactive girls positive images of women as physically strong, economically independent, sexually self-fulfilled, occupationally competent, and acting with *real* power, therapists can encourage them to give up the "pseudo-power" of sexually abusing others and increase their self-esteem so they are less likely to be further abused.[51]

Male victims of sexual molestation also are barraged by societal messages from media, family, and peers: "men are strong," "don't be weak," "protect." As a result of the repeated reinforcement of these societal images of maleness, male victims tend to feel shame and guilt that they weren't "strong enough" to prevent or stop their own molestation. Male victims also hear emerging therapeutic messages: "sexual molestation is not your fault" and "tell and you'll get help." Unfortunately, when male victims tell family, neighbors, and/or peers, they may be labeled as "gay" or "weird" or blamed for being victimized. When the abuser was female, others may deny that boys' early sexual experiences were abusive.

Male and female victims both get negative, dysfunctional, and destructive messages about themselves from sex-role stereotypes. Likewise each gender gets unrealistic and dysfunctional images of the opposite gender. Males learn to regard women as weak, "natural" victims and to exploit that "weakness," while females learn to rely on "macho" males to protect them, trading sex for fulfillment of survival needs.

Abuse-reactive children are even more confused. Their sexual acting out is out of control. Because the reasons behind the sexual acting out are not understood by the child or his/her parent, the child's worst fears become real. The family has begun to regard the child as "gay," a "pervert," a "slut," or a "tramp."

The task for the therapist is continually to clarify the child's misconceptions about his/her sexuality and sexual identity. This may include helping the children to explore and expose their fears about homosexuality and loss of virginity, along with assisting them to understand how sexual victimization can affect sexual identity. The family belief system also needs to be explored. In addition to issues of homosexuality, the societal and family pressures on the male victim to be "macho" should be explored. When working with abuse-reactive boys, it is helpful to have a male therapist who can model strength, vulnerability, and gentleness.

The following are structured activities in the area of sex-role stereotyping and sexual identity. It is important to remember that this is a very sensitive area. In order to reduce anxiety, it is helpful to proceed slowly, and move from general to specific.

---

[51] Such images for women are admittedly rare in mainstream media, but may be found. Editor Euan Bear, who contributed this discussion of female sex-role stereotyping and victimization (Bear, 1990), offers this analysis as food for thought in observing how much attention is paid in the literature and in clinical practice to the effect of victimization on boys. In contrast, it is widely accepted, both clinically and socially, that the feminine identity *encompasses* the role of victim. For help in discussing sex-role stereotyping, see the classic book and storytelling tape *Free to Be You and Me* by Marlo Thomas, and *Macho: Is That What I Really Want?* by Py Bateman and Bill Mahoney (both listed in Resources).

Activity: **A Man Can Be**

Ages: *5-8*

Materials: *The book* A Man Can Be *(by Susan Kempler; see Resources)*

Procedure: Read the story *A Man Can Be*. Ask the children if it is okay for a man or boy to cry and feel sad. Explore with both boys' and girls' groups how the messages we get from TV, parents, and friends can influence how we act.

Discussion: This is an excellent book for helping the younger child to understand sex roles. This book could be used in a family session or family group where the subject of sex roles could be discussed with both the parent and child present.

Activity: **The Paper Bag Princess**

Ages: *5-13*

Materials: *The book The Paper Bag Princess (by Robert N. Munsch; see Resources)*

Procedure: Read the story of the Paper Bag Princess. Talk about how Elizabeth must have felt right after she rescued the prince and then how she felt after he spoke to her. Why do you think they didn't get married after all? What lesson should Ronald learn from his experience?

Discussion: This book is a wonderful twist on the usual Prince-Princess-Dragon tale. Topics for discussion might include: Why are boys/men usually shown doing all the rescuing/adventure? Elizabeth saved Ronald by using her brain instead of her muscles (and even Ronald wouldn't have been strong enough). Why did it matter to Ronald what she looked like after she saved him? Do looks matter more to boys? What does this story tell girls about what they are capable of doing?

Activity: **Tough Eddie**

Ages: *5-7*

Materials: *The book Tough Eddie (by Elizabeth Winthrop; see Resources)*

Procedure: Read the book *Tough Eddie* out loud to the group. Ask the children if it is possible for Eddie to still be strong even if he likes to play with dolls or stuffed animals. Ask the children to tell you what "strong" means. Do boys always have to be strong? Can girls be strong?

Discussion: Again, this book is an excellent springboard for discussion about roles and pressure of being male or female. Whether or not you read this story with a group of girls, you might also discuss female roles. Is it okay for girls to play football or baseball? After a general discussion, move from general to specific. Bring up the children's victimization and explore the issue of feeling "weak" because the victimization took place. Discuss other ways for girls to feel strong than by victimizing others.

Activity: ***The Perfect Male/Female***

Ages: *7-12*

Materials: *Magazines; scissors; paste; paper for mounting*

Procedure: Have children look through magazines and pick out images they see as embodying "the perfect male" or "the perfect female." Have them cut the pictures out and make a group collage.

Discussion: Discuss their images of the perfect man or perfect woman. Are they very realistic? Explore with the children what stereotypes are evident. Ask them if their parents fit the perfect male or perfect female. Ask them how they are similar to or different from the pictures that they selected.

Activity: ***Stereotyping in Music***

Ages: *11-12*

Materials: *Tape Recorder*

Procedure: Have the group members bring in a song on a cassette tape that illustrates sex-role stereotyping. Have the children play the songs for each other. Elicit comments from other group members.

Discussion: This is a favorite activity for early teenagers who are into music. Many songs illustrate using women as sex objects and encourage violence of all kinds including sexual violence. Making young people aware of the messages that they receive from the media and from music is important.

Activity: ***Willy the Champ*** 📖

Ages: *5-10*

Materials: *The book Willy the Champ (by Anthony Browne; see Resources)*

Procedure: Read the story to the group. Talk about Willy's feelings when he tries very hard to be good at sports and isn't as good as the others. Ask the children if that makes Willy less of a male.

Discussion: This is an excellent book to explore sex roles with younger children. At the end of the story, Willy uses his small size to his advantage, and finds his own power. Explore the issue of power with the group. Is power *always* equated with aggression? With size? What are the implications of this kind of power for girls? This is an extremely important concept for the abuse-reactive child who uses power inappropriately.

Activity: ***Gilbert and the Color Orange***

Ages: *6-12*

Materials: *Story: "Gilbert and the Color Orange" (following)*

Procedure: Read the story of Gilbert and the Color Orange (below). Ask the children to make a list of as many orange things as they can think of that Gilbert missed out on. Talk about labeling and how labeling people or prejudging them can hurt them. Explore with children times that they have labeled others, perhaps because of skin color, appearance, etc. Also ask the children if they feel labeled both as a victim and a perpetrator.

Discussion: This is an excellent springboard to begin to deal with fears regarding being labeled for sexual acting out. In addition, this is an excellent exercise to bring up the issue of homosexuality. Explain that sexual orientation is an identity one *discovers* in examining who one feels closest to and sexual about as one grows older. Suggest that many young adults try out sexual relationships with partners of both genders as part of the discovery process, and that being gay can be okay too.

Gilbert and the Color Orange[52]

Gilbert hated the color orange. He learned to hate it as a young child. In fact, he couldn't remember a time when he didn't hate it.

Now, Gilbert had never actually been around anything that was orange. He certainly didn't have anything orange in his house. But his parents hated orange and so did the rest of his family, so Gilbert knew the color orange was not to be trusted.

Gilbert went through his life avoiding orange. He never tasted the juicy sections of the orange fruit or smelled an orange flower. He never drew with an orange crayon or wore an orange shirt. He never carved an orange pumpkin or watched the sun set in an orange sky. For Gilbert, orange soda pop, orange flavored sherbet, and orange candy were out.

In high school, the rest of Gilbert's friends signed up for the basketball team, but Gilbert stayed home. The idea of dribbling an orange basketball down the court made him shudder. "Why don't the others understand how horrible orange is?" Gilbert thought.

Because Gilbert hated orange, he missed out on a lot. He feared the color and kept away from it whenever he could. In fact, Gilbert grew to be an old man without ever really tasting or touching or smelling any of the enjoyable orange things in the world.

Gilbert's attitude toward the color orange in the story above is called *prejudice*—that is, Gilbert "pre-judged" the color orange before he ever had a chance to know, from experience, what it was like.

Sometimes we have *prejudice* toward other people or groups of people. We "pre-judge" them without any evidence from personal experience to tell us what they're really like. Our prejudices are unreasoned and sometimes unreasonable. They can hurt us and others.

Can you remember a time when someone "pre-judged" you wrongly? How did you feel? What happened?

---

[52] Excerpted from *Teaching Peace* by Ruth Fletcher. Copyright © 1987 by Ruth Fletcher. Reprinted by permission of HarperCollins Publishers.

Activity: *The Truth about Alex* 📖

Ages: *11-12*

Materials: *The book* **The Truth about Alex** *(by Ann Snyder; see Resources)*

Procedure: Read the book to the group. This is likely to take several sessions to complete. This novel was made as a TV special for young people. Explore labeling and "homophobia" with the children. Do they think that Brad should drop Alex just because he is gay? Can a star quarterback be gay?

Discussion: This is an excellent story to address labeling and prejudice. Many of these children have been labeled as "perverts" or as "sick," yet they still label others. It would be very helpful to point out the relationship between being labeled and labeling others. This is also a good exercise for exploring homophobia, as well as addressing the issue of stereotyping, i.e., what does a gay person look and act like? Use Alex as a example of how damaging stereotyping can be.

This chapter focused on sexuality, sex roles, and stereotyping. It is essential that a thorough sex education program become a vital part of a program for abuse-reactive kids. Such a program should include: names and functions of body parts, reproduction, contraception (for older children), and AIDS education. If most of the children in the group are victims of sexual abuse, discussing their bodies may be extremely anxiety provoking. It is important to present a little information at a time rather than "bombarding" the child with too much information.

It is also essential to the program that while you are working with the children, you work with the parents too. Their feelings about such issues as AIDS, first sexual experiences, masturbation, and homosexuality will give you crucial information that will help you to understand and educate abuse-reactive children and their caregivers.

Activity: *Dealing with Homophobia* 📖

Ages: *6 and up*

Materials: *The book,* **Uncle What Is It Is Coming To Visit** *by Michael Willhoite (AlysonPublications, 1993; see Resources).*

Procedure: Read and discuss the book Uncle What Is It Is Coming to Visit, which relates to children's fears of what homosexuality is. Issues that children often have who have been molested and are abusing others and/or setting fires is that they have may have sexual urges that are same-sex. These urges may be deviant or they may have both. Because of these urges they may feel that they are gay and may become homophobic. Discuss that same-sex urges are normal and that even if they have them it doesn't mean homosexuality. After reading the book, discuss the word homophobic and talk about the prejudices around homosexuality.

Discussion: This book is a wonderful lead-in to discussing homosexuality and sexual thoughts. It is important to be honest with children with this issue. Telling children that they won't be homosexual may not be true. Explaining to children that we don't know why some people are heterosexual and some are homosexual is an honest explanation. Some people fall in love with the same sex rather than the opposite sex and many gay people know this at a very young age. Can be the beginnings of a discussion. Beginning to discuss sexual urges at this point is indicated.

PART III

MEASURING PROGRESS

CHAPTER TWELVE

Evaluating Children's Progress

It is important to follow the progress of each child in your group on a regular basis. A checklist enables group leaders to track individual progress and stay focused on the goals of the group process. A weekly checklist evaluation encourages discussion among co-therapists and helps the group leaders to identify at a glance the areas that need work for individual children and for the group as a whole.

The weekly evaluation form that follows is a short behavioral assessment to be completed on each child following a group session. Therapists can use it to record amounts of acting out; positive relationships with staff and peers; and the child's ability to problem-solve, use internal controls, and confront victimization and perpetration. It also is designed to delineate weekly "red flag" indicators of problems occurring in a child's life that may be affecting behavior in the group. The weekly evaluation could be used as the basis for feedback given to parents or their therapists concerning issues requiring immediate or ongoing attention.

Finally, the weekly form provides a space for monthly assessment of the child's continuing risk to others, i.e., his/her continuing propensity to act out sexually or reabuse.[53] This evaluation form is concise, easy to complete, and serves as a visual tool for the therapist to measure children's growth or decline in each area.

The second form is a more comprehensive assessment tool, designed to be completed on a less frequent basis (e.g., semi-annually or at the end of a treatment cycle) but still intended to be simple in its application. It focuses on social interaction, problem-solving, decision-making, behavior, feelings, and most of the issues/goals addressed in treatment sessions. It can also be used as a guide to help therapists structure group activities. For example, if group members are all having difficulty in the area of problem-solving, activities can be scheduled to address the objectives in that category.

Without a formal evaluation period, it becomes difficult to stay focused on both group and individual needs. Also, when new therapists enter the group, up-to-date checklist evaluations can quickly enable them to see children's progress, as well as gain an understanding of the group's goals and objectives.

---

[53] While "risk" is difficult to quantify, the attempt helps therapists to focus on this most important treatment issue and identifies children who are not responding to intervention or who need more attention than group treatment can offer.

Weekly Evaluation Form: Children's Group

Child's Name _____ Current Age _____

Group Identification _____ Began Treatment _____

Therapist's Name _____ Current Year _____

Scoring Key: +   =   Achieved; 80% or better frequency of occurrance

               V   =   In progress; 50-79% frequency of occurrence

               O   =   Not achieved; less than 50% frequency of occurrence

1. *Amount of Acting Out* (Aggressiveness toward peers; misbehavior during group; destruction of property; need for restraint)

Week	Jan.	Feb.	Mar.	Apr.	May	Jun.	Jul.	Aug.	Sept.	Oct.	Nov.	Dec.
1.												
2.												
3.												
4.												
5.												

2. *Amount of Sexual Acting Out* (sexual preoccupation; sexualized behavior, touching self or others, lewd gestures, etc.)

Week	Jan.	Feb.	Mar.	Apr.	May	Jun.	Jul.	Aug.	Sept.	Oct.	Nov.	Dec.
1.												
2.												
3.												
4.												
5.												

Adapted by C. Cunningham and K. MacFarlane, 1987, from Individual Implementation Plan Assessment Sheet developed by G. Freitag, Ph.D. and D. Kingdon, Ph.D., Dubnoff Center for Child Development and Educational Therapy, 1986, North Hollywood, CA 91606.

Weekly Evaluation Form: Children's Group

3. *Ability to Express Feelings Appropriately* (identifies/verbalizes range of feelings; affect consistent with feelings; respect others' feelings)

Week	Jan.	Feb.	Mar.	Apr.	May	Jun.	Jul.	Aug.	Sept.	Oct.	Nov.	Dec.
1.												
2.												
3.												
4.												
5.												

4. *Ability to Utilize Internal Controls* (containment in groups; impulse control; explosiveness/hypersensitivity; removal or flight from room, etc.)

Week	Jan.	Feb.	Mar.	Apr.	May	Jun.	Jul.	Aug.	Sept.	Oct.	Nov.	Dec.
1.												
2.												
3.												
4.												
5.												

5. *Degree of Positive Relationships with Peers* (shares time and attention; bullies or scapegoats others; cooperation/tolerance/empathy, etc.)

Week	Jan.	Feb.	Mar.	Apr.	May	Jun.	Jul.	Aug.	Sept.	Oct.	Nov.	Dec.
1.												
2.												
3.												
4.												
5.												

Adapted by C. Cunningham and K. MacFarlane, 1987, from Individual Implementation Plan Assessment Sheet developed by G. Freitag, Ph.D. and D. Kingdon, Ph.D., Dubnoff Center for Child Development and Educational Therapy, 1986, North Hollywood, CA 91606.

Weekly Evaluation Form: Children's Group

6. *Degree of Positive Relationships with Staff* (problems with authority; complies with requests; listens to directions; argues; shows respect, etc.)

Week	Jan.	Feb.	Mar.	Apr.	May	Jun.	Jul.	Aug.	Sept.	Oct.	Nov.	Dec.
1.												
2.												
3.												
4.												
5.												

7. *Ability to Problem Solve Successfully* (recognizes problems and consequences; accepts responsibility when appropriate; creates alternative solutions, etc.)

Week	Jan.	Feb.	Mar.	Apr.	May	Jun.	Jul.	Aug.	Sept.	Oct.	Nov.	Dec.
1.												
2.												
3.												
4.												
5.												

8. *Ability to Confront Victimization* (can talk about own victimization; exhibits appropriate affect and feelings; degree of repression/self-blame, etc.)

Week	Jan.	Feb.	Mar.	Apr.	May	Jun.	Jul.	Aug.	Sept.	Oct.	Nov.	Dec.
1.												
2.												
3.												
4.												
5.												

Adapted by C. Cunningham and K. MacFarlane, 1987, from Individual Implementation Plan Assessment Sheet developed by G. Freitag, Ph.D. and D. Kingdon, Ph.D., Dubnoff Center for Child Development and Educational Therapy, 1986, North Hollywood, CA 91606.

Weekly Evaluation Form: Children's Group

9. *Ability to Acknowledge Perpetration* (accepts responsibility; denial/minimization/projected blame/willing to discuss; appropriate affect and feelings, etc.)

Week	Jan.	Feb.	Mar.	Apr.	May	Jun.	Jul.	Aug.	Sept.	Oct.	Nov.	Dec.
1.												
2.												
3.												
4.												
5.												

10. *Degree of Current Family Problems* (verbalizes problems at home; family discord/stress/disruption of routine; parental conflict; discipline issues, etc.)

Week	Jan.	Feb.	Mar.	Apr.	May	Jun.	Jul.	Aug.	Sept.	Oct.	Nov.	Dec.
1.												
2.												
3.												
4.												
5.												

11. *Degree of Continuing Risk to Others* (recognizes severity of problem; exhibits remorse/regret/responsibility; recognizes feelings/needs/rights of others; capacity for empathy with victim; degree of self-control; willingness to acknowledge potential for recidivism; attempted reabuse, etc.)

Jan.	Feb.	Mar.	Apr.	May	Jun.	Jul.	Aug.	Sept.	Oct.	Nov.	Dec.

Adapted by C. Cunningham and K. MacFarlane, 1987, from Individual Implementation Plan Assessment Sheet developed by G. Freitag, Ph.D. and D. Kingdon, Ph.D., Dubnoff Center for Child Development and Educational Therapy, 1986, North Hollywood, CA 91606.

Progress Evaluation and Treatment Needs: Children's Group

Child's Name _____ Current Age _____

Group Identification _____ Began Treatment _____

Therapist's Name _____ Today's Date _____

Scoring Key:
+ = Achieved; 80% or better frequency of occurrence
V = In progress; 50-79% frequency of occurrence
O = Not achieved; less than 50% frequency of occurrence

Feelings Identification

____ 1. Can identify different feelings

____ 2. Is able to differentiate feelings from thoughts

____ 3. Can identify own feelings

____ 4. Can identify feelings in others

____ 5. Can express own feelings

____ 6. Understands that people feel & express feelings differently

____ 7. Accepts/respects other people's feelings when different from own

Areas Needing Improvement

_____

_____

Self Esteem

____ 1. Can identify personal strengths

____ 2. Can identify personal weakness

____ 3. Can identify strengths & weakness in others

____ 4. Can tolerate mistakes without undue self-blame

____ 5. Can accept he/she is not all good or all bad (ambivalence)

____ 6. Had developed a sense of trust in others

____ 7. Has developed a sense of mastery over tasks

Areas Needing Improvement

_____

_____

Self-Control

____ 1. Can wait for his/her turn

____ 2. Can relate action to outcomes

____ 3. Can tolerate making mistakes

____ 4. Can express feelings of frustration appropriately

____ 5. Can respond to feedback and interpretation

____ 6. Can tolerate obstacles and disappointments

____ 7. Has developed coping skills to deal with difficult situations

____ 8. Controls sexual acting out in group

Areas Needing Improvement

_____

_____

Adapted by C. Cunningham and K. MacFarlane, 1987, from Individual Implementation Plan Assessment Sheet developed by G. Freitag, Ph.D. and D. Kingdon, Ph.D., Dubnoff Center for Child Development and Educational Therapy, 1986, North Hollywood, CA 91606.

Progress Evaluation and Treatment Needs: Children's Group

Problem Solving

— 1. Recognizes when problems occur

— 2. Correctly labels problem and consequences

— 3. Expresses feelings related to problem

— 4. Accepts own responsibility for problem

— 5. Creates alternatives

— 6. Decides on appropriate plan for solution

— 7. Follows through on selected alternatives

— 8. Can negotiate with others

Areas Needing Improvement

Authority Issues

— 1. Shows respect for authority figures

— 2. Has reduced # of power struggles that occur with authority figures

— 3. Can accept feedback/criticism from authority figures

— 4. Can accept limit setting from adult

— 5. Can ask for what he/she needs

— 6. Exhibits less need to control peers, siblings, etc.

— 7. Can disagree without power struggle

— 8. Reduced need for discipline

Areas Needing Improvement

Anger/Aggression

— 1. Can identify feelings of anger

— 2. Can identify aggressive acts exhibited by self and others

— 3. Can identify the potential consequences of aggressive behavior

— 4. Can identify self-destructive behavior

— 5. Can identify thoughts that occur prior to aggressive acts

— 6. Can recognize & relate internal cues to feelings of anger

— 7. Has developed coping mechanisms to deal with anger/aggression

— 8. Can express anger without loss of control

Areas Needing Improvement

Adapted by C. Cunningham and K. MacFarlane, 1987, from Individual Implementation Plan Assessment Sheet developed by G. Freitag, Ph.D. and D. Kingdon, Ph.D., Dubnoff Center for Child Development and Educational Therapy, 1986, North Hollywood, CA 91606.

Progress Evaluation and Treatment Needs: Children's Group

Social Interaction

_____ 1. Recognizes feelings, needs, behavior of others

_____ 2. Responds appropriately to peers

_____ 3. Initiates/maintains appropriate interactions

_____ 4. Shows respect for others' person, rights, property

_____ 5. Uses positive self-assertion

_____ 6. Handles interpersonal conflicts positively

_____ 7. Shares time and attention

_____ 8. Exhibits tolerance/empathy for others

Areas Needing Improvement

_____
_____
_____
_____
_____
_____
_____

Sexuality

_____ 1. Knows and uses correct names for body parts

_____ 2. Understands the reproduction cycle

_____ 3. Can differentiate appropriate sexual fantasies from inappropriate fantasies

_____ 4. Understands homosexuality

_____ 5. Can differentiate appropriate sex from inappropriate sexual acting out

_____ 6. Understands the importance of sexual hygiene

_____ 7. Can differentiate sexual intimacy from coercive sex

Areas Needing Improvement

_____
_____
_____
_____

Decision Making

_____ 1. Recognizes opportunity for decision making

_____ 2. Correctly labels

_____ 3. Discusses choices

_____ 4. Evaluates alternatives

_____ 5. Uses good judgement in choosing among alternatives

_____ 6. Makes decisions independently

_____ 7. Follows through on decisions

_____ 8. Other: _____

Areas Needing Improvement

_____
_____
_____
_____
_____
_____
_____

Adapted by C. Cunningham and K. MacFarlane, 1987, from Individual Implementation Plan Assessment Sheet developed by G. Freitag, Ph.D. and D. Kingdon, Ph.D., Dubnoff Center for Child Development and Educational Therapy, 1986, North Hollywood, CA 91606.

Progress Evaluation and Treatment Needs: Children's Group

Victimization

—— 1. Acknowledges own victimization

—— 2. Can talk about the specific incident(s)

—— 3. Can verbalize anger and/or ambivalence toward the offender

—— 4. Has verbalized feelings of guilt and/or self blame

—— 5. Recognizes that the abuse is not his/her fault but is the responsibility of the offender

—— 6. Has developed appropriate physical boundaries with others

—— 7. Has developed sexual abuse prevention skills

—— 8. Has developed a support system

—— 9. Comprehends that there is a relationship between victimization and perpetration

Perpetration

—— 1. Acknowledges molestation took place

—— 2. Assumes responsibility for molestation

—— 3. Does not blame victim for any of the abusive behavior

—— 4. Understands rape cycle

—— 5. Can identify thought & feelings that occurred prior to sexual acting out

—— 6. Shows empathy for the victim

—— 7. Understands consequence of repeated molestation

—— 8. Can identify inappropriate masturbatory fantasies

—— 9. Has developed coping mechanisms to lessen anxiety

Empathy/Morality

—— 1. Can identify feelings in others

—— 2. Can show concerns for others' feelings

—— 3. Can identify others' needs

—— 4. Attempts to satisfy others needs in appropriate ways

—— 5. Shows respect for property, rights, privacy

—— 6. Can understand how wrong doing & inappropriate behavior affects others

—— 7. Can acknowledge wrong doing

—— 8. Shows guilt and/or remorse for wrong doing

—— 9. Can identify how his/her victim felt after the molestation

Areas Needing Improvement

Areas Needing Improvement

Areas Needing Improvement

Adapted by C. Cunningham and K. MacFarlane, 1987, from Individual Implementation Plan Assessment Sheet developed by G. Freitag, Ph.D. and D. Kingdon, Ph.D., Dubnoff Center for Child Development and Educational Therapy, 1986, North Hollywood, CA 91606.

Epilogue

We live in a society that would like to believe that the children who are the subject of this manual do not exist. Perhaps we would all rather pretend that sex offenders and other abusive adults are alien beings who arrive, full grown, from another planet. Often the implausible is easier to accept than the unthinkable. Certainly none of us wants to look into the eyes of young children and see the seeds of potential destructiveness. Even when we do see it, we are naturally reluctant to affix the labels of deviance and criminality onto ones so young.

We did not write this manual to label, categorize, or predict the future of children with sexual behavior and other impulse control problems. As pioneers in a still-young field, neither we nor anyone else can yet responsibly promise cures, reliably estimate how many abusive incidents any treatment program will prevent, or reassuringly provide scientifically sound outcome data.

If you have found yourself uncomfortable with our structured activity format, or experience the manual as foreign or incomplete, we remind you of three points stressed in the Preface to the First Edition and mentioned throughout the text. First, in choosing to focus on *group* activities, we never intended *When Children Abuse* to represent an all-inclusive approach to treatment or to replace individual or family therapy. Second, our experience has shaped our firm opinion that structure helps impulsive children bind their anxiety in ways that free them (and their therapists) to deal with their difficult underlying issues. Finally, you are free to modify the concepts, language, and activities we've presented to fit any child's developmental needs.

As mentioned in the Preface to the First Edition, *When Children Abuse* represents a *beginning*, an affirmative approach to addressing the issues that appear to underlie the behavior of abuse-reactive youngsters. It is our hope that the resources it offers will alleviate some of the struggle we experienced in our own search to find techniques that reached these kids. We also hope that by providing practical, issue-specific tools for working with this population, clinicians will be a little more comfortable with the task of identifying and treating them. Perhaps it will even help to remind us all that sex offenders come from somewhere, and that, if we ignore them in their youth, they will likely revisit us in their adulthood when they will be harder to reach and when the results of their behavior will have left its painful mark on other young lives.

References and Recommended Readings

Abel, G.G., Becker, J., Cunningham-Rathner, J., Rouleau, J., Kaplan, M., & Reich, J. (1984). *The treatment of child molesters.* Unpublished manuscript, Columbia University, New York (available from SBC-TM, 722 W. 168th St., Box 17, New York, NY 10032).

Allen, J. (1988). *Inscapes of the child's world.* Dallas, TX: Spring Publications, Inc.

American Psychiatric Association. (1987). *Diagnostic and statistical manual of mental disorders* (3rd Ed., rev.). Washington, DC: Author.

Ballester, S., & Pierre, F. (1989, September). *Monster therapy.* Presented at the Second Annual Male Survivor Conference, Atlanta Coalition of Sexual Abuse Professionals, Atlanta, GA.

Bash, M.A.S., & Camp, B.W. (1985). *Think aloud classroom program, grades 5-6.* Champaign, IL: Research Press.

Bays, L., & Freeman-Longo, R. (1989). *Why did I do it again? Understanding my cycle of problem behaviors.* Orwell, VT: The Safer Society Press.

Bays, L., Freeman-Longo, R., & Hildebran, D. (1990). *How can I stop? Breaking my deviant cycle.* Orwell, VT: The Safer Society Press.

Bear, E. (1990, December). Personal communication.

Bera, W. (1990). The systemic/attributional model: Victim-sensitive offender therapy. In J.M. Yokley (Ed.), *The use of victim-offender communication in the treatment of sexual abuse: Three intervention models.* Orwell, VT: The Safer Society Press.

Berliner, L., Manaois, O., & Monastersky, C. (1986). *Child sexual behavior disturbance: An assessment and treatment model.* Seattle, WA: Harborview Sexual Assault Center.

Biele, N., & Plotkin, S. (1985, May). Taped site interview by F.H. Knopp. Quoted in E. Porter (1986), *Treating the young male victim of sexual assault.* Orwell, VT: The Safer Society Press.

Boat, B.W., & Everson, M.D. (1986). *Using anatomical dolls: Guidelines for interviewing young children in sexual abuse investigations.* Chapel Hill, NC: University of North Carolina Press.

Borba, M., & Borba, G. (1978). *Self-esteem, a classroom affair* (Vol. 2). New York: Harper & Row.

Bowlby, J. (1969) *Attachment & Loss: Vol. 1, Attachment.* New York: Basic Books.

Bowlby, J. (1973). *Attachment & Loss: Vol 2, Separation: Anxiety & anger.* New York: Basic Books.

Bowlby, J. (1980). *Attachment & Loss: Vol 3, Loss, sadness & depression.* New York: Basic Books.

Bradshaw, J. (1988). *On the family.* Deerfield Beach, FL: Health Communications.

Breer, W. (1987). *The adolescent molester.* Springfield, IL: Charles C Thomas.

Briere, J. (1989). *Therapy for adults molested as children: Beyond survival.* New York: Springer.

Briere, J., & Runtz, M. (1988). Symptomology associated with childhood sexual victimization in a non-clinical adult sample. *Child Abuse and Neglect, 12,* 51-59.

C.G. Jung Institute of San Francisco. (1981). *Sandplay studies: Origins, theory and practice.* San Francisco, CA: Author.

Camp, B.W., & Bash, M.A.S. (1981). *Think aloud primary level.* Champaign, IL: Research Press.

Carnes, P. (1983). *Out of the shadows: Understanding sexual addiction.* Minneapolis: CompCare.

Clarity Collective. (1983). *Taught not caught.* Fitzroy, Australia: Spiral Education Resources.

Committee for Children. (1988). *Second step: A violence prevention curriculum,* Grades 1-3, 4-5, 6-8. Seattle, WA: Author.

Conte, J., & Berliner, L. (1988). The impact of sexual abuse on children: Empirical findings. In L. Walker (Ed.), *Handbook on sexual abuse of children* (pp.72-93). New York: Springer.

Delaney, R. (1991) *Fostering Changes.* Fort Collins, CO: Walter Abbott.

Eth, S., & Pynoos, R. (Eds.). (1985). *Post-traumatic stress disorder in children.* Washington, DC: American Psychiatric Press.

Feindler, E.L., & Ecton, R.B. (1986). *Adolescent anger control.* Elmsford, NY: Pergamon.

Feshbach, N.D., & Feshbach, S. (1969). The relationship between empathy & aggression in two age groups. *Developmental Psychology.* Cited in *Second Step: A violence prevention curriculum,* Grades 1-3. Seattle, WA: Committee for Children.

Feshbach, N.D., Feshbach, S., Fauvre, M., & Ballard-Campbell, M. (1983). *Learning to care.* Glenview, IL: Scott, Foresman and Company.

Finkelhor, D. (1984). Four preconditions of abuse: A model. In D. Finkelhor, *Child sexual abuse: New theory & research* (pp. 53-68). New York: Free Press.

Finkelhor, D., & Browne, A. (1986). Initial and long-term effects: A conceptual framework. In D. Finkelhor (Ed.), *A sourcebook on child sexual abuse* (pp. 180-198). Beverly Hills, CA: Sage.

Finkelhor, D., & Russell, D.E.H. (1984). Women as perpetrators: Review of the evidence. In D. Finkelhor, *Child sexual abuse: New theory & research* (pp. 171-187). New York: Free Press.

Friedrich, W.N., Grambsch, P., Broughton, D., & Kuiper, J. (in press). Normative sexual behavior in children. *Pediatrics.*

Green, A. (1985). Children traumatized by physical abuse. In S. Eth & R. Pynoos (Eds.), *Post-traumatic stress disorder in children* (pp. 133-154). Washington, DC: American Psychiatric Press.

Groth, A.N. (1979). Sexual trauma in the life histories of rapists and child molesters. *Victimology: An International Journal, 4*(1), 10-16.

Heinz, J.W., Gargaro, S., & Kelly, K.G. (1987). *A model residential juvenile sex-offender treatment program: The Hennepin County Home School.* Orwell, VT: The Safer Society Press.

Hindman, J. (1990). The restitution model: The restitution treatment and training program. In J.M. Yokley (Ed.), *The use of victim-offender communication in the treatment of sexual abuse: Three intervention models.* Orwell, VT: The Safer Society Press.

Hoghughi, M. (1988). *Treating problem children: Issues, methods and practice.* London: Sage.

Ilg, F., & Ames, L. (1982). *Child behavior.* New York: Harper & Row.

Isaac, C., & Lane, S. (1990). *The sexual abuse cycle in the treatment of adolescent sexual abusers* (Videotape or audio cassette & reference materials). Orwell, VT: The Safer Society Press.

James, B. (1989). *Treating traumatized children.* Lexington, MA: Lexington Books.

Jensen, L.C., & Hughston, K.M. (1979). *Responsibility and morality.* Provo, UT: Brigham Young University Press.

Johnson, T.C. (1988). Child perpetrators—children who molest other children: Preliminary findings. *Child Abuse and Neglect, 12,* 219-229.

Johnson, T.C., & Berry, C. (1989). Children who molest: A treatment program. *Journal of Interpersonal Violence, 4,* 185-203.

Jones, D.P.H., & Macquiston, M. (Eds.). (1985). *Interviewing the sexually abused child.* Denver, CO: Kempe Center Publications.

Kahn, J. (1989). *The use of the sandtray in psychotherapy with children and their parents.* Petaluma, CA: Playrooms.

Kahn, T.J. (1990). *Pathways: A guided workbook for youth beginning treatment.* Orwell, VT: The Safer Society Press.

Kahn, T.J. (1990). *Pathways guide for parents of youth beginning treatment.* Orwell, VT: The Safer Society Press.

Kalff, D. (1980). *Sandplay: A psychotherapeutic approach to the psyche.* Santa Monica, CA: Sigo Press.

Kendall, P.C. (1991). *Child and Adolescent Therapy: Cognitive Behavioral Procedures.* NY: Guilford Press.

Kinsey, A., Pomeroy, W.B., Martin, C.E., & Gebhard, P.H. (1953). *Sexual behavior in the human female.* Philadelphia: WB Saunders.

Kluft, R.B. (Ed.). (1985). *Childhood antecedents of multiple personality.* Washington, DC: American Psychiatric Press.

Knopp, F.H. (1982). *Remedial intervention in adolescent sex offenses: Nine program descriptions.* Orwell, VT: The Safer Society Press.

Knopp, F.H. (1985). *The youthful sex offender: The rationale & goals of early intervention and treatment.* Orwell, VT: The Safer Society Press.

Kreisman, J., & Straus, H. (1989). *I hate you—don't leave me: Understanding the borderline personality.* Los Angeles: Price Stern Sloan, Inc.

Kubler-Ross, E. (1969). *On death and dying.* New York: MacMillan.

Lane, S. (1991). The sexual abuse cycle. In G.D. Ryan & S. Lane (Eds.), *Juvenile sexual offending: Causes, consequences, and correction.* Lexington, MA: D.C. Heath.

Lew, M. (1990). *Victims no longer.* (Reprint; originally published 1988 by Nevraumont). New York: Harper & Row.

Longo, R.E., & Groth, A.N. (1983). Juvenile sexual offenses in the histories of adult rapists and child molesters. *International Journal of Offender Therapy and Comparative Criminology, 27,* 150-155.

Longo, R.E., & McFadin, B. (1981, December). Sexually inappropriate behavior: Development of the sexual offender. *Law and Order,* pp. 21-23.

Lusk, R., & Waterman, J. (1986). Effects of sexual abuse on children. In K. MacFarlane & J. Waterman, *Sexual abuse of young children* (pp. 101-118). New York: Guilford.

MacFarlane, K. (1986). *Response to child sexual abuse: The clinical interview* (Videotape). New York: Guilford.

MacFarlane, K., Cockriel, M., & Dugan, M. (1990). Treating young victims of incest. In R.K. Oates (Ed.), *Understanding and managing child sexual abuse* (pp. 149-177). Sydney: Harcourt Brace Jovanovich.

MacFarlane, K., & Cunningham, C. (1988). *Steps to healthy touching.* Mount Dora, FL: Kidsrights.

MacFarlane, K., & Feldmeth, J.R. (1989). *Response to child sexual abuse: The clinical interview* (Syllabus). New York: Guilford.

MacFarlane, K., & Waterman, J., with Connerly, S., Damon, L., Durfee, M., & Long, S. (1986). *Sexual abuse of young children.* New York: Guilford.

Maltz, W., & Holman, B. (1987). *Incest and sexuality: A guide to understanding and healing.* Lexington, MA: Lexington Books.

Marshall, Hudson, & Hodkinson (1993). The importance of attachment bonds in the development of juvenile sex offending. In Barbaree, Marshall, & Hudson (Eds.), *The Juvenile Sex Offender* (pp. 164-181). New York: Guilford.

Mathews, R., Matthews, J.K., & Speltz, K. (1989). *Female sexual offenders: An exploratory study.* Orwell, VT: The Safer Society Press.

McGinnis, E., & Goldstein, A.P. (1984). *Skill streaming the elementary school child* (Program Forms). Champaign, IL: Research Press.

Meichenbaum, D.H., & Asarnov, J. (1979). Cognitive behavioral modifications and metacognitive development. In P.C. Kendall & S.D. Holton (Eds.), *Cognitive behavioral intervention: Theory, research and procedures.* New York: Academic Press.

Murdock, J. (1991). *Counseling children: Basic principles for helping the troubled or defiant child.* New York: Continuum.

Namka, L. (1994) Shame busting: Incorporating group social skill training, shame release,and play therapy with a child who was sexually abused. In *I Stop My Bully Behavior Kit.* Tucson, AZ: Talk, Trust & Feel Therapeutics.

National Adolescent Perpetrator Network (1988). Preliminary report from the National Task Force on Juvenile Sexual Offending 1988. *Juvenile & Family Court Journal, 39*(2).

Novaco, R. (1975). *Anger control: The development and evaluation of an experimental treatment.* Lexington, MA: D.C. Heath.

Palmer, P. (1977). *Liking myself.* San Luis Obispo, CA: Impact.

Peters, S.D., Wyatt, G.E., & Finkelhor, D. (1986). Prevalence. In D. Finkelhor (Ed.), *A sourcebook on child sexual abuse* (pp. 15-39). Beverly Hills, CA: Sage.

Porter, E. (1986). *Treating the young male victim of sexual assault: Issues & intervention strategies.* Orwell, VT: The Safer Society Press.

Pynoos, R., & Eth, S. (1986). Witness to violence: The child interview. *Journal of the American Academy of Child Psychiatry, 25,* 306-319.

Russell, D.E.H. (1984). *Sexual exploitation.* Beverly Hills, CA: Sage.

Ryan, G.D. (1989). Victim to victimizer: Rethinking victim treatment. *Journal of Interpersonal Violence 4,* 325-341.

Ryan, G.D., & Lane, S. (Eds.). (1991). *Juvenile sexual offending: Causes, consequences, and correction.* Lexington, MA: D.C. Heath.

Salter, A.C. (1988). *Treating child sex offenders and victims.* Newbury Park, CA: Sage.

Seidman, Marshall, Hudson & Robertson (1994). An examination of intimacy & loneliness in sex offenders. *Journal of Interpersonal Violence,* 9(4) 518-534.

Selman, R.L. (1980). *The growth of interpersonal understanding.* New York: Academic Press.

Sgroi, S. (1988). *Vulnerable populations: Evaluation and treatment of sexually abused children and adult survivors* (Vol. 1). Lexington, MA: Lexington Books.

Sharmet, M. (1991). *I'm the best.* New York: Holiday House.

Spivak, G., Platt, J., & Shure, M. (1976). *The problem-solving approach to adjustment.* San Francisco: Jossey-Bass.

Steen, C., & Monnette, B. (1989). *Treating adolescent sex offenders in the community.* Springfield, IL: Charles C Thomas.

Stickrod, A., Hamer, J., & Janes, B. (1984). *Informational guide on the juvenile sexual offender.* Eugene, OR: Adolescent Sex Offender Treatment Network.

Summit, R. (1983). The child sexual abuse accommodation syndrome. *Child Abuse and Neglect, 7,* 177-193.

Terr, L. (1990). *Too scared to cry: Psychic trauma in childhood.* New York: Harper & Row.

Thompson, C.L., & Rudolph, L.B. (1982). *Counseling Children* (3rd ed.). Pacific Grove, CA: Brooks Cole.

van der Kolk, B.A. (1987). *Psychological trauma.* Washington, DC: American Psychiatric Press.

White, S., Strom, G.A., Santilli, G., & Halpin, B.M. (1986). Interviewing young sexual abuse victims with anatomically correct dolls. *Child Abuse and Neglect, 10,* 519-540.

Wolpe, J., & Lazarus, A.A. (1966). *Behavior therapy techniques: A guide to the treatment of neurosis.* Oxford: Pergamon.

Wyatt, G.E., & Powell, G. (Eds.). (1988). *Lasting effects of child sexual abuse.* Newbury Park, CA: Sage.

Resources

Ballester, S., & Pierre, F. (1989). *A matter of control.* Monsterworks Publications, 2171 Torrance Blvd. #8, Torrance, CA 90501 / phone: (213) 782-0041.

Bash, M.A.S., & Camp, B.W. (1985). *Think aloud classroom program, grades 5-6.* Champaign, IL: Research Press.

Bateman, P., & Mahoney, B. (1986). *Macho: Is that what I really want?* Youth Education Systems, Box 223, Scarborough, NY 10510.

Borba, M. (1989). *Esteem builders.* B.L. Winch and Associates / Jalmar Press, 45 Hitching Post Drive, Bldg. 2, Rolling Hills Estates, CA 90274.

Borba, M., & Borba, G. (1978). *Self-esteem, a classroom affair* (Vol. 2). New York: Harper & Row.

Browne, A. (1985). *Willy the champ.* New York: Alfred Knopf.

C. Henry Kempe National Center for the Prevention of Child Abuse and Neglect, 1205 Oneida St., Denver, CO 80220 / phone: (303) 321-3963.

Camp, B.W., & Bash, M.A.S. (1981). *Think aloud primary level.* Champaign, IL: Research Press.

Caruso, K.R., & Pulcini, R. *Projective storytelling cards.* Available in minority and nonminority sets from Northwest Psychological Publishers, Inc., PO Box 494958, Redding, CA 96049-4958 / phone: (916) 223-4735.

Cerio, J. (1983). *Explore.* DOK Publications, PO Box 1099, Buffalo, NY 14224 / phone: (800) 458-7900.

Childswork/Childsplay *The Angry Monster Machine*, 307 East Church Road, Suite 1, King of Prussia, PA 19406 / phone: (610) 277-4020.

Clarity Collective. (1983). *Taught not caught.* Spiral Education Resources, 269 Smith Street, Fitzroy, Australia 3065.

Committee for Children. (1988). *Second step: A violence prevention curriculum*, Grade 1-3, 4-5, 6-8; and *Talking about touching.* Committee for Children, 172 20th Ave., Seattle, WA 98122 / phone: (206) 322-5050.

Crary, E. (1984). *Kids can cooperate.* Parenting Press, PO Box 75267, Seattle, WA 98125 / phone: (800) 992-6657.

Cunningham, C. (1988). *All kinds of separation.* Kidsrights, PO Box 851, Mount Dora, FL 32757 / phone: (800) 892-5437.

Doleski, T. (1983). *The hurt.* Paulist Press, 997 MacArthur Blvd., Mahwah, NJ 07430 / phone: (201) 825-7300.

Drake, E., & Nelson, A.G. (1986). *Working together/Getting together* (Pamphlets). Child Care Publications, 221 Calexico Way S., St. Petersburg, FL 33712 / phone: (813) 867-7647.

Duling, G.A. (1983). *Creative problem solving for an Eency Weency Spider.* DOK Publications, PO Box 1099, Buffalo, NY 14224 / phone: (800) 458-7900.

Edwards J. A. (1989). *Mandy.* New York: Harper & Row.

Fletcher, R. (1987). *Teaching peace.* New York: HarperCollins.

Gibbs, J. (1987). *Tribes—A process for social development and cooperative learning.* Center Source Publications, 862 3rd St., Santa Rosa, CA 95404 / phone: (707) 578-0223.

Groth, A.N. (1984). *Anatomical drawings for use in the investigation and intervention of child sexual abuse.* Forensic Mental Health Associates, 2688 Crystal Circle, Dunedin, FL 34698 / phone: (813) 786-5576.

Hazen, B. (1987). *The knight who was afraid of the dark.* New York: Dial Press.

Herzfeld, G., & Powell, R. (1986). *Coping for kids.* West Nyack, NY: The Center for Applied Research in Education. Order from Prentice Hall, Prentice Hall Bldg., Englewood Cliffs, NJ 07632 / phone: (201) 767-5030.

Isaac, C., & Lane, S. (1990). *The sexual abuse cycle in the treatment of adolescent sexual abusers* (Videotape or audio cassette with reference materials). The Safer Society Press, RR #1, Box 24-B, Orwell, VT 05760-9756 / phone: (802) 897-7541.

Jensen, L.C. (1977). *That's not fair.* Provo, UT: Brigham Young University Press.

Jensen, L.C., & Hughston, K.M. (1979). *Responsibility and morality.* Provo, UT: Brigham Young University Press.

Johnson, T.C. (1989). *Human sexuality: Curriculum for parents and children in troubled families.* Available from Children's Institute International, Marshal Resource Library, 711 S. New Hampshire Ave., Los Angeles, CA 90005 / phone: (213) 385-5104.

Kahn, T.J. (1990). *Pathways: A guided workbook for youth beginning treatment.* The Safer Society Press.

Kempler, S. (1987). *A man can be.* Human Sciences Press, Inc., 72 Fifth Ave., New York, NY 10011.

Kreidler, W.J. (1984). *Creative conflict resolution.* Scott, Foresman and Company, 1900 E. Lake Ave., Glenview, IL 60025 / phone: (708) 729-3000.

MacFarlane, K., & Cunningham, C. (1988). *Steps to healthy touching.* Kidsrights, PO Box 851, Mount Dora, FL 32757 / phone: (800) 892-5437.

McElmurry, M.A. (1986). *Caring.* Good Apple Press, 1204 Buchanan St., Box 299, Carthage, IL 62321-0299 / phone: (800) 435-7234.

McGinnis, E., & Goldstein, A.P. (1984). *Skill streaming the elementary school child.* Champaign, IL: Research Press.

Munsch, R.N. (1980). *The paper bag princess.* Toronto: Annick Press, Ltd. Available from Firefly Books, Ltd., 250 Sparks Ave., Willowdale, Ontario M2H 2S4, Canada.

Namka, L. (1993). *I Stop My Bully Behavior Kit.* Talk Trust Feel Therapeutics, 1120 Buchanan Ave., Charleston, IL 61929 /phone: (217) 345-2982.

Narimanian, R. (1990). *Secret feelings and thoughts.* Philly Kids Play It Safe, 1421 Arch St., Philadelphia, PA 19102-1582 / phone: (215) 686-8785.

Network Publications/ETR Associates (ask for the Family Life Education materials catalogue), PO Box 1830, Santa Cruz, CA 95061-1830 / phone: (800) 321-4407.

Palmer, P. (1977). *Liking myself.* Impact Press, San Luis Obispo, CA 93046.

Playrooms (for sandtrays and figures), PO Box 2660, Petaluma, CA 94953.

Porter, E. (1986). *Treating the young male victim of sexual assault.* The Safer Society Press.

Satullo, J.A.W., Russell, R., & Bradway, P.A. (1987). *It happens to boys too.* Rape Crisis Center of Berkshire County, Inc., 18 Charles St., Pittsfield, MA 01201.

Schmidt, F., & Friedman, A. (1985). *Creative conflict solving for kids.* Grace Contrino Abrams Peace Education Foundation, Inc., 3550 Biscayne Blvd., Suite 400, Miami, FL 33137 / phone: (305) 576-5075.

Sharmet M.W. (1991) *I'm the Best.* Holiday House, 425 Madison Ave., New York, NY 10017/ phone: (212) 688-0085.

Simon, N. (1984). *Nobody's perfect: Not even my mother.* Albert Whitman and Company, 6340 Oakton St., Morton Grove, IL 60053 / phone: (708) 647-1355.

Simon, N. (1987). *Children do, grownups don't.* Albert Whitman and Company, 6340 Oakton St., Morton Grove, IL 60053 / phone: (708) 647-1355.

Snyder, A. (1981). *The truth about Alex.* New York: Signet Press.

Thomas, M. (1987). *Free to be you and me* (Book and audio cassette). Order from McGraw-Hill, Princeton Road, Hightstown, NJ 08520 / phone: (800) 722-4726.

Vernon, A. (1988). *Helping yourself to a healthier you.* Burgess International Group, Inc., 7110 Ohms Lane, Edina, MN 55439 / phone: (612) 831-1344.

Vernon, A. (1989). *Thinking, feeling, and behaving.* Champaign, IL: Research Press.

Waters, V. (1979). *Color us rational.* Institute for Rational Living, 45 East 65th St., New York, NY 10021.

Wilhoite, M. (1993). *Uncle What Is it Is Coming to Visit.* Alyson Publications, PO Box 4371, Los Angeles, CA 90078 /phone: (800) 525-9766.

Winthrop, E. (1985). *Tough Eddie.* New York: Dutton Press.

Select Safer Society Publications

37 to One: Living as an Integrated Multiple by Phoenix J. Hocking (1996). $12.00.

The Brother / Sister Hurt: Recognizing the Effects of Sibling Abuse by Vernon Wiehe, PhD (1996) $10.00.

Adult Sex Offender Assessment Packet by Mark Carich & Donya Adkerson (1995). $8.00.

Empathy and Compassionate Action: Issues & Exercises: A Workbook for Clients in Treatment by Robert Freeman-Longo, Laren Bays, & Euan Bear (1995). $12.00.

The Difficult Connection: The Therapeutic Relationship in Sex Offender Treatment by Geral T. Blanchard (1995). $10.00.

Men & Anger: A Relapse Prevention Guide to Understanding and Managing Your Anger by Murray Cullen & Rob Freeman-Longo (1995). $15.00.

Shining Through: Pulling It Together After Sexual Abuse by Mindy Loiselle & Leslie Bailey Wright (1995). $12.00. A workbook especially for girls ages 10 through 16.

From Trauma to Understanding: A Guide for Parents of Children with Sexual Behavior Problems by William D. Pithers, Alison S. Gray, Carolyn Cunningham, & Sandy Lane (1993). $5.00.

Adolescent Sexual Offender Assessment Packet by Alison Stickrod Gray & Randy Wallace (1992). $8.00.

The Relapse Prevention Workbook for Youth in Treatment by Charlene Steen (1993). $15.00.

Pathways: A Guided Workbook for Youth Beginning Treatment by Timothy J. Kahn (1990; revised 1992; 3rd printing). $15.00.

Pathways Guide for Parents of Youth Beginning Treatment by Timothy J. Kahn (1990). $7.50.

Man-to-Man, When Your Partner Says NO: Pressured Sex & Date Rape by Scott Allen Johnson (1992). $6.50.

When Your Wife Says No: Forced Sex in Marriage by Fay Honey Knopp (1994). $7.00.

Female Adolescent Sexual Abusers: An Exploratory Study of Mother-Daughter Dynamics with Implications for Treatment by Marcia T. Turner & Tracey N. Turner (1994). $18.00.

Who Am I & Why Am I in Treatment? A Guided Workbook for Clients in Evaluation and Beginning Treatment by Robert Freeman-Longo & Laren Bays (1988; 7th printing). $12.00.

Why Did I Do It Again? Understanding My Cycle of Problem Behaviors by Laren Bays & Robert Freeman-Longo (1989; 5th printing). $12.00.

How Can I Stop? Breaking My Deviant Cycle by Laren Bays, Robert Freeman-Longo, & Diane Hildebran (1990; 4th printing). $12.00.

Adults Molested As Children: A Survivor's Manual for Women & Men by Euan Bear with Peter Dimock (1988; 4th printing). $12.95.

Family Fallout: A Handbook for Families of Adult Sexual Abuse Survivors by Dorothy Beaulieu Landry, Med. (1991). $12.95.

Embodying Healing: Integrating Bodywork and Psychotherapy in Recovery from Childhood Sexual Abuse by Robert J. Timms, PhD, and Patrick Connors, CMT. (1992). $15.00.

The Safer Society Press publishes additional books, audiocassettes, and training videos related to the treatment of sexual abuse. For a catalog of our complete listings, please write or call The Safer Society Press, PO Box 340, Brandon, VT 05733-0340 / phone: 802-247-3132.

Order Form

Date: _____

Shipping Address:

☐ **Please send a catalog.**

Name and/or Agency _____

Address (No P.O. Boxes) _____

City _____ State_____ Zip _____

Billing Address (if different from shipping address):

Address _____

City _____ State_____ Zip _____

Daytime Phone (_____)_____

P.O. No. _____

Qty	Title	Unit Price	Total Cost

Make checks payable to:
SAFER SOCIETY PRESS

Sub Total	
VT residents add sales tax	
Shipping	
TOTAL	

US FUNDS ONLY. All prices subject to change without notice.
Phone orders accepted with Visa/MasterCard

Mail to:

**Add 8% to all orders
for shipping & handling**

**Bulk order discounts available
Rush Orders – add $10.00**

SaferSocietyPress PO BOX 340 • BRANDON, VT 05733-0340
PHONE: (802) 247-3132